NAPOLEON AT WAR

NAPOLEON AT WAR

Selected Writings of F. Loraine Petre

Edited and with an Introduction by
Albert A. Nofi

HIPPOCRENE
BOOKS, INC.

For information, address: Hippocrene Books, Inc.,
171 Madison Avenue, New York, New York 10016.

Manufactured in the United States of America.

Library of Congress Cataloging in Publication Data

Petre, F. Loraine (Francis Loraine), 1852–1925.
    Napoleon at war.

    Bibliography: p. 279
    1. Napoléon I, Emperor of the French, 1765–1821—
Military leadership—Addresses, essays, lectures.
2. Military art and science—France—History—18th
century—Addresses, essays, lectures. 3. Military art
and science—France—History—19th century—Addresses,
essays, lectures. 4. Strategy—History—18th century—
Addresses, essays, lectures. 5. Strategy—History—19th
century—Addresses, essays, lectures. 6. Napoleonic Wars,
1800–1814—Campaigns—Addresses, essays, lectures.
7. First Coalition, War of the, 1792–1797—Campaigns—
Addresses, essays, lectures. 8. Second Coalition, War of
the, 1798–1801—Campaigns—Addresses, essays, lectures.
I. Nofi, Albert A. II. Title.
DC203.9.P58   1983   355.4′8′0924   83-26678
ISBN 0-88254-805-0

Contents

Preface

Napoleon's greatness as a soldier was evident virtually from the start of his remarkable career. Victory followed upon victory for over a decade. Yet if Napoleon's genius was obvious, his method was not. Nor was he particularly helpful in the matter. A man of action, Napoleon committed to paper neither the principles that guided his conduct of operations nor the techniques that he employed to implement those principles. As a result, even before his ambitions led him to his ultimate destiny, military commentators undertook the difficult task of explaining his ways of war. Thus began a seemingly endless flood of books and pamphlets and articles. Several years ago it was calculated that perhaps a half-million works existed on the various aspects of Napoleon's life and empire. Nor does it seem likely that the pace set by this voluminous output will slacken, given the productivity of the last twenty years.

Some particularly notable individuals have endeavored to elucidate the Napoleonic style of warfare. They range from men who were talented soldiers in their own right, such as Henri Jomini and Carl von Clausewitz, veterans of the Napoleonic Wars themselves, to the current batch of very capable academic scholars, such as David Chandler and Gunther E. Rothenberg. Yet few have approached the analytic incisiveness, the careful scholarship, and the clarity of presentation of one who was neither a professional soldier nor a professional scholar, F. Loraine Petre.

F. Loraine Petre (1852–1925), scion of an aristocratic English family, was a civil servant with over twenty years of service in India at the height of the British Raj. Not until his retirement in 1900 did he embark upon a career as a military historian, concentrating on Napoleon. Petre's purpose was not merely to help explain the career of Napoleon. He was convinced that the practice of war was undergoing fundamental changes as demonstrated by Britain's relatively poor performance in The Boer War (1899–1902) and the mutual disasters of The Russo-Japanese War (1904–1905). Petre saw military history as a way of awakening more serious study of the ways in which war was changing so that the British Army might be better prepared. Over the next fourteen years Petre produced five notable volumes on the campaigns of 1806–1807, 1809, 1813, and 1814. Only the advent of a newer and greater war in 1914 seems to have prevented the publication of additional works devoted to the balance of Napoleon's career. During World War I Petre returned to public service, spending five years in the Ministry of Munitions. Upon his second retirement in 1920 he resumed writing, but abandoned himself to the writing of regimental histories, to the great loss of Napoleonic studies.

Petre's approach to military history owed much to the development of a serious analytic school of military writers in both Great Britain and Germany during the late nineteenth century. Men such as Spenser Wilkinson, Charles Oman, and Major A. H. Burne in Britain, and Hans Delbrück and General Yorck von Wartenburg in Germany, among many others, were part of a revolution in the writing of military history. Disregarding tradition and polemic, they sought to impose objective, scientific standards to the evaluation of events in military history. This meant personal examination of the terrain, careful analysis of the tactics employed, and considerable criticism of sources. Ultimately, their approach was rooted in the basic realities of human existence and of war: men can run only so fast, armies must consume certain amounts of food and fodder, weapons can only fire at given rates. If an existing account of an engagement is inadequate, legitimate conclusions may still be drawn on the basis of "inherent military probability," reasoned comparison with standard contemporary practice, minute examination of the terrain, and the application of common sense. This type of analysis was not always welcome. Military history had hitherto been largely inspirational, heavily larded with words like "glory" and "gallantry," and therefore generally weak in practical details. Debate was often acrimonious, frequently silly. But in the end the innovative school succeeded in establishing itself.

Armed with notebooks and camera and astride his bicycle, Petre managed to tour the site of virtually every battle described in his works. It was perhaps the last decade in which it was possible to conduct such a terrain analysis, for the increasing industrialization of rural Europe had not yet destroyed many of the features with which Napoleon would have been familiar. His analysis of the terrain was supplemented by careful reading of the often voluminous literature on each campaign. Personally acquainted with both French and German, Petre strove to make as complete a survey of the available literary and documentary resources as possible. The end product has well withstood the test of time. One can fault Petre on some matters. He had a tendency to see everything from the top, which is understandable given his essentially didactic purpose. He also was disinclined to tell a good tale, even a true one, thus omitting many a good soldier's story. However, it is difficult to find serious flaws in his works, though he does have a clear bias against the French, despite considerable admiration for Napoleon as a soldier. Otherwise, his principal faults are a tendency to inflate casualty figures and some occasionally confusing descriptions of tactical maneuvers. Nevertheless, like many gifted amateurs, Petre often saw things more clearly than did the soldiers. Thus, as early as 1907, for example, he advanced the then almost heretical notion that cavalry was incapable of confronting entrenched infantry.

Petre's books on Napoleon have become collector's items. The original editions, published between 1901 and 1914, command considerable sums. Not reissued again until the mid-1970s, they quickly went out of print once more. Individual volumes of that edition have been known to change hands at several times the original price. Requests for copies continue to arrive at the publishers—Arms & Armour Press

in Britain and Hippocrene Books in the United States—at a
modest but steady rate. Given the prohibitive cost of reissu-
ing the entire series in the present difficult condition of the
Western economies, Hippocrene Books made the decision in
late 1982 to produce an anthology of some particularly interesting, informative, and useful selections from the entire five
volumes. Knowing of the present writer's interest and experience in the field of Napoleonic studies, the Editors at Hippocrene Books very kindly suggested that he undertake to
make the selections and to prepare a general introduction.
The end result is the volume which you now hold in your
hands.

Preparing *Napoleon at War* was neither a simple nor a bur-
densome task. It necessitated many hours of pleasurable re-
reading of the Petre series for the purpose of selecting
passages best suited to illustrate Napoleon's "mind and
method." This was somewhat complicated by the fact that
Petre had not dealt with any of Napoleon's remarkable campaigns before 1806, nor with those of 1812 and 1815, which,
aside from including his most famous battles—Arcole, The
Pyramids, Marengo, Austerlitz, Borodino, and Waterloo—
provided notable examples of various strategic concepts in
action, such as the *manoeuvre sur les derrières* and the strategy
of the central position. They also featured some particularly
fine examples of French tactical flexibility, such as the operations of V Corps at Austerlitz, and of ultimate French tactical
decay, as exemplified by D'Erlon's corps at Waterloo. Nevertheless, suitable substitutes were found. In writing the in-
troductory essay, "The Art of War in the Age of Napoleon,"
every effort was made to tie the text into the various selections so as to provide illustrative materials. This essay utilizes
a "modular" approach to the presentation of materials.
Thus, the body of the essay deals with general background,
strategy, and tactics, and is fully capable of standing alone.
Supplementing this essay, however, is a series of technical
discussions on specialized matters, such as musketry and artillery.

Each of the selections from Petre has been edited carefully, so as to retain the critically important aspects of the
operation under consideration. Each selection is preceded by

a summary of the circumstances leading up to the operation. In the selections themselves, Petre's text has been presented just as it appears in the original, save for the insertion of an occasional line to clarify matters referring to materials not included in *Napoleon at War*. In addition, Petre's footnotes have generally been omitted. Aside from this, the only changes have been the correction of minor typographical errors. For reasons of clarity, Petre's maps, quite good in their day, have all been replaced. A bibliography, added by the Editor, includes a selection of materials which postdate Petre.

The Editor wishes to thank the staff of Hippocrene Books for making this volume possible. Thanks are also in order to R.L.DiN., J.F.D., D.C.I., J.E.K., and J.C.S., for their assistance and advice in the preparation of this volume, and most particularly to M.S.N. and M.J.S., for their patience during that preparation.

Albert A. Nofi

Brooklyn, New York
December 2, 1983

NAPOLEON AT WAR

INTRODUCTION

Napoleon at War
By Albert A. Nofi

Napoleon Bonaparte has few peers in the art of war. For more than a decade he led the armies of Revolutionary and Imperial France from victory to victory, rising to the mastery of almost all of Europe. Then, his ambition growing boundless, he undertook to complete the subjugation of the Continent, leading to reverses in Spain and Russia, which sparked a general rising against him. A series of disasters ensued, leading to final defeat at Waterloo and exile for life on St. Helena. Yet even in the years of defeat Napoleon proved a resourceful, imaginative, and unpredictable commander. His enemies could not match his skills nor those of his armies. Their victories were due more to overwhelming numbers than to the talents of their generals.

THE OLD REGIME

In the late seventeenth century and for much of the eighteenth as well the conduct of war was rather formal and stylized. Limited war for limited objectives was the rule. It was the "sport of kings," a dispassionate, carefully calculated undertaking designed to secure relatively modest

3

gains at minimal cost. There were many reasons for this. It
was, after all, the time of the Enlightenment, when men saw
a new age of reason and justice dawning. More pointedly,
the excesses perpetrated upon civilians during The Thirty
Years' War (1618–1648) had provoked a widespread reaction against armies living off the land. Thus, armies acquired lengthy and clumsy logistical trains. Simultaneously,
the art of fortification rose to remarkable new levels of technical sophistication, resulting in the proliferation of
fortified places for defense and for the protection of the
vulnerable lines of supply, and in the necessity of dragging
ponderous siege guns about. And armies themselves became more skilled, necessitating long years of meticulous
and expensive training and maintenance. The net result
was that the tempo at which war was conducted slowed.
Bold strategic strokes were unusual. Battles became rare, if
only because they consumed vast amounts of valuable manpower. Sieges became the norm, as armies endeavored to
strike at each others' cumbersome lines of supply based on
fortified depots, magazines, and entrenched camps. When
battles did occur they were almost invariably the result of an
attempt to relieve a siege. The greatest generals were those
who could force their enemy into honorable surrender
through pure maneuver.

Soldiers tended to see themselves as part of a supranal-
tional brotherhood which transcended all loyalty and pas-
sion. Professional ritual developed to a remarkable degree,
with detailed prescriptions for the formal conduct of a
siege, for the conclusion of an honorable peace, for the
treatment of prisoners. One could serve in a foreign army
with little stigma, and many rose to high rank fighting
against their native land, such as Eugène of Savoy, a French
Savoyard who attained supreme command in Austrian service, or Maurice de Saxe, a Saxon who became
Maréchal-général of France, or the Duke of Berwick, illegiti-
mate son of James II of England, who rose to high rank in
France.

Some generals failed to play by the rules. England's Duke
of Marlborough conceived and executed a remarkably bold
march from the Netherlands to the Danube in 1705 result-

ing in a magnificent victory at Blenheim in cooperation with Eugène of Savoy. Similar in scope and spirit was George Washington's brilliant march from New York to Virginia in 1781 leading to the crowning victory at Yorktown. Marlborough, Washington, Prince Eugène, Prussia's Frederick the Great, and Marshal Saxe all knew how to fight a battle when necessary. But even these unusually able commanders did so relatively rarely. Saxe managed to fight, and win, but three pitched battles in a career that encompassed some 150 sieges. Men of their times, they were but rarely able to rise above the current professional, cultural, political, economic, and logistical limitations on the conduct of war. Nevertheless, their example helped point the way for reform. By the mid-eighteenth century the system was beginning to be questioned. Then came general dissatisfaction over the conduct and conclusion of The Seven Years' War (1756–1763), which sparked an enormous outpouring of creative military thought.

REFORM AND REVOLUTION

Even before The Seven Years' War some professional soldiers had begun to question contemporary practice and even to make suggestions for reform. The experience of the war greatly strengthened this trend. While men all over Europe made contributions to the intellectual fermentation in the period, it was the French who were particularly innovative, for victory had not crowned French efforts. A great many ideas were advanced. Not all of the numerous suggestions and systems and reforms proposed were necessarily constructive. Many were little more than half-baked notions, such as pleas for the restoration of the pike, or suggestions for a return to Roman patterns of organization, or proposals to replace existing battlefield maneuvers with still more meticulously choreographed drill. Yet even the most ridiculous suggestions were frequently useful. The very existence of some of the more *outré* ideas ensured that nothing in the existing military system would remain unquestioned. Moreover, the vast literary effort had the useful effect of establishing a unified terminology. Thus did such terms as "tactics," "strategy," and "line of operations" acquire their present meanings. But this intellectual ferment produced more than just a general agreement on terminology. It sparked genuine progress. And it was in France most particularly that substantive developments occurred.

Merely noting the contributions of the various individuals involved gives some idea of the scale and scope of the reforms undertaken by the French. Thus, Marshal Victor de Broglie, a veteran commander of The Seven Years' War, developed the idea of the division as an administrative and tactical formation and introduced the use of light infantry and skirmish tactics into the French service. Jacques de Guibert, scion of a military family, wrote extensively on tactics, proposing reliance not on column or on line, but rather a series of flexible tactical formations, each suited to particular circumstances. De Guibert supported the idea of light infantry and skirmish tactics and advocated reform of the artillery and the establishment of permanent divisions. He also advanced the revolutionary notion that all citizens were liable for military service. Jean Baptiste de Gribeauval, a seasoned gunner, sparked and sponsored a total reorganization and reform of the French artillery upon attaining the lofty status of Inspector General of that arm. He promoted the redesign of guns and carriages, standardized calibers, and introduced new approaches to tactical deployment. To foster increased professionalism and reliability De Gribeauval secured the replacement of the customary civilian contractor gunners with trained soldiers. Jean DuTeil and his younger brother Jean-Pierre, both artillerymen, advocated increased mobility on the battlefield, the use of artillery as an offensive arm, to prepare and support infantry attacks, and sounder preparation for officers. And Pierre Joseph de Bourcet, a seasoned campaigner and military educator, wrote extensively on organization and strategy, advocating the permanent division of armies into self-contained, relatively large subordinate bodies of all arms capable of undertaking limited independent operations for short periods. De Bourcet suggested that in this fashion an army of considerable size could advance with great speed, agility, and flexibility, for each body of the army—*corps d'armée*—could move along parallel routes of march toward the same objective, while remaining within supporting distance of the balance of the army. Operationally, De Bourcet advocated unusual strategic approaches, such as "the maneuver of the central position" and "the maneuver about the rear."

None of these changes came easily. Resistance was strong. The top-heavy French officer corps was dominated by members of the nobility intent upon maintaining their prerogatives. The struggle was hard. Nevertheless, the reforms made progress. The obvious value of many greatly facilitated their adoption. Experiments and maneuvers served to establish the usefulness of others. The experience of The American Revolution (1775–1783) greatly facilitated matters, for the French Army performed with greater credit than it had for many decades. And the popularity of things American sparked renewed interest in light infantry, skirmish tactics, and citizen armies. The war also provided a new generation of soldiers with considerable practical experience, among them the Marquis de Lafayette and the Count de Rochambeau, who quickly added their voices to the chorus of reformers. The net result of the quarter century following The Seven Years' War was that by 1789 France possessed a much reformed army. Then came the Revolution.

Most of the reformers believed that France's weakness was not merely the result of the inadequacy of her military institutions, but was due also to her antiquated political, social, and economic institutions. So most of them supported the Revolution when it came in 1789. In the process of rebuilding France, the Revolutionary government put the finishing touches on the military reforms. The initial effect of the increasing radicalization of the Revolution in 1791–1792 was a rapid deterioration in the quality of the army, as numerous officers abandoned France, including some of the reformers. Discipline disappeared, morale fell, desertions rose to alarming levels. Nevertheless, the Revolution brought forth hidden strengths. The National Guard, a

militia, was formed. Deserving men of the lower classes attained higher rank. When war came against the powers of
reaction, the resources of patriotism were tapped, yielding
the "Volunteers of '92." And when they proved insufficient,
the ultra-radical Jacobins came to power, unleashing the
"Reign of Terror" and proclaiming the *levée en masse*, con-
scripting the entire nation to its own defense. Lazare Carnot, de facto minister of war in the ruling "Committee of
Public Safety," became the "Organizer of Victory."

Carnot was an organizational genius. He established a
general staff to facilitate planning and coordination for the
armies; he set up a nationwide semaphore telegraph system,
permitting more rapid communications; and he created the
first unified engineering corps. Lacking time to train the
vast masses of conscripts and volunteers, Carnot fostered
the *amalgame*, which used the old Royal Army as the hard
core around which new regiments were formed, thereby
greatly facilitating the implementation of the new tactics;
the recruits could be used in column attack, where spirit
was more vital than meticulous training, while the seasoned
veterans could be used in line and as skirmishers, where
discipline and training were more important than élan.
Everything was in short supply, so the armies did without
tents, trains, and similar impedimenta, learning to live off
the land, and were thus able to move more rapidly than
their foes.

Carnot was also ruthless. Trusting no one, he used a system of political commissars, the "Deputies on Mission," to
keep an eye on the reliability of generals. Failure, whether
political or military, was not permitted. Fully 680 generals
were dismissed during the height of the Revolution, many
going to the guillotine. Success was the only criterion for
rank. As younger, more capable generals were found, the
armies of France advanced to greater and greater victories.
Among these new men was a young Corsican, Napoleon
Bonaparte.

Napoleon Bonaparte was a product of his times. He had
been a cadet at the height of the controversies generated by
the reformers. A voracious reader, particularly of history,
he studied the numerous suggestions for reform, the his-

tory of past campaigns, and the lives of the great commanders. He acquired a vast store of miscellaneous information on the politics, geography, military institutions, customs and traditions, religion and superstitions, and fundamental character of virtually every country in the world, but particularly of those of Europe. Under the guidance of Jean-Pierre DuTeil he absorbed much of what was valuable in the ideas of the reformers, particularly De Bourcet's novel strategic notions. He also learned from the innovations of the Revolutionary armies, while gaining valuable experience with the troops. His personal courage and skill quickly brought him to the attention of well placed individuals. Success in the field, and in supporting the right political faction at the right moment, brought him a generalship at 24 and command of the Army of Italy at 26. And it was in Italy that the world began to notice that Bonaparte was more than just an ordinary commander.

Napoleon's genius was not that of a creator. Indeed, he made few practical reforms or innovations in the military art. His talents lay elsewhere, in the strategic and administrative areas of war. Napoleon had the ability to visualize with great clarity the military situation confronting him and to determine the most profitable course of action. He could conceive the most remarkably bold undertakings, and then execute them, making full use of the considerable abilities of the reformed French Army. He developed an aggressive strategic style based largely on De Bourcet's proposals. And he used the Republic as a model in his ability to tap the ultimate resources of France, frequently stamping whole new armies out of the ground in the face of disaster. Thus, Napoleon's genius lay in the fact that he saw the ways in which all of the innovations of the late eighteenth century could be orchestrated into a virtually invincible military system.

ORGANIZATION FOR WAR

The Revolutionary and Napoleonic periods marked a significant milestone in the development of military organization, resulting in great innovations not merely in administrative structures and operational forces, but also in terms of fundamental national military policies as well. In a very real sense the period marks the beginning of what may be termed modern military organization, with developments since being essentially refinements.

Fundamental Policy—Under the *Ancien Régime* most states recognized some degree of universal obligation for military service on the part of their subjects, at least in theory. But no state was inclined to implement such a policy in practice. While conscription was used to fill the ranks, it was usually confined to the lowest classes, and even then resorted to minimally. Exemptions were liberal, with the object of sparing "useful" citizens the drudgeries of military life. For instance, in Prussia, the most militarized state in Europe, there were 500,000 legal exemptions in 1789, with an army of some 200,000 men, about 50% of whom were not Prussians at all, but foreigners attracted or coerced into Prussian service. The net result was that the average man was virtually immune to military service, unless he belonged to the Prussian nobility, which, as a group, carried a heavier burden of compulsory military service than any other European group. This policy fitted well with the political premises of the Old Regime—royal absolutism. War was the king's business, not the people's. The French Revolution changed all that.

Confronted by what it perceived to be a universal conspiracy to restore the Old Regime, Revolutionary France resorted to arms on April 20, 1792. The regular army was weak and suspect, many aristocratic officers had fled, others remained in the ranks. The enthusiasm of the Revolutionary masses was tapped through a call for volunteers, which produced an agreeable response, filling the ranks with willing if unskilled men. It was the remnants of the old Royal Army and the "Volunteers of '92" who secured the first victories of the Revolution. But as more and more states became involved in the war against France, the situation began to grow serious. This led to the stern, even excessive measures of "The Terror." And it led also to the first national compulsory military service law in modern times, the *levée en masse,* proclaimed on August 23, 1793:

From this moment until that in which the enemy shall have been driven from the soil of the Republic, all Frenchmen are in permanent requisition for the service of the armies.
The young men shall fight; the married men shall forge arms and transport provisions; the women shall make tents and clothing and serve in the hospitals; the children shall turn old linen into bandages; the aged shall betake themselves to public places to arouse the courage of the soldiers and preach the hatred of kings and the unity of the Republic.

There was more, for not only did the decree order all unmarried men of ages 18–25 into the army, it also conscripted horses, weapons, factories, rations, and literally all France for the prosecution of the war. Within a month nearly a half-million additional men were under arms. Over the next year nearly a million. None of France's enemies could match this vast outpouring of manpower, since all continued to recruit by more traditional methods. With such manpower resources, the French armies could prosecute the war with a far greater chance of success.

Napoleon made the *levée en masse* the fundamental basis of his armies, recruiting men almost exclusively through conscription. With populous France as his base he was always assured of sufficient manpower to overwhelm his enemies so long as his own losses did not become enormous or his enemies did not resort to similar measures. By 1812 both of these conditions could no longer be met. The Revolution and Napoleon drew some 3,000,000 men from France, some 12% of the total population, strength peaking in 1798 at 1,100,000, or 4.6% of the total population. This was close to the limit of France's resources. Though about a million eligible men still remained uncalled in 1812–1814, Napoleon could not tap this last reserve lest the French economy collapse. Meanwhile, having learned their lessons in the hard school of war, France's enemies resorted to universal military service. Though never quite as sweeping as French efforts, Austria, Prussia, and Russia were able to greatly enlarge their armies by the implementation of realistic conscription policies. And as their combined population was far greater than that of France, the balance of forces turned decisively in their favor.

National Military Administration—A rather chaotic situation prevailed at the highest administrative levels in all armies prior to the Revolution. Typically, the head of the armed forces was the chief of state; in the name of the Crown, a war council formulated policy and supervised its implementation. A war department handled administrative details through a series of bureaus, each charged with a particular set of duties. Unfortunately there was little organizational logic to the bureaucratic structure, and no trained staff officers to develop any. In France, for example, three of the eight bureaus of the Department of War dealt with pay and pensions, and each had other, totally unrelated duties as well. Thus, the "Second Bureau" handled officers' pensions, vacancies, and decorations, while the "Fourth" dealt with troops' pay and pensions, and officers' brevets, and the "Fifth Bureau" dealt with officers' pay. This sort of structure had just grown over the years, largely as a result of the bureaucratic combativeness of the various nobles directing particular bureaus; thus the "Eighth Department" handled such unrelated matters as artillery, fortifications, hospitals, equipment, and quarters. The bureau system was not administratively sound.

When the Revolution came, the administrative structure of the Royal Army collapsed due partially to the emigration of numerous noble officers and to the unprecedented demands placed on it by the hordes generated by the *levée en masse*. Lazare Carnot, a captain of engineers of bourgeois orgins, was named to head "La section de la guerre" of the Committee of Public Safety at the time the *levée en masse* was proclaimed. Confronted with imminent administrative collapse, Carnot began a total reorganization of the administrative structure of the army. Much of his work was on an ad hoc basis: something had to be done, so it was done. Many existing agencies were dissolved, particularly those dealing with relatively minor matters dear to the hearts of the aristocracy. In the end, Carnot supervised two departments, the Bureau Topographique, which oversaw plans and operations, and the Intendance, which supervised all aspects of supply, quartering, and maintenance. To maintain close supervision over the armies in the field, Carnot instituted the "Representatives of the People on Mission," a system of political commissars posted with each army and reporting back to him independently.

Napoleon made significant changes in Carnot's system, partially out of administrative necessity and partially due to the fact that he did not merely direct military operations from Paris, as Carnot had done, but actually conducted them in the field, while supervising all other French military activities, and simultaneously running the government. Thus, Napoleon's administrative machinery tended to be larger and somewhat clumsier than Carnot's.

A Ministry of War handled the "civil" functions of the army, such as conscription, pay, and record keeping. Napoleon himself headed *Grand-Quartier-Général*, which actually supervised the army. Under him was his personal staff, *La Maison*, which included an operational headquarters, a traveling cabinet for France, and the Bureau Topographique, his intelligence and planning staff. The two principal subordinate agencies of *G-Q-G* were the "General Commissariat of Army Stores," which supervised all types of supply, and "General Headquarters of the Army," under Marshal Louis-Alexandre Berthier, a particularly talented chief-of-staff, though an inept general in his own right. Berthier directed the "General Staff," which had several distinct sections and departments, each dealing with a well defined area of responsibility, such as troop movements and intelligence, personnel and records, and legal affairs, plus special staffs for each arm of service. Napoleon's staff organization was quite efficient, but had certain limitations, the principal ones being Napoleon and Berthier themselves. Having worked so long together, the two became incapable of working efficiently with anyone else. Napoleon had but to utter a few words for Berthier to comprehend his meaning and frame pages of clear, accurate orders. No one else could do

Organization of *Grand-Quartier-General*

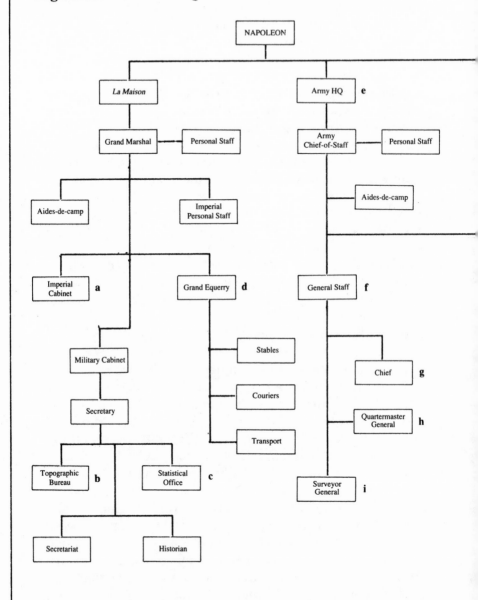

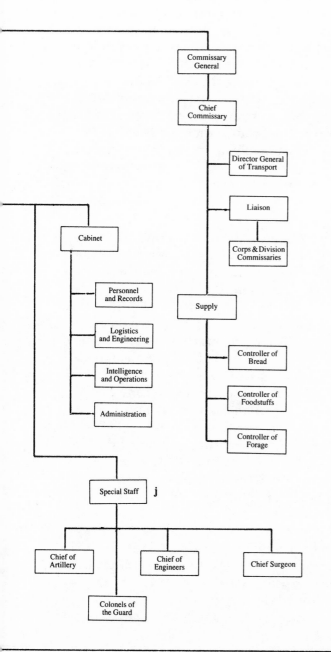

Notes:

a Civil and diplomatic affairs of France.

b Plans.

c Intelligence.

d Movement and Lodgings of *G-Q-G.*

e Direct Supervision of Administration and Operations.

f Correspondence and Chain of Command.

g Administration and Organization.

h Accommodations and Line of March.

i Intelligence and Topography.

j Liaison and Technical Advice.

that. In effect, Napoleon's staff organization was a personal staff, rather than a genuine general staff. A further problem was that Napoleon's staff tended to grow, for he was not merely running *his* army, but all the other armies of France and the government as well. When G-Q-G was paraded just prior to the invasion of Russia in 1812 someone remarked that it looked like an army corps, for it numbered over 4500 men, including the staff itself, administrative and service troops, civil and diplomatic officials, and headquarters guards. Nevertheless, the French example was far superior to any other and began to be adopted rather widely, notably in Prussia, where certain refinements were introduced, increasing specialization and laying the foundations for the evolution of the modern military staff.

Logistics—Pre-Revolutionary supply practice had been tied to a system of fixed magazines established in fortified places on the frontiers. Here rations and other supplies were accumulated in peacetime and forwarded to the armies by wagon train in war. This tended to slow the movement of armies considerably, for not only were they tied to their magazines, but their supply trains were vulnerable to raids by enemy forces, which could fall upon them from fortified places. Thus, it was necessary to reduce all fortified places in the path of an army before it could advance. Further slowing the pace of an army was the necessity of making a halt every three or four days to set up field ovens and bake fresh bread, which was the mainstay of the military ration. As an army slowly advanced, its magazines were moved forward and supplies were also requisitioned from the surrounding area. All of this further slowed the rather ponderous rate of advance.

The Revolution brought significant changes to this system. To begin with, armies grew larger while at the same time they grew leaner, for the Revolutionary forces abandoned the practice of using tents, which required an enormous number of hungry horses to transport, and also eliminated the luxurious standard of living enjoyed by officers under the *Ancien Régime,* who thought nothing of going to war with several wagons laden with fine linen, table silver, rare vintages, servants, and mistresses. This enabled armies to move faster, which was useful, for they had to move in order to eat: their size rapidly outstripped the ability of the magazine/wagon system to keep them fed. So the Revolutionary armies learned to live off the land. Initially this was quite informal, but a measure of organization was soon imposed. As the armies advanced, special officers were placed in charge of locating, securing, and distributing food and fodder. This practice placed some hardship on the local citizenry, but not an impossible one, for it was soon recognized that a given region can usually support two or three times its normal population for short periods of time without starvation resulting.

Napoleon refined this system. He included food stocks among the items on which his intelligence service was required to gather data prior to a campaign. He sometimes arranged for supplies to be purchased and stockpiled in the enemy's country before a campaign began. He relied heavily on hardtack rather than fresh bread as the mainstay of the daily ration, for it was just as nutritious and considerably lighter than bread, and could be stored indefinitely. When a campaign began, Napoleon made certain that every man had several days' hardtack in his pack, along with additional items of uniform and equipment, usually including a spare pair of shoes. As his armies advanced, Napoleon's agents would scour the countryside for food stocks, collect them at forward depots, and distribute them to the troops as required.

This system worked remarkably well, but it had its limitations. A policy of living off the land could only work efficiently where the local resources were extensive. In France itself, in South Germany, and in Italy, populous, relatively prosperous agricultural regions, armies of considerable size could be supported. But in impoverished regions, such as Spain, Poland, and Russia, a large army could quickly starve. Although Napoleon attempted to reinstitute a magazine/wagon system for his campaign in Russia, the attempt failed and that failure was one cause of the disaster which overtook him there.

DAILY FORAGE AND RATION REQUIREMENTS DURING THE REVOLUTIONARY AND NAPOLEONIC WARS

Ration allotment per man
ca. .5 kg bread or hardtack
ca. .5 kg meat or dried fish
ca. .5 kg potatoes, peas, or other staple
ca. 1 liter beer or wine
small amounts of sugar, salt, etc.

Fodder and feed allotment per horse
ca. 12 kg cut fodder
ca. 12 kg feed

On the basis of these figures, it is fairly easy to establish the daily requirements of an army of 100,000 men with 250 cannon and 40,000 horses. Rations for the troops would be about 335 tons per day, including the weight of the barrels much of it would come in. The horses would require about 600 additional tons. Thus the total daily food and fodder requirement was about 935 tons, which would require 625 wagons to transport, each of which required four to six horses and two men, for some 1250 teamsters and over 3100 horses, plus additional personnel and horses as escorts, thus further increasing food and fodder requirements. To sustain an army of these proportions at a distance of 50 miles from its base by the magazine/wagon system would thus have required some 3100 wagons, with over 15,500 horses, and a minimum of 6200 men. Moreover, 50 miles would be the outer limit at which such a supply system could operate, for the horses and men transporting the goods would soon be consuming most of the loads being carried, for after covering a distance of approximately 50 miles one third the load is consumed in transporting it. When foraging using Napoleon's well organized techniques, such an army could be sustained in an area of about 65 miles across in Northern Italy, Eastern

France, or South Germany, but about 105 in Poland, Spain, or Russia. Ammunition supply would not be a serious problem. An army of this size would have about 1700 tons of shot and powder, roughly 1135 wagon loads, representing some 20,000 artillery rounds and perhaps two million musket rounds, more than sufficient for one or two major battles.

Infantry—The infantry was the backbone of all armies during the Revolutionary and Napoleonic periods. In most armies there were technically three types of infantry: line, light, and heavy. Line infantry was composed of the regular troops, capable of all infantry missions. Light infantry, often gloriously known as *voltigeurs, velites, jägers,* or *chasseurs,* included the most agile and valiant men in the army, usually outfitted in the flashiest uniforms, with light equipment, for service in skirmishing, raiding, river crossings, and flank protection, and in some armies they were equipped with rifles. Heavy infantry, usually known as grenadiers, was also impressively uniformed and received special privileges in most armies. It included the bravest and sturdiest men, earmarked for the most dangerous missions, such as storming parties and leading infantry assault columns. In practice, however, these distinctions were often academic, showing up primarily as differences in uniform rather than function. Upward of a third of an army might be light infantry, while no more than one tenth consisted of grenadiers. Whole regiments of grenadiers were rare, but in many armies independent battalions of grenadiers were common, and some "converged" regimental grenadier companies into ad hoc battalions. In all armies, the infantry was organized into regiments and companies for administrative purposes, but in most the actual tactical units were the battalion and platoon. Organization varied greatly from country to country.

The old French Royal Army had regiments of about 1300 men with two battalions, each comprising one grenadier and eight line companies. These were dissolved into their component battalions in the early days of the Revolution and were sent into the field as stiffening for the numerous battalions of volunteers and conscripts. It soon became the practice to combine one old regular battalion with two new Revolutionary ones, often throwing in a battery of six 4-pounders to provide some extra firepower. In this way the old regulars helped accommodate the greenhorns to the military persuasion while the latter imparted some Revolutionary fervor to the former. This process was formalized in the *amalgame* of January 8, 1794, which set up the *demi-brigade*, of three 748-man battalions, each consisting of one grenadier and eight line companies, with a battery and a small staff. Needless to say, Revolutionary organization was never very neat, but the demi-brigade on this model became standard. The demi-brigade was essentially a regiment and was thus renamed by Napoleon in 1803. Napoleon gradually introduced certain refinements into his regimental organization. A company in each battalion was converted into light infantry and company strength was raised by eliminating three line companies. The regimental battery was dropped, only to be restored in 1809, and then dropped again in 1812, even before most regiments had received one. Meanwhile the number of battalions rose. Napoleon ultimately proposed that regiments be abolished in favor of administrative "legions" composed of eight battalions and a centralized depot, with the battalions operating independently in the field. He approached this policy by 1808, when he authorized the creation of regiments of seven line battalions and a depot. No more than three battalions ever actually served together in the field, and it was not uncommon for a regiment to have two battalions serving together in Spain, two more with the *Grande Armée* in Germany, the fifth on garrison duty elsewhere, and the depot stationed somewhere in France and forwarding recruits as needed. The French system proved quite effective and was eventually adopted by most of Napoleon's satellites. The infantry organization of other powers was actually not dissimilar to that of France.

The accompanying table, "Infantry Organization, 1789–1815," summarizes the principal organizational features of the various armies in the period.

INFANTRY ORGANIZATION, 1789–1815

POWER	BATTNS = COMPANIES				NOTES
		Line	*Gren*	*Light*	
AUSTRIA					
1789	3 (1092)	6 (182)			A
1805	5 (688)	4 (182)			B
	1 (688)		2 (182)	2 (182)	
1809	3 (1308)	6 (218)			C
GREAT BRITAIN	1 (950)	8 (86)	1 (112)	1 (112)	D
FRANCE					
1789	3 (650)	8 (72)	1 (72)		E
1790	2 (692)	4 (173)			F
1793	3 (746)	8 (83)	1 (83)		G
1803	3 (1107)	7 (123)	1 (123)	1 (123)	
1807	4 (738)	4 (123)	1 (123)	1 (123)	H
PRUSSIA					
1789	2 (850)	5 (170)			I
1808	2 (600)	4 (140)			J
	1 (600)			4 (140)	
RUSSIA	2 (738)	3 (182)	1 (191)		K
	1 (764)		3 (191)	1 (191)	

The table compares the general regimental organization of the principal armies of Europe during the Revolutionary and Napoleonic Wars. Years are those in which new regimental organizations were introduced. Where no date is indicated, the organization shown prevailed through the entire period. *Battns* is the number of battalions per regiment, with paper strength in parentheses. *Companies* is the number of companies of each type per battalion, with strength in parentheses. Where a second line has been given for a particular year, it indicates that regiments contained more than one type of battalion. *Notes* refers to the lettered explanations which follow below.

A—two grenadier companies and a depot of four companies attached.

B—a depot of four companies and a battery of 3- or 6-pounders attached.

C—two 145-man grenadier companies and a depot of four companies attached.

D—a battery of two 4-pounders with 13 men attached, in use until 1801.

E—this system was revived in 1791.

F—a 107-man grenadier company and a 123-man light company were attached. This organization was official, but never fully implemented.

G—a battery of six 4-pounders with 70 men was officially attached, though not always present.

H—a depot of four companies was attached. From 1805 the number of battalions tended to rise, reaching seven by 1809. Between 1809 and 1812 many regiments in the field had a battery of four light field pieces attached.

I—two 170-man grenadier companies and a reserve company were attached.

J—separate grenadier battalions followed a similar table of organization.

K—the same basic organization was maintained for the numerous types of infantry which Russia fielded, including line, light, and various types of heavy infantry.

Cavalry—Like the infantry, the cavalry was divided into several types, notably light, heavy, and dragoons. Light cavalry—variously designated as *chasseurs, jägers, hussars,* light dragoons, *uhlans,* and lancers—was supposed to be assigned to reconnaissance, screening, foraging, pursuit, and sometimes shock action, for which they were normally equipped with a saber and carbine, though the use of the lance grew popular. Heavy cavalry—horse grenadiers, *cuirassiers,* carabiniers, dragoon guards—was primarily designed for shock action, and was generally composed of bigger men on large horses, equipped with heavy swords, carbines, and often breastplates and helmets. Dragoons were originally mounted infantry, designed primarily to use their horses to get to where they could fight on foot. They gradually evolved into another branch of the cavalry, fulfilling a variety of roles and, in most armies, rarely serving dismounted. The French, however, not only preserved the older practice of using dragoons as mounted infantry, but also gave all of their cavalrymen some training as infantry, a measure which proved quite useful at times. Some armies, notably the Russian and Austrian, made use of ultra-light irregular cavalry, such as cossacks, which functioned primarily as raiders and skirmishers, having little inclination or skill relative to more serious combat. Napoleon found this type of trooper useful and raised several regiments in the period 1812–1814.

Cavalry was at once the most expensive and least flexible of the arms. In some armies its strength was disproportionate to its role. The French cavalry was actually relatively poor, the long-term effects of the Revolution not being fully overcome until about 1808 or so. But French cavalry, though neither as well trained nor as splendidly mounted as the British, Prussian, Russian, or Austrian, was well disciplined, which made it far easier for Napoleon to make more effective use of the arm than anyone else. His cavalry suffered a devastating blow in Russia, from which it proved incapable of recovering. Many of Napoleon's problems in the campaign of 1813 can be directly attributable to a severe shortage of cavalry.

Cavalry organization varied greatly throughout the wars and among the various powers, there being little standardization in the arm except at the lowest levels. Two troops of 50 to 100 men usually made up a squadron. Most French regiments ran to three or four squadrons, for a total of 600 to 800 men, as did heavy regiments in general in most armies. In many armies, however, light regiments could run upward of 1500 sabers in five or six squadrons.

Guards—Guards were the elite formations of the armies of the period. Normally an army possessed a few guards units in each arm, recruited from the bravest, most experienced men. The primary mission of guards formations was not the security of the sovereign, but rather to provide an absolutely reliable battlefield resource. Napoleon, for example, invariably held the *Garde Impérial* out as part of the reserve, preferring to commit it only in the most critical moments of a battle. Guards were of mixed value. While they frequently earned their extra pay in battle, and while they did provide a mark for all soldiers to emulate, they were not necessarily cost-effective, for they consumed inordinate amounts of superior manpower, which, if spread among the line troops, might have considerably improved their quality. The British Army possessed very few guards units and does not seem to have been the worse for it, and the Austrians managed without any at all. The *Garde Impérial* tended to grow as time went on, for Napoleon incorporated the best of his recruits into the "Young Guard," partially because the overall quality of his manpower was declining and partially as a device to boost the morale of the unfortunate conscripts of 1813–1814.

Higher Formations—Before the Revolution the French Army was the only one to accept the notion of using divisional organization on campaign and actually had a perma-

French Army Corps Organization

St. Cyr's XIV. Corps at Dresden
August 26-27 1813

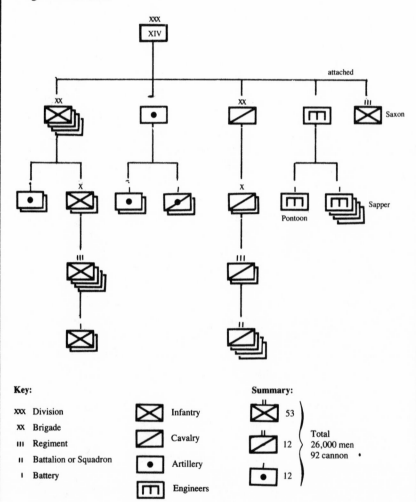

Key:

xxx	Division		
xx	Brigade		
iii	Regiment		
ii	Battalion or Squadron		
i	Battery		

Infantry
Cavalry
Artillery
Engineers

Summary:

53
12
12

Total
26,000 men
92 cannon •

Notes: St. Cyr's XIV. Corps was fairly typical of French corps organization in the latter period of the wars. By this time, Napoleon's armies had grown so large that it had become convenient to number divisions serially through the army, rather than identify them by division commander; St. Cyr thus had the 42nd, 43rd, 44th, and 45th Divisions of Infantry and the 10th of Cavalry. Note that one infantry brigade in each division had only three regiments, and that one regiment in each brigade had but one battalion. Similarly, one brigade of the cavalry division had only one regiment.

nent peacetime organization based on brigades and divisions, with two regiments to a brigade and two brigades to a division. This greatly facilitated training and other preparations for war, since higher organizations did not have to be improvised at the last moment. But the use of brigades and divisions also made battlefield command and control easier, for it reduced the number of people in direct communication with the commanding officer. One reason for the French success in the Revolutionary Wars was this organizational advantage, for all French field forces were organized as divisions, though few actually conformed to the authorized table of organization, with two demi-brigades of line infantry and one of light, for about 7500 men and 18 cannon. None of France's enemies managed any formal organization above the brigade. Moreover French organization got better. By the late 1790s French field commanders were informally grouping divisions into yet higher commands, usually dubbing the grouping a "wing-" or "body-of-the-army," which latter term became permanent, *corps d'armée*. Napoleon adopted the corps as a formal command echelon on a permanent basis, and eventually introduced divisional and corps organization for cavalry as well.

The army corps varied between two and four divisions, plus a detachment of medium artillery, and usually a little cavalry, some engineers, and some train personnel as well. Each division generally had two brigades and a battery or two of lighter guns, for a paper total of eight or twelve battalions, some 4000 to 10,000 men, and six or twelve cannon. Napoleon maintained his corps, and particularly his divisions, on a fairly permanent basis, keeping the same regiments together for years at a time, usually under the same commanders. By tailoring the command of each marshal to his particular talents, Napoleon further improved his already excellent organization. It was not before 1805 that France's enemies began adopting the division as a normal command echelon, and several years more before the corps became common, but even then Allied use of army corps was never as sophisticated as that of France.

GRAND STRATEGY

Grand strategy deals with the fundamental question of why a nation takes up arms. Under the Old Regime the answer was simple, for war was an instrument of the Crown, to be used in order to gain a disputed province or to secure some commercial advantage or to establish the rights of the sovereign, all essentially limited objectives. The advent of the French Revolution brought about a significant change, for the enemies of France sought not limited gains but rather the cancellation of the Revolution and the restoration of the Old Regime. This made the wars of Revolutionary France struggles for survival, obliging the Republic to tap the full resources of the most populous and powerful nation in Europe. This led to France's triumphs in the period 1794 through 1798. But with the threat of imminent disaster removed, France faltered. Seizing power in 1799, Napoleon restored firm central direction to France and soon restored luster to her arms once more.

Napoleon initially undertook wars in the spirit of, and as the heir to, the Revolution. The frontiers attained by France during the Consulate (1799–1804) had to be secured by force of arms during the early years of the Empire (1804–1807). But victory is a heady brew and Napoleon soon became intoxicated with it. His ambitions alone became sufficient grounds for war. The invasion of Spain, the campaign of 1809 against Austria, and the invasion of Russia, were all dictated by his personal ambition rather than the genuine needs of France. His regime grew oppressive just as men throughout Europe were imbibing the ideals of the Revolution—*liberté, égalité, fraternité*. The Revolution and the Empire inspired reform among France's opponents and they too soon began to tap the tremendous potential of nationalism. As late as 1813 and 1814, in the face of a united Europe and after massive defeats, Napoleon could have had peace with enlarged frontiers. But even in defeat his ambition knew no bounds, and he refused to settle for anything less than the Grand Empire of 1809–1812. And thus, desiring all, he ended with nothing.

STRATEGY

Napoleon recognized that victory lay in the destruction of the enemy's will to resist. Success on the battlefield was the quickest way to attain this goal. To assure success in the field required careful planning and, especially, careful conduct of operations. Napoleon used five quite simple principles to guide the development of his operational plans designed to hasten the attainment of victory.

- The primary objective is the destruction of the enemy's armies.
- All forces must concentrate on the task of attaining the objective.
- Operations must be designed to surprise and confuse the enemy.
- Every effort must be made to render the enemy helpless through the severance of his lines of supply, communications, and retreat.
- The security of French forces must be carefully guarded to prevent surprise.

When preparing for a campaign Napoleon sought to gather as much information as possible. In the months and weeks before operations actually commenced he would begin to collect information. In addition to reading an enormous number and variety of books bearing on the enemy and the theater of operations, he studied the copious volumes of intelligence reports forwarded by the agents that he had scattered throughout Europe. Nothing escaped his attention, for he believed firmly that everything had an effect on the conduct of war. Thus he would peruse works of military and political history, accounts of the state of roads and bridges in the proposed area of operations, reports on the personalities and habits of the principal enemy commanders, studies of the religion and folklore of the enemy, data on local patterns of food stockpiling and distribution. He sought not merely to understand the material resources of his foe and the nature of the theater of operations, but also to comprehend the character of the enemy,

French Strategic March Order
The *Bataillon Carré* in Action

The *bataillon carré,* or "battalion square," was Napoleon's preferred formation for the advance, permitting the use of parallel roads which greatly facilitated rapid movement, yet did not dangerously disperse the army.

Phase I. The army, advancing in the direction of the presumed location of the enemy (1) behind a screen of cavalry (2), is deployed so that each corps is not more than one or two days' march from its neighbor, and each is assigned a specific role, such as Advanced Guard (3), Right (4) and Left (5) Flank Guard, and Reserve (6), the "front" of the army covering some 50 to 60 kilometers.

Phase II. The location of the enemy being reported on the right flank of the army (1), the cavalry shifts (2) around to screen that flank more effectively, while the entire army changes direction of march to the right, and the corps change their roles, so that there is a new Advanced Guard (3), new Right (4) and Left (5) Flank Guards, and a new Reserve (6), the "front" of the army beginning to narrow to about 40 to 50 kilometers.

Phase III. The location of the enemy being confirmed as on the (new) right flank (1), the cavalry shifts around the perimeter of the army once more (2), and the corps again change roles, so that there is again a new Advanced Guard (3), new Right (4) and new Left (5) Flank Guards, and a new Reserve (6), which all advance to contact along a "front" which has already narrowed to 30 or 40 kilometers, and is growing narrower still.

Alternative Modes of Advance. The *bataillon carré* permitted a variety of alternative deployments on the line of advance; thus the army could advance in a lozenge, as illustrated in the example, or in a wedge formation, or in a right or left echelon, or frontally, with the center or the right or the left strengthened. The critical elements in the use of the *bataillon carré* was that the entire advance be screened by the cavalry and that the individual army corps be no more than 20 to 40 kilometers apart, which could be covered easily in one or two days of marching, and less by forced marches.

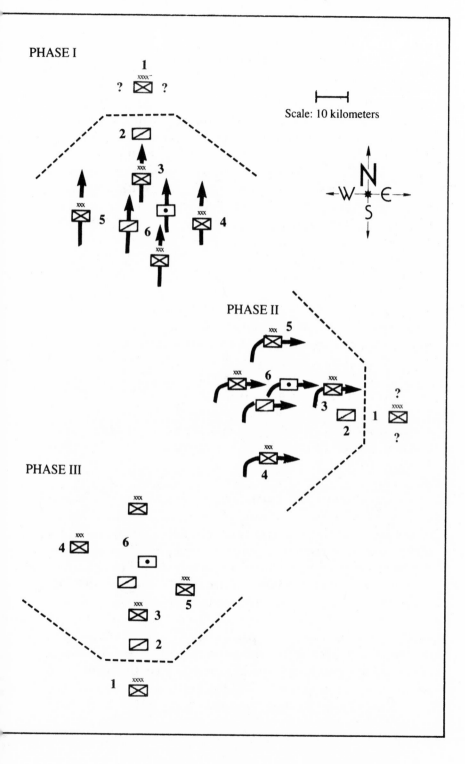

from the lowest soldier to the highest commander, realizing
that war is not merely a clash of physical resources, but also
one of character and will.

Napoleon used this mass of information to formulate the
general outlines of his plans, all within the framework of his
basic principles. With a full understanding that war, more
than any other human endeavor, is subject to chance, Napoleon avoided meticulous planning. His instructions were
general directives to his subordinates. After outlining the
expected course and objectives of the campaign, he would
indicate the particular missions of the various corps commanders, arrange command and communications relation-
ships, and establish lines of advance. With an unusually
keen awareness of the character and talents of his marshals
and generals, Napoleon tried to assign to each a mission
and a command best suited to his abilities. Thus, Marshal
Ney could be trusted to do a fine job if assigned no more
than 5000 or 10,000 men and a mission calling for absolute
courage and little cerebration, while Marshal Davout could
be confidently entrusted with a command of any size and a
mission of any nature, and Murat, while totally unsuited for
virtually anything else, was a remarkable cavalry commander once his mission had been explained to him. This
customizing of command and mission also served the useful
function of confusing the enemy, for in a given campaign
the size of the corps often varied considerably.

The creation of permanent army corps enabled Napoleon
to practice what may be termed "dispersed concentration"
of his forces. As each corps was essentially a small army of
all arms, it was capable of considerable operational independence. This was particularly useful with regard to Napoleon's techniques of strategic approach. During the advance
to contact, each corps was assigned a separate route of
march insofar as this was possible. Care was taken so that all
such lines of advance were parallel and no more than one
or two days' march apart, this being the essence of de Bourcet's strategic proposals. During the advance, the army
would rapidly converge toward the generally assumed location of the enemy. During the Jena Campaign of 1806, for

example, Napoleon's front was reduced from some 200 miles on October 6 to little more than 40 miles by October 12 while the army advanced over 100 miles into enemy territory; in the same period the Prussian Army had actually increased its dispersal! This sort of lightning movement to concentration frequently discomforted his enemies.

The advance of the army would take place behind a screen of light cavalry, with some stiffening from more heavily armed troopers. Their mission was twofold, to seek out the enemy and to deny him information. When the enemy's main body had been located, the nearest corps would advance to contact, becoming the advanced guard. Its function would be to hold the enemy in place until the main body of the army arrived. Generally a single army corps was sufficiently strong to exert considerable pressure for at least a day, ample time for the adjacent corps to move up to its support. As these corps arrived they would be fed into the battle, while the cavalry regrouped in the rear to become part of the reserve. A full-scale battle would then be possible.

While a straightforward advance to contact with the enemy was always a viable option, Napoleon much preferred more creative strategies. He had two favorites, the "Strategy of the Central Position" and the "*manoeuvre sur les derrières*—the maneuver about the rear." Each was suited to different circumstances and Napoleon used each throughout his career, though the latter, more commonly known as the "Strategy of the Indirect Approach," was undoubtedly his favorite.

The Strategy of the Indirect Approach—This could be termed Napoleon's "strategy of superiority," to be used when Napoleon had plenty of manpower and maneuvering room. It was simultaneously more sophisticated and more dangerous than "the central position." Essentially it entailed a vast turning movement in the face of the enemy. One or two corps would be detached to pin the attention of the enemy to his front. Meanwhile, Napoleon would take the bulk of his army on a swift, wide march around one of the enemy's

Napoleonic Strategic Concepts

The map and diagrams in this section are designed to illustrate Napoleon's favorite strategic maneuvers. In practice, of course, Napoleon suited his strategic designs to the particular situation confronting him, so these diagrams should be taken as general guides only.

Key to Strategic Diagrams

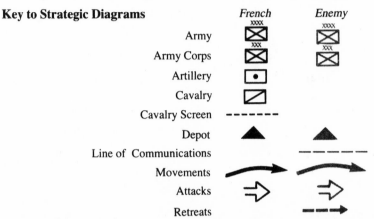

	French	Enemy
Army		
Army Corps		
Artillery		
Cavalry		
Cavalry Screen		
Depot		
Line of Communications		
Movements		
Attacks		
Retreats		

The Campaign against Prussia in October of 1806 is one of the finest examples of Napoleon's use of the *manoeuvre sur les derrières*, or indirect approach. By October 6 Napoleon had established his base of operations at Würzburg, and had concentrated some 180,000 men in an area only some 95 miles across and about 75 miles deep in northern Bavaria (1 on the map), at a time when the Prussians and their Saxon allies had not yet completed their concentration, having some 90,000 men north of the Thuringian Forest (2), a further 40,000 southeastward of that, in Saxony, and some deep in the rear, along with large Russian armies which had barely begun moving. The Prussians expected that Napoleon would move directly upon them from his base area. Instead, forming a *bataillon carré* of three major groups (A 40,000 man Left Flank, a 50,000 strong Right Flank, and a 70,000 strong Main Body), he pushed his forces northeastward behind a thick screen of cavalry along three roughly parallel routes (3), using the Thuringian Forest as a "curtain of maneuver," to mask and screen the operation. The movement was conducted with almost total immunity, combat occurring only on October 10, when a division under Prince Louis Ferdinand of Prussia was soundly thrashed at Saalfeld, the Prince losing his life in the process. This incident served to alert the Prussians to the French maneuver and they attempted to shift front, fall back, and reconcentrate at the same time. This proved impossible, as Napoleon's army began turning northward and then westward (4), threatening the Prussians' communications with their depots. On October 13 Marshal Jean Lannes, one of the finest advanced guardsmen in the French Army, encountered the Prussians in the vicinity of Jena, pinning them, and sending riders spurring back to report to Napoleon. Next day saw the overwhelming French victories of Jena and Auerstädt.

The Strategy of the Indirect Approach as illustrated by the Campaign Against Prussia in 1806

Situation and General Outline of Movements October 6 through October 13.

The Strategy of the Central Position

The Strategy of the Central Position was Napoleon's "strategy of inferiority." When confronted with two separate enemy forces of equal or greater strength he strove to get between the enemy armies to prevent their juncture, and then, turning first on one and then on the other, to defeat them in separate battles. This strategy fitted well with the Allied preference for the so-called "Concentric Advance," in which several armies converge toward a particular objective from widely dispersed points of origin. It was used with tremendous effect in Italy in 1796, during the Campaign of 1805, and during the opening phases of the Campaigns of 1809, 1813, and 1814, but failed disastrously at Waterloo.

Phase I. Having located the enemy armies (1a . . . 1b), the French cavalry (2) presses into the void between them, closely followed by their Advanced Guard (3), while the Main Body of their army (4) moves up behind a thick screen of cavalry (5), with the last arriving elements constituting the Reserve (6).

Phase II. While cavalry forces (1) prevent contact between the two enemy armies, Napoleon dispatches a strong force as a "Corps of Observation" (2) to keep the morally or materially weaker enemy army occupied, while he takes the bulk of the Main Body (3) and the Reserve (4) and engages the stronger enemy army in battle, defeating it.

Phase III. As the defeated stronger enemy force attempts to retreat (1), Napoleon assigns a reinforced corps or two (2) to pursue it and prevent it from coming to the aid of the weaker enemy, while he takes the Main Body (3) to the support of the "Corps of Observation" (4) confronting the other enemy army, inflicting a second defeat on the foe (5).

Phase IV. With both enemy armies in retreat (1a . . . 1b), Napoleon throws his cavalry and additional forces (2a . . . 2b) after them in pursuit, while regrouping the balance of his army with the intention of pressing them forward as quickly as possible (3).

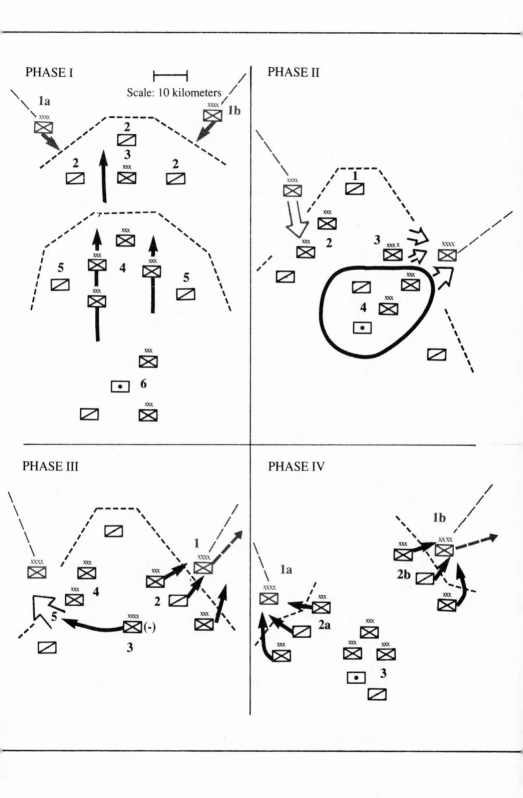

PHASE I

Scale: 10 kilometers

PHASE II

PHASE III

PHASE IV

strategic flanks, behind a thick screen of cavalry, optimally
with some substantial geographic feature providing a "curtain of maneuver." As he advanced toward the enemy's
rear, he would thrust a corps or two and some cavalry forward to prevent reinforcements from coming up, and then
fall upon the enemy from the rear, having severed his lines
of communication and retreat, and hopefully annihilating
his forces. It was this maneuver which brought about the
smashing strategic victories of Ulm in 1805, Jena-Auerstädt
in 1806, and Friedland in 1807. There was great risk in this
strategy. Only bold execution, swift movement, and aggressive use of the pinning forces and the cavalry could make it
work. If the enemy gained any notion of what was afoot, as
in 1807 when the Russians intercepted an order revealing
Napoleon's intentions before Eylau, he might slip away, or
even attack the relatively vulnerable marching columns.

The Strategy of the Central Position—This strategy may be
termed Napoleon's "strategy of inferiority," used in situations where the French Army was weaker than its enemy,
but the latter was dispersed in two or more rather widely
separated concentrations, such as during the opening
phases of both the Campaign of 1809 and that of Waterloo,
and with remarkable brilliance in the face of overwhelming
odds in 1814, culminating in the triple victories of Champ-
paubert, Montmirail, and Vauchamps. This strategy necessitated bold leadership, careful timing, and aggressive
movement, for it required the army to get *between* the
enemy concentrations, thereby preventing them from
uniting. By moving swiftly into the central position, Napoleon could concentrate the bulk of his forces against the
more threatening enemy contingent and seek a decisive battle, while a corps or two undertook to hold off the other
enemy contingent for as long as possible. When the first
body was defeated, a corps or two would be sent in pursuit,
while Napoleon shifted the attentions of the rest of the
army to the support of the probably hard-pressed screening
forces before the balance of the enemy. A second decisive
engagement, a second pursuit, and the campaign would be
well on the road to a successful conclusion. Things could go

wrong, of course. The enemy could discern the French intentions and withdraw, as occurred in April 1809, or a battle might not turn out as decisively as expected or the pursuit might be poorly handled, allowing a defeated contingent to march to the support of its comrades, both of which occurred in 1815 before Waterloo.

Napoleon often used his two favorite strategies interchangeably. In 1805, for example, he used the indirect approach to place himself in the central position between the Austrian and Russian armies. During the Jena Campaign the following year he did it again. In 1813 he took advantage of his central position to undertake a series of indirect approaches, though his victories at Lützen and Bautzen were by no means as decisive as he had hoped. To be truly decisive, a victory had to result not merely in the defeat of the enemy, but also in pursuing him *à outrance* to total destruction. This desirable goal was but rarely achieved operationally. In Italy in March and April of 1797 he managed to chase the Austrians almost all the way back to Vienna, and in 1806, in the 23 days following the Prussian disaster at Jena-Auerstädt, French armies totally overran Prussia against trifling resistance. A few weeks more and the French were knocking at the gates of Warsaw. The opportunities for such a stupendous pursuit came but rarely, for the foe had to be smashed with minimal damage to one's own forces, which would have to lose no time in undertaking a renewed advance.

Allied strategy in the long wars pales beside that of Napoleon. The bulk of his opponents were able, but unspectacular. The Duke of Wellington was the one exception, being superb at comprehending the overall strategic picture, having some skill at executing the indirect approach, and being a master of retreat, always one of the truest tests of generalship. Austria's Archduke Charles was able, but uninspired. Before Ratisbon on April 19, 1809, he passed up a perfect opportunity to use the strategy of the central position against Napoleon. The best strategy most of Napoleon's opponents could come up with was to shove armies in his direction. Indeed, given endless manpower, this strategy of

The Napoleonic Battle

Napoleon's two basic battle plans are illustrated here. As always, the actual details of his use of either plan were dictated by the nature of the tactical situation.

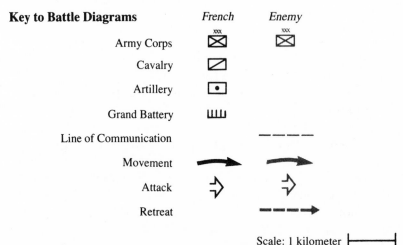

Key to Battle Diagrams

	French	Enemy
Army Corps		
Cavalry		
Artillery		
Grand Battery		
Line of Communication		
Movement		
Attack		
Retreat		

Scale: 1 kilometer

The Battle of Maneuver

Napoleon's favorite battlefield tactic, the Battle of Maneuver, maximized French superiority in artillery and at executing rapid movements. Austerlitz, Jena, and Eylau, three of his greatest victories, were all essentially battles of maneuver, as was Auerstädt, Marshal Davout's brilliant triumph over the Prussians on the day of Jena.

Phase I. As soon as contact is made with the enemy (1), the French Advanced Guard (2) engages them, in order to pin the foe in place. As the Main Body of the Army arrives (3), its component corps are fed into the fight to establish a strong battleline, while Napoleon constitutes a reserve out of the later arriving corps, the Guard, and elements of the cavalry and artillery (4).

Phase II. With a major frontal action developing (1), Napoleon concentrates a "Grand Battery" (2), which commences a severe bombardment of what appears to be the weaker enemy flank, while shifting strong forces (3) in a maneuver against and around that same flank, and keeping some forces—usually the Guard and the bulk of the Cavalry—in Reserve (4).

Phase III. When the enemy withdraws his flank under the bombardment of the "Grand Battery" and the threat of envelopment (1) and begins to shift his Reserve (2) to support it, Napoleon throws his Reserve in against the strained portion of the enemy's lines (3), supported by a general advance of all his forces (4), while holding out considerable light cavalry and some infantry as a *corps de chasse* (5), with which to pursue the foe when he breaks.

Phase IV. With the enemy broken and streaming away in retreat (1) behind its rear guards (2a . . . 2b), Napoleon begins a pursuit with the *corps de chasse* (3) and other relatively unbattered portions of his army, while resting and reconcentrating the balance of his forces (4) in order to resume the advance with them as quickly as possible.

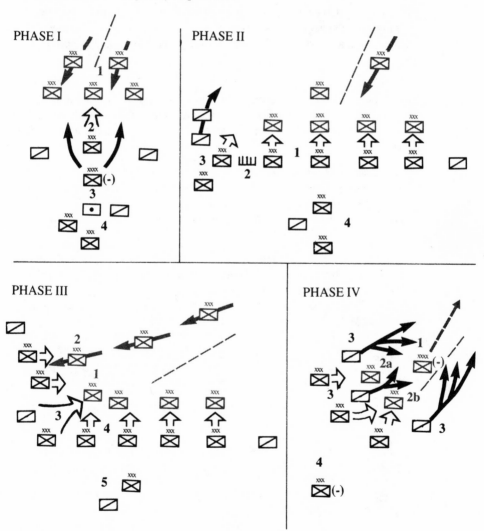

The Battle of Attrition

The battle of attrition, a costly, frontal slugging-match, was not Napoleon's preferred battlefield tactic, but was often forced upon him by circumstances, such as failure in an attempt at a battle of maneuver, or where the terrain was unsuited to one, or the troops were insufficiently skilled to execute one. The result was always a bloody battle, sometimes a great victory such as Wagram, but more often a marginal success such as Borodino, or even a disastrous defeat such as Waterloo.

Phase I. Confronting the enemy (1) with his full strength, Napoleon commences a general action (2) while concentrating a "Grand Battery" (3) against what appears to be a weaker portion of their front, and gathering his Reserves, the Guard, and Cavalry (4).

Phase II. With both sides heavily engaged (1), Napoleon undertakes localized attacks (2) to pin enemy forces in place, divert their attention, "feel out" their positions, and to draw their reserves into action (3) while concentrating the Reserve (4) for an attack, though still holding out a *corps de chasse* (5).

Phase III. While the enemy position weakened (1) by the constant artillery pounding, Napoleon throws in the bulk of his Reserve infantry or cavalry, or sometimes both (2) in a powerful frontal attack, which smashes into and through the enemy lines (3), while the *corps de chasse* (4) prepares to advance.

Phase IV. With the enemy broken into two separate wings and streaming away in retreat (1a . . . 1b), Napoleon begins a pursuit with the *corps de chasse* and the less exhausted elements of the army (2), while resting and reconcentrating the bulk of his forces in order to resume the advance as soon as possible (3).

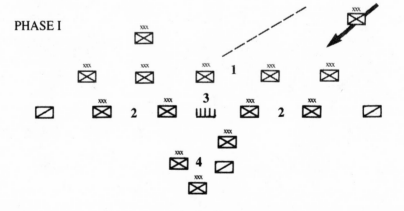

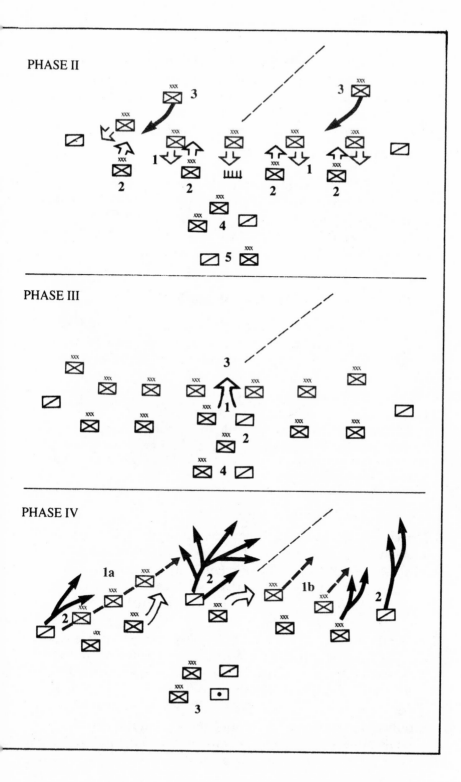

the concentric advance—advancing armies from all directions—ultimately led to Napoleon's defeat in 1813 in Germany and again in 1814 in France. For although this strategy enabled Napoleon to win numerous victories using the central position, practically conceded to him, his increasingly outnumbered forces could not win every battle. Moreover, Napoleon's enemies grew wary. The more often he defeated them, the more they learned how to avoid those defeats. If the concentric advance was an uninspired strategy, it was one that they had confidence in, for Napoleon might win some battles, but could not be everywhere at once, and they would surely win the last battle.

CONDUCT OF BATTLE

Once the strategy had brought the enemy to the battlefield, Napoleon had but one purpose: destruction. He preferred to fight offensively under all circumstances, even when on the defensive. Normally he began to plan his battles even as the reinforcing army corps were marching up to the support of the advanced guard on the firing line. He had only two basic battle plans, the "Battle of Maneuver" and the "Battle of Attrition," shifting easily from one to the other as the circumstances dictated, even in the midst of combat itself.

The Battle of Maneuver—Napoleon's favorite grand tactical device, the battle of maneuver was characterized by movement supported by massive firepower, While the main body of the French army held the enemy's attention to his front, strong forces supported by a "Grand Battery" of dozens of heavy cannon fell upon one of his flanks, crushing it, and then rolling up the rest of his line, and throwing in cavalry to begin the pursuit. Normally the development of this type of operation required some superiority in numbers, but at Auerstädt (October 14, 1806) Marshal Davout managed to roll up *both* Prussian flanks although outnumbered by over 40%. The primary advantage of this type of battle was that it inflicted a major defeat on the enemy at minimal cost, such as those at Austerlitz (December 2, 1805) and Friedland (June 14, 1807). But things could go wrong. A quick movement of reserves in the enemy's rear could thicken up his threatened flank. And an enemy deployed with strong natural supports on his flanks would be relatively immune to such a tactic. In such a case brute force would have to prevail.

The Battle of Attrition—The battle of attrition was a frontal slugging match in which firepower was poured into the enemy in enormous amounts until he appeared to be weakening, and then great masses of men would be thrown in to smash their way through his lines. Victory was secured by sheer weight of shot and shell and manpower. When the enemy crumbled, additional forces would be pushed forward, to complete and exploit the victory. Such a battle was costly, and not merely to the loser. Indeed, the victor could easily come away as battered as the vanquished. But there were times when no other course was possible. Napoleon opted for the battle of attrition in about a third of his battles. Some were smashing victories such as Wagram (July 5–6, 1809), others were marginal successes at best, such as Borodino (September 7, 1812), and several were disastrous defeats, such as Waterloo (June 18, 1815). There was much that could go wrong in such a battle. The enemy might prove stronger, or more resilient than anticipated; the infantry and cavalry might be thrown in too soon; or the enemy might have a trick or two up his sleeve, such as Wellington's reverse slope defenses, which put the bulk of his forces behind convenient hills and ridges, screening them from the brunt of the fire of a French "Grand Battery," so that he could commit them only when the French cavalry and infantry approached, as he did with remarkable skill at Waterloo, the only time the two best generals of the age confronted each other.

TACTICS

Regardless of the type of battle he chose to fight, Napoleon made use of essentially the same set of tactics, inherited

French Tactical Formations

The following diagrams are designed to illustrate the basic tactical formations employed by the French during the Revolutionary and Napoleonic Wars. As variations on the formations were common, it should be realized that the deployments depicted are idealized. Note also that the diagrams assume that the French regimental table of organization of 1807 is used.

Scale: 35 meters ├──┤

Key

Location of the Enemy	_____/	*Voltigeur* Company	▮ V
Skirmishers	– – – – – –	Battalion	⊔
Line Infantry Company	▮	Regiment	⊔
Grenadier Company	▮ G	Regimental Guns	⊔⊔

Ordre Profond
Regimental Attack in Battalion Columns

The regiment deploys in three battalion columns on an overall front of about 350 meters or less, depending upon intervals.

A-A-A: Voltigeur companies deployed in skirmish order.

B-B-B: The battalions are deployed as columns as much as 70 meters apart, providing room to deploy into line if necessary. Each battalion is deployed in a "column of divisions" of two companies abreast, one division three meters behind the other. Each division is approximately 75 men wide and three deep, occupying approximately 75 meters of front and three of depth, for a battalion "block" of 450 men.

C-C-C: Grenadier companies held in reserve.

D-D-D: Regroupment positions for the Voltigeurs when the columns make their attack.

Variants: Battalions in company columns, with one company behind the other on a front of about 35 meters three ranks deep, with perhaps five paces between companies. Grenadiers might be distributed by platoons as an additional rank of the first division, lending their greater courage and steadiness to the assault, and raising battalion strength to about 565. Both Grenadier and Voltigeur companies could be constituted as an additional "division," forming the front of the battalion, raising the strength to about 675 men. Regimental guns, when available, could be deployed singly on the flanks of the regiment and between the battalions, or in pairs between the battalions, or held in reserve. One battalion could be deployed somewhat forward and two drawn back to form a "broad arrow."

Note on Massive Columns: from 1809 onward Napoleon made increasing use of large columns comprising entire regiments and brigades, and eventually even whole divisions and corps. At Waterloo, for example, one division of seven battalions was deployed as a column, with each battalion formed in line, one behind the other at four pace intervals, forming a massive block of 4,200 men some 180 meters wide and 50 deep, presenting an enormous target for Allied artillery. Massive columns were necessitated by the declining quality of Napoleon's manpower and, while they could bring victory, their use only furthered the deterioration of his human resources.

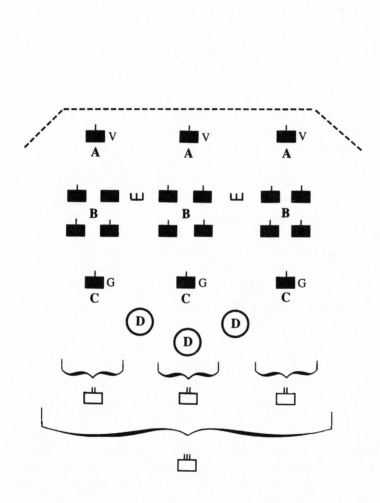

from the Republic, which had adopted and polished the
final reforms under the Monarchy.

As in every period in history, tactics during the Napoleonic Wars were dictated by the nature of the arms available. For the entire eighteenth century the standard
infantry arm was the musket, with its low rate of fire and
poor accuracy. The evolution of tactics in the period had
engendered considerable controversy. In the period before
the French Revolution a remarkably flexible system of tactics had been worked out. These were the basis of the tremendous tactical superiority of the armies of Revolutionary
and Imperial France. Reflecting the experience of the
Seven Years' War, all combined fire and movement in varying degrees.

One of the most critically important aspects of French
tactics was the use of skirmishers. A portion of each regiment was supposed to be trained as light infantry, and a
number of entire regiments were also assigned this role. At
the onset of a battle, the light infantry would spread themselves thinly across the front of the army and, making use
of available cover, maintain a harassing fire against the
enemy. The Austrians and the British also made considerable use of light troops, though rarely on the scale that
the French achieved on occasion. Frequently as many as a
third of the troops available to a commander would be put
out as skirmishers, while he deployed the balance of his
forces in anticipation of more serious combat, using one of
the preferred tactical orders.

Column—Column, or *ordre profond,* grouped the troops
into a massed block to be used in shock action, as a battering ram to smash into the enemy. A regiment in column
could have three battalion blocks with a front of ten men
and a depth of five, separated by several yards, with the
whole formation having a frontage and depth of no more
than ten meters by five, or some similar arrangement, such
as a solid regimental block, or a column of battalions in line.
A column could move rapidly under virtually any conditions of ground or combat. It had the advantage of being

Ordre Mince

Regimental Deployment in Line.

The regiment deploys in one line on a front of approximately 420 to 500 meters.

A-A-A: Voltigeur companies deployed in skirmish order.

B-B-B: Line companies deployed in three ranks of approximately 35 men each, on a frontage of 35 meters with a depth of three, for a battalion front of about 150 meters with 450 men.

C-C-C: Grenadier companies held in reserve.

D-D-D: Regroupment positions for Voltigeurs.

Variants: Grenadier companies could take their place in the line, raising battalion frontage to about 185 meters and strength to about 565, with regimental frontage rising to about 600 meters. Voltigeur companies could do likewise, raising battalion frontage to about 220 meters with some 675 men, and regimental frontage to about 700 meters. Should regimental guns be available, they deploy in pairs on the flanks of the regiment unless held in reserve, or placed in pairs in the line between the battalions.

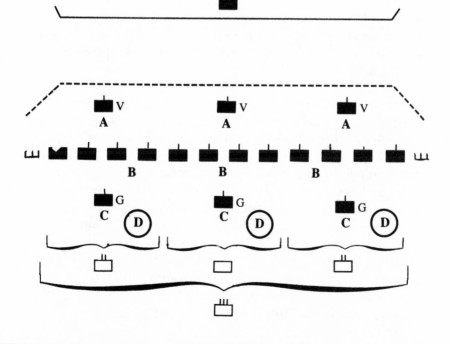

useful for green troops, since the demands on training and
discipline were minimal. Column was the ideal tool for
smashing enemy formations rapidly after having softened
them up with firepower. But it had severe disadvantages as
well, for it was incapable of being engaged in sustained fire
combat, being able to deliver no more than 40 to 60 rounds
a minute to its front, and perhaps 60 to 90 on the flank.
Moreover, it presented a considerable target, particularly to
the artillery, which could tear great swaths through the formation.

Line—Line, or *ordre mince*, was the usual formation for
protracted combat. The troops would be deployed on a
broad front in two or three lines, permitting each to fire his
musket at the enemy. Given a regiment of 1500 men deployed in line, some 3000 rounds a minute could be maintained in combat on a front of about 700 meters, making
the formation ideal for developing sustained firepower in
great volume. But line was highly vulnerable to flank attacks, able to concentrate not more than eight to twelve
rounds a minute on the flanks. Moreover, line was ill-suited
to rapid battlefield maneuvers, since it was difficult to maintain alignments while maneuvering. It was also quite useless
for green troops, since it required considerable training and
discipline when used in combat.

Mixed Order—Mixed order, or *ordre mixte*, was a combination of line and column, and the best French troops were
capable of using it with considerable skill. Mixed order normally involved deploying one battalion of a regiment in line
between two in column. The line battalion developed the
sustained firepower necessary to soften up the enemy, and
the battalions in column prepared to attack with the bayonet at the opportune moment. In battle, a well-trained
regiment, such as those Napoleon had in the period 1805–
1807, could switch from one to either of the other two orders quite handily. At Auerstädt, Morand's division
changed its deployment five times in the course of about as
many hours, going from columns of march to a line of bat-

Ordre Mixte
Regiment in Mixed Order

In mixed order, a regiment was deployed both in line and in column, occupying a front of about 300 meters.

A-A-A: Voltigeur companies deployed in skirmish order.

B-B-B: battalions deployed in "columns of divisions," as in *ordre profond*.

C-C-C: battalion deployed in line as in *ordre mince*.

D-D-D: Grenadier companies held in reserve.

E-E-E: Regroupment positions for Voltigeurs.

Variants: As for both *ordre profond* and *ordre mince*. In addition there was occasionally found a variant in which one battalion was deployed in column between two in line, for a regimental frontage of about 375 meters. When regimental guns were available, they were usually deployed in pairs between the battalions or held in reserve.

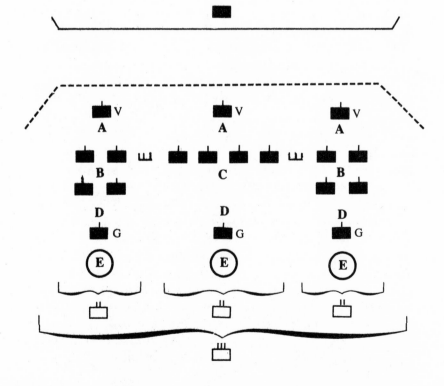

talion columns to line proper to square and then back to a line of battalion columns.

As the infantry was the queen of the battlefield, the tactics of the other arms were essentially designed to support the infantry. The artillery's principal functions were to prepare for the attack of the infantry by battering the enemy's formations, and to assist in the defense of the infantry by smashing the enemy's attacking forces. A variety of different types of ammunition were available to permit the artillery to fulfill its role. The battlefield role of the cavalry was rather restricted. It could be used in the charge, as a massed battering ram designed to smash through the enemy, but that was practically its only tactical function and it could be frustrated by the use of square, whereby the infantry presented a solid wall of muskets and bayonets bolstered by artillery. Though squares could break, it was the cavalry which did so more frequently.

The flexible French tactics were remarkably effective in action. However, their use required experienced personnel. So long as Napoleon's wars were both short and victorious, the butcher's bills did not seriously impair the quality of his manpower. Through the ongoing *amalgame,* the veteran cadres could easily absorb the new recruits and acclimate them to the vagaries of military life and practice with little difficulty. But after 1807 both the wars and the casualty lists got longer. The Spanish adventure which Napoleon launched in 1808 began a hemorrhage of seasoned manpower which he could not staunch and which grew worse and worse as time went on. As the irreplaceable cadres were lost, the overall quality of the army began to decline. By 1809 the French skirmishing capabilities had begun to slip. Tactical finesse gave way to brute force as Napoleon had to rely more heavily on the free expenditure of manpower. At Wagram he essayed the first massive column, a hollow square of some 28 battalions in column. It achieved a breakthrough, but at considerable cost. Nevertheless, Napoleon was forced to make use of massive columns with increasing frequency in the closing days of the Empire. With the veterans scattered dead from Lisbon to Moscow, it was the best he could do.

MUSKETRY

The musket was the principal military firearm of the Revolutionary and Napoleonic Wars. A smooth-bore, muzzle-loading piece, the musket had been introduced in the early part of the sixteenth century, but it did not attain perfection until the middle of the eighteenth, after the development of the socket bayonet, the flintlock firing mechanism, and the iron ramrod, coupled with the discovery of cheaper sources of nitrates and more efficient processes for the production of gunpowder, which permitted greater reliance on firepower. Thereafter, the musket became the dominant battlefield arm, rendering excellent service until well into the nineteenth century. Nevertheless, the musket had severe limitations, for it was difficult to handle, had a poor rate of fire, and was remarkably inaccurate.

Loading the long (from 95 to 150 cm) and heavy (from 4.5 to 7 kg) weapon was by no means a simple task. Under ideal circumstances a well-trained man could manage up to six rounds a minute. In combat one or two was more likely. The procedure may be summarized in far less time than it actually consumed.

Grounding his piece, the musketeer held it steady with one hand while taking one of the 50 to 60 heavy (from 30 to 40 gram) paper-wrapped cartridges from his ammunition pouch. Biting the ball end of the cartridge off and retaining it in his teeth, the man would pour the powder down the barrel, tapping the butt of his piece on the ground once or twice in the process, to insure that some powder filled the priming cavity at the base of the tube. Then, spitting the ball into the barrel and jamming the paper wrapping in after it, he would take his ramrod and vigorously tamp everything down. Replacing the ramrod in its slot under the barrel, he then lifted the piece to his shoulder, cocked the flintlock mechanism, aimed, and fired.

Even without the pressures and panic of battle, this was a complicated process to follow. In the heat of battle much could go wrong. One could spill the powder on the ground or forget to ram the charge home or, having done so, neglect to remove the ramrod from the tube. One's powder could be damp or the flint worn. Misfires were common, and it was not unusual for a man to accidentally double or even triple-load a piece in the heat of battle, only to have it blow up in his face. Even in the best of circumstances a piece would begin to foul after ten or a dozen rounds, due partially to the uneven quality of gunpowder and also to the poor fit of ball to barrel.

Under the best conditions musketry was inaccurate. In battle it became even more so. In 1790, the Prussian Army conducted firing tests with its 1782 musket. The results were hardly impressive, given that the target, supposed to represent the front of an infantry company (32 m by 1.8 m) was actually a solid framework covering roughly 42% more surface area than would actually be occupied by the troops (30 m^2 rather than 52 m^2). Moreover, the firing troops were performing under ideal conditions, with no one shooting back.

PRUSSIAN MUSKETRY TRIALS OF 1790

RANGE	HITS
300 m	20%
200	25
140	40
70	70

More practical statistics suggest that in actual combat no more than 15% of the rounds fired hit anyone in actual combat, and frequently far fewer. It was this basic fact that molded tactics. Firepower could be lethal only if delivered in great volume on a relatively narrow front. By forming troops up virtually shoulder to shoulder in two or three lines one could maximize their fire effectiveness. If a regiment in line massed 1500 muskets, that would mean 3000 rounds a minute, which theoretically could be expected to inflict upward of 450 wounds at ranges under 70 meters, though some analysts have suggested that as few as six rounds were likely to be lethal. Moreover, 70 meters could be covered by troops at a fast walk in about a minute.

Far more accurate than the musket was the rifle. At the start of the wars all armies made some use of rifles, particularly by their light infantry. The rifle could be deadly at far greater ranges than the musket. But although considerably

Density of Front
Manpower and Firepower per Five Meters of Front

Order	Ranks	Men	RPM (Br)
Skirmish Line	1	1-2	2-4 (3-6)
Firing Line	1-2	4-8	8-16 (12-24)
Battle Line	2-3	15 +	30 (45 +)

Notes: *Order* is the type of action for which the troops are deployed; *Ranks* indicates the number of successive lines into which the troops so deployed were normally grouped; *Men* is the actual number of troops committed per five meters of front; *RPM* is the number of rounds per minute that could be expected from each five meters of front at least in the initial moments of an action, with *Br* indicating the number which British regulars could deliver; note that for rifles all figures should be halved. Skirmish order was designed to harass and annoy the enemy, softening him up for further action, but was incapable of resistng all but the feeblest attacks. Firing line was useful for providing security and could be used in sustained combat, being capable of resisting fairly serious attacks. Battle line was dense enough to engage in sustained, heavy fire or shock combat, whether as defender or attacker.

lighter than the contemporary musket, the rifle was even
more difficult to use and maintain, with a considerably
lower rate of fire, due to difficulties in loading properly to
attain the neccessary tight fit between barrel and bullet: in
some models one had to shove the bullet down the barrel
with a mallet! The British made the most extensive use of
rifles, equipping entire battalions with them for service as
skirmishers, but they had a particularly fine rifle, the Baker,
one of the first machined and mass-produced firearms in
history. The French abandoned their use of the rifle in
1807 by order of Napoleon himself, who thought them un-
necessarily expensive. Most other armies, however, continued to maintain some rifle-armed troops for special
duties.

There were several interesting aspects to the entire question of infantry firepower in the period. The British relied
heavily on meticulously trained manpower well supplied
with what must be termed "sporting" grade powder and
flints, and were thus able to develop and sustain a volume
of fire upward of 50% greater than anyone else. The Russians, plagued by a plethora of miscellanous types of equipment, inferior training, and poor quality powder, plus a
positive bias against firepower in favor of the bayonet, usually maintained a rate of fire considerably lower than the
contemporary norm, though their musket and rifle were
technically at least as good as anyone else's when used
properly. French muskets fouled more frequently than
British ones due to a coarser powder, but they were easier
to repair if seriously damaged, having a detachable barrel.
All armies, of course, relied on the bayonet for close combat, though it appears to have been far more important and
effective psychologically than in terms of actual casualty
causation.

ARTILLERY

Artillery became a maneuverable battlefield asset during the
wars of the Revolution, due largely to the reforms of
Gribeauval and men like the DuTeils, who redesigned guns
and carriages, reduced the weight of the pieces, reduced

MUSKETS AND RIFLES OF THE REVOLUTIONARY AND NAPOLEONIC WARS

COUNTRY	PIECE	CAL	WT	RPM	RANGE
Au	Musket, 1770/1798	17.5 mm	6.8 kg	2/4	70/140 m
Au	Jäger-Grenzer Rifle, 1795	15.0	3.6	.5/1	140/275
Au	Girondoni Air Rifle, 1795	12.7	5.0	3/6	80/120
Br	Tower Musket Mark III, *by* 1700	18.7	5.0	3/6	70/140
Br	Baker Rifle, 1800	16.2	4.3	1/2	140/275
Fr	Charleroi Musket, 1777	17.2	4.8	2/4	70/140
Pr	Potsdam Musket, 1782	19.5	5.7	2/4	70/140
Pr	Silesian Rifle	15.0	3.6	.5/1	140/275
Ru	Musket, 1805	19.1	5.2	1/2	80/150
Ru	Jäger Rifle, 1805	16.5	4.3	.5/1	150/250

Key: *Country: Au,* Austria; *Br,* Britain; *Fr,* France; *Pr,* Prussia; *Ru,* Russia. *Piece,* the customary name of the weapon, with the year of introduction where available. *Cal* is caliber in mm. *Wt* is weight of the piece in kg, without bayonet, which added an additional .5 to .8 kg depending upon country in question. *RPM* is rounds per minute, with sustainable given before maximum; note that the rate of fire of the Baker Rifle is for patched bullets; with unpatched ones the rate doubled but the effective range was halved. *Range* in meters, with normal effective given before maximum. The Girondoni air rifle was a radical innovation in infantry arms, being used to equip some Austrian light troops. It was approximately as effective as the contemporary musket and had the added advantage of being virtually silent in combat, but its use required carefully trained troops, a commodity which could not be provided under the pressures of sustained combat, resulting in its withdrawal in 1801.

and standardized the number of calibers, developed innovative tactics, and fostered the creation of a professional corps of artillerymen within the army. As the arm of service least affected by the initially unsettling effects of the Revolution, the artillery was the backbone of the Revolutionary Armies in the early part of the wars. Indeed, the great victory over the Prussians at Valmy (September 20, 1792), generally believed to have "saved" the Revolution, was essentially a demonstration of the superiority of the reformed French artillery.

Napoleon was himself a gunner, having entered the
Royal Army in 1784, serving under the younger DuTeil.
The training and experience he gained in this period
proved useful throughout his career, for Napoleon was the
first general to see the possibilities of using artillery in mass.
His first essay in the battlefield employment of Grand Battery tactics occurred at Castiglione (August 5, 1796), when
he massed little more than a dozen guns, a modest harbin-
ger of the scores which he would frequently employ later.
Upon attaining supreme power, Napoleon promoted
further reform in the artillery. He militarized the transpor-
tation of the guns, increased the proportion of horse artillery, which had become popular during the Republic, and
began the practice of retaining a fair proportion of his artillery at his direct disposal when on campaign. Throughout
his career he paid close attention to the condition of the
artillery, pressing for ever more effective reforms, such as
an even further reduction in the number of calibers, while
almost constantly increasing the strength of the arm. In
1805 he possessed a total of some 23,000 guns, howitzers,
and mortars, of which about 70% were in his favorite
battlefield calibers: 12-, 8-, and 4-pounders, plus 6" (24-
pounder) howitzers. In 1803 Napoleon decided that he
could eliminate both the 8-pounders and the 4-pounders in
favor of a new 6-pounder and subsequently made serious
efforts to do so, in order to facilitate still further the standardization of ammunition supply, equipment, and training, while permitting the savings realized by the reduction
to be translated into additional pieces. This decision was
dictated not merely by a belief that fewer calibers were
more desirable. He needed more guns, for he believed that
as the quality of his infantry declined the amount of
firepower required to support it had to be increased to attain the same degree of success. He believed that the op-
timum ratio of guns to troops was five per thousand,
though he was never able to do better than three per
thousand due to high losses, notably in his later campaigns,
a situation which also frustrated his efforts to further reduce the number of calibers.

Most armies eventually imitated French practice, though

BRITISH AND FRENCH FIELD ARTILLERY

PIECE	WT	LN	PRO	CHG	RNG	RPM	CREW	TEAM
Fr 12-Pdr	2.0	2.3	5.9	1.9	1.8	1	15	12
Br 12-Pdr	1.6	2.0	5.5	1.8	1.4	1	15	8–10
Br 9-Pdr	1.5	1.8	4.1	1.3	1.4	2	12	6–8
Fr 8-Pdr	1.4	2.0	3.9	1.3	1.5	2	13	8
Fr 6-Pdr	1.2	1.8	3.0	1.0	1.35	2–3	10	6
Br 6-Pdr	0.75	1.5	2.7	0.7	1.1	2–3	8	6
Fr 4-Pdr	0.95	1.6	1.9	0.7	1.2	2–3	8	6
Br 3-Pdr	0.4	1.1	1.3	0.4	1.2	3–4	6	2
Fr 6" Hwtzr	1.2	0.7	10.9	1.4	1.2	1	13	8
Br 5.5" Hwtzr	0.7	0.6	7.2	0.5	1.2	1	10	6

NOTES: The artillery of other powers was not generally dissimilar in characteristics. *Piece,* is the standard identification for the weapon. *Wt* is weight in metric ton. *Ln* is length of the barrel, or chase, in meters. *Pro,* projectile weight in kilograms, with shot for guns and shell for howitzers; note that the "poundage" ratings of the pieces are not useful guides to projectile weight, due to differences in the definition of the pound from country to country, as, for example, in the case of the old French pound which was actually about 8.3% heavier than the English pound. *Chg,* normal powder charge in kilograms required to fire the projectile its effective battlefield range. *Rng,* maximum range in kilometers, with shot and shell being effective at between half and two-thirds the indicated distance, but canister at no more than a third of it. *RPM,* sustainable number of rounds per minute. *Crew,* the normal complement of men required to serve the piece, its animals, and ammunition wagons. *Team,* the number of horses required to draw the piece efficiently. Ammunition: a 12-pounder usually had about 75 rounds at hand between immediate and reserve supplies. For lighter pieces, the amount was greater, a 3- or 4-pounder usually having upward of 150–175 rounds available. Normally, about a third of the ammunition available was canister.

few ever became as efficient with the arm as did the French. The British artillery was certainly the technical equal of the French during most of the wars, and indeed carried the reduction in calibers even further, by going from three types of guns (12-, 6-, and 3-pounders) plus one howitzer (5.5"/16 pounder) to a train of mostly 9-pounders plus howitzers after 1808. But British employment of artillery was hampered by an overall shortage of pieces, which never permitted the development of massed firepower. The result was that despite excellent personnel and equipment, the arm never realized its potential. Other armies were not as efficient as the British or the French. Most suffered from a plethora of calibers, though, of course, both the French and the British sometimes had to make do with odd pieces as well.

Organization—Although all armies maintained battalions and regiments of artillery for administrative purposes, these never served in the field, the tactical unit always being the battery. Almost universally, foot batteries fielded six guns and two howitzers while horse batteries had four guns and two howitzers, though the Russians favored eight guns and two howitzers for their foot artillery. A battery was actually composed of two elements: the battery proper, which comprised the guns with between 100 and 150 artillerymen, and a separate train squadron, of 75 to 150 men, which transported the spare ammunition, repair facilities, and extra equipment. The use of half-batteries was quite common in all armies, and Napoleon himself is said to have favored the permanent establishment of batteries at four guns and two howitzers, though he was unable to carry this notion into practice due to the difficulty of securing sufficient numbers of properly trained artillerymen.

Napoleon normally retained upward of 25% of his artillery in the general reserve, including a significant number of his beloved 12-pounders. He normally tried to attach a battery of 8- or 6-pounders to each infantry division and, from 1809, a detachment of two to four 4-pounders to each regiment as well. Cavalry divisions occasionally were assigned a battery of horse artillery but not always, these being normally retained as part of the reserve or assigned to the overall cavalry command. Army corps customarily had a battery or two of 12-pounders, plus one 6-pounder of the horse artillery as a mobile reserve. Wellington, though consistently short of artillery, tried to assign one or two batteries to each division, and usually gave considerable freedom to his gunners. The Russians normally assigned from three to six batteries of various types to each division throughout the wars, while the Austrians and Prussians initially assigned a battery to each brigade, leaving them with little tactical flexibility in the employment of artillery. They eventually streamlined their artillery, the Austrians by assigning two or three batteries to each division and the Prussians placing all eight or ten batteries in a corps directly under the corps commander. However, neither the Russian, nor the Austrian, nor the Prussian system permitted employment of artillery on the scale and with the degree of effectiveness realized by the French.

Serving the Guns—The actual working of the guns was in the hands of enlisted men. Having arrived at a suitable position, a seasoned gun crew could unhitch the gun teams, unlimber their piece, site it, load, and get off their first round in one minute, and maintain that rate of fire or better for some time. An entire battery could manage the task in two or three minutes. Getting away required a few minutes longer. Each man in a gun crew had a specific task assigned, but was "cross-trained" so as to be able to serve in almost any capacity. The procedure was complex.

As the piece recoiled from its last round, the Spongemen damp-swabbed the tube to quench any live embers, while the Ammunition Handlers brought up a felt- or serge-wrapped powder bag and the type of round indicated by the Gunner. The Loader inserted the powder charge into the tube and the Spongeman shoved it home with the ram end of his swab, while the Ventman placed his leather-cased thumb over the vent as further insurance against premature explosion due to unextinguished embers. The Loader then placed the projectile with its loosely attached wooden wad into the tube. As the Spongeman shoved this down, the Ventman jabbed a "pricker" through the vent into the powder bag to tear it, and then shoved a light metal or goose quill primer filled with high quality powder into the tear. The Gunner then relaid the piece, adjusting elevation and deflection by the use of wedges, screws, or main force. A slow match was then applied to the primer, discharging the piece.

The normal projectile for guns, which had relatively long barrels and could attain considerable range with a flat trajectory, was shot, or ball. This was a solid sphere of metal designed to smash into things. If fired properly so that it struck relatively hard ground in front of a target, such as a mass of troops, it could be particularly devastating, since the impact would throw rocks and gravel at the troops and, moreover, the ball would ricochet, or bounce. Ideally a shot could bounce along for some time, each leap covering slightly less than half the distance made by the former, until it bounced to a halt, unless, of course, it hit something. Under any circumstances shot tore great gaps in the ranks, which was one reason for the popularity of line formations and for the British reverse-slope defensive tactics, which massed the troops out of the line of fire.

Howitzers had a short barrel and were designed for high-angle fire. Their normal projectile was the shell, a hollow metal sphere filled with powder and provided with a fuse. Before inserting the shell in the tube the Loader had to cut the fuse to a length suited to the range required and, usually, apply a match to it too, making his job considerably more hazardous than under normal circumstances. Howitzers were particularly useful for getting at places behind obstacles, such as villages, forests, and hills, thereby making them the best weapon for dealing with normal British defensive tactics. Howitzers could also be used to drop shells into the midst of large masses of troops. Both guns and howitzers were also provided with canister, sometimes called grapeshot, for situations where the enemy was literally at point-blank range. Canister was aptly named, for it was essentially a package which released numerous small lead balls upon leaving the barrel. A "taste" or two of grapeshot discharged into the head of a charging column could cause horrendous damage and quite possibly result in the failure of the attack. During the wars the British introduced shrapnel, which was a combination of shell and canister, and proved particularly effective against massed bodies of troops.

Tactics—The French favored the aggressive use of artillery. Even a Grand Battery could be expected to limber up and advance upon command, as at Friedland (June 14, 1807) when some 30 guns deployed initially at some 600 meters from the Russian lines closed the range to some 60 meters in three bounds, unlimbering and firing a few rounds at each halt. Most other armies dispersed their artillery. Since Napoleon was usually on the offensive, his predilection for massed batteries and aggressive handling is understandable. His opponents, who usually fought defensively, favored greater dispersal of their batteries and more autonomy for them in action.

Offensively, Napoleon used his artillery to batter the enemy's infantry, pounding them with shot and shell until he was ready to send in his own foot soldiers, accompanied by regimental guns to give close support.

In defense, artillery could be quite effective. Counterbattery fire was not considered worth the effort, so one kept one's guns relatively uncommitted until the enemy put in his infantry and cavalry. When the enemy was within 1000 to 1,200 meters' range, one opened up, concentrating solid shot immediately in front of the advancing troops to attain maximum ricochet effect while showering them with shells. At about 300 or 400 meters one went over to direct canister fire with both guns and howitzers, double-shotting the last round or two for good measure. Some idea of the potency of such may be gained by considering the capacity of a single unsupported battery of six 8- or 9-pounders and two howitzers to resist a frontal attack at 1,200 meters, which can be covered by cavalry in three to five minutes and by infantry in seven to ten minutes, depending upon the nature of the ground and the condition of the troops.

ARTILLERY VOLUME OF FIRE

ATTACKER	BALLS	SHELLS	CANISTERS	TOTAL
Cavalry	24–36	3–5	12–24	39–65
Infantry	48–60	8–10	36–48	92–118

In view of these statistics Napoleon's reliance upon artillery to pound his enemy into senselessness before committing his own infantry and cavalry becomes quite understandable. Certainly the few times he suffered tactical defeats, such as at Waterloo, were primarily the result of committing the troops before the artillery had done its work.

NAPOLEON THE COMMANDER

Few generals can be compared favorably with Napoleon. Before his time perhaps only Alexander, Hannibal, Caesar,

Belisarius, Genghis Khan, Gustavus Adolphus, and Frederick the Great can be considered his peers. Certainly none since his time approach his reputation even remotely. A deadly foe, Napoleon sought to destroy his enemies by bringing them to battle at the earliest opportunity. To be sure, he had a superb military instrument, brought to perfection by the Revolution. But the armies of Revolutionary France lacked adequate direction and guidance. It was Napoleon who provided those.

Looking back upon Napoleon's career, one finds it difficult to compare his campaigns. He personally appears to have viewed that of 1809 as his finest effort. Yet, while the quality of the French Army had begun to slip and the Austrians proved a doughty foe, one must dismiss this evalution. The consensus among historians is that Napoleon was at his peak during the Italian Campaign of 1796–1797 and again during the Campaign in France in 1814. In both, but particularly in the latter, he faced a considerably superior foe while having available inferior resources within the framework of an unfavorable political and strategic situation. The Italian Campaign, of course, turned out successfully, while that in France did not. Nevertheless, on balance, the Campaign of 1814 must be considered the most brilliant demonstration of Napoleon's military talents. That he lost should not obscure its remarkable conduct.

For a perfect campaign, we need look no further than that of 1806. The French Army, honed to a fine edge by the brilliantly conducted Campaign of 1805 in Germany and Bohemia, secured the total annihilation of the Prussian Army and state in precisely one month, from October 6 to November 6. It was a remarkable demonstration of what the French military system could accomplish under Napoleon's guidance. But the achievement was flawed in that the foe was ill-led and poorly prepared for a struggle to the death.

Napoleon had an enormous capacity for hard work, a remarkable ability to comprehend his opponents' intentions through the fog of war, a tremendous ability to develop and carry out highly sophisticated, yet eminently practical plans of campaign, an instinctive ability to inspire his troops, and

a marvelous skill at leading, all combined with an incredible
ambition to pursue his destiny. In the end, of course, it was
this ambition that brought him low. Intoxicated by his victories, he failed to fully understand the limitations of
France's physical and spiritual resources, the character and
motivation of Great Britain, his principal foe, and the nature of the forces that the French Revolution had unleashed
and that he himself had helped to spread throughout
Europe—nationalism.

Napoleon's effect on the conduct of war has been pro-
found. His fundamental strategies have been replicated often. Thus, the indirect approach was essayed during the
Peninsular, Chancellorsville, and Vicksburg Campaigns of
1862 and 1863 in The American Civil War and in the In-
chon Landings in 1950 in Korea; also, the German defense
of East Prussia in 1914 during World War I was a fine example of the strategy of the central position. Such efforts
have not always been crowned by victory, for they require
not merely Napoleonic vision to conceive, but also Napoleonic audacity and courage to execute. Nevertheless, a soldier could do worse than to endeavor to emulate Napoleon.

SELECTIONS
FROM THE WORKS
OF F. LORAINE PETRE

I

The Politics of War

Wars are fought for political purposes, a point frequently ignored in many works of history. F. Loraine Petre's works on Napoleon, however, do not suffer from this flaw. Petre fully comprehended the importance of the political framework to the conduct of a war, and was careful to place military events in their proper political setting. This is of considerable importance when treating of Napoleon, for it was his astute understanding of the political currents of his times which lay at the foundation of his ability to dominate Europe for over a decade.

The two selections which follow illustrate the political environment within which Napoleon functioned, as well as his ability to manipulate the politics of the age in his favor. In addition, they demonstrate Petre's understanding of the relationship of politics to war and his considerable capacities as an analyst of international affairs, while at the same time they give a general picture of the overall political setting of the period.

"The State of Europe," from *Napoleon's Campaign in Poland, 1806–1807*

The Napoleonic Wars were not necessarily a logical extension of the wars of the Republic. But the conservative states of Europe certainly were hostile to France, even after General Bonaparte had seized power in 1799, paving the way for a general peace by 1802, for the sentiments of "Liberty, Equality, Fraternity" were infectious, and dangerous. Moreover, the settlement of 1802 had been greatly favorable to France, planting a desire for vengeance in some. Plots and conspiracies were numerous, including attempts on the life of the First Consul of the Republic, Napoleon Bonaparte. After one of these, some of his agents, acting under their own initiative, arranged to kidnap from the independent state of Baden the Duke of Enghien, hope and scion of the discredited and dethroned Royal Family, subject him to a drumhead court-martial for plots against France, and shoot him. It was this violation of the sovereignty of Baden and the consequent "spilling of Royal Blood" which brought everything to a head in Europe and launched the seemingly interminable series of wars.

Shortly after the tragic death of the duc d'Enghien, on the 21st of March, 1804, Napoleon, then first consul for life, took measures to induce the French senate to propose his elevation to the Imperial dignity. With the senate he found no difficulty. On the 18th May, that subservient body declared him Emperor of the French. With regard to his wish to make the title hereditary, he had recourse to a plebiscite, the result of which was an overwhelming majority in his favour. On the 2nd December, 1804, he was crowned, or rather crowned himself, amidst a scene of unrivalled pomp, surrounded by a brilliant court and by the marshals whom he had recently appointed. The Pope himself had been induced, or compelled, to attend the ceremony and confer his benediction on the new sovereign.

If this revival of the sovereignty was received with resignation, rather than with enthusiasm, by the bulk of the populace, such was not the case with the army. It was by his matchless military talents, and by the brilliant victories to which he had so often led the soldiers of the republic, that Napoleon had become their idol and, with them at his back, had risen from a humble lieutenant of artillery to be the greatest personality in France and in Europe.

It was as much by the necessity for retaining the favour of the army as by his own boundless ambition, and his schemes for an universal empire, that the Emperor was impelled to enter upon a continued career of conquest. His designs he cloaked by pretended overtures to England, with whom he had been again at war since May, 1803. He neither believed nor hoped that peace would follow, but the negotiations served to reveal to him the existence of an alliance between England and Russia. Austria too, he knew, was labouring to repair the losses she had suffered in recent campaigns. Prussia, confident in the strength of an army which was believed to be as invincible as those of the great Frederick, was bent on playing her own game rather than that of Europe generally. She offered a splendid opportunity for the exercise of the diplomatic talents of Talleyrand and his master who soon saw that, by judicious treatment, she could be kept out of the field, until it was too late for her to enter it with powerful allies.

Whether Napoleon really ever intended seriously to attempt the invasion of England or not, his avowed intentions enabled him to train, on his northern coasts, the finest army he ever commanded. At that distance, his preparations were far removed from the view of Austria, who little thought that an army collected at a point so remote from her frontier could be used against her with such rapidity and deadly effect as it presently was.

At the same time, the Emperor was busy strengthening himself on his continental frontier. Holland, soon to be erected into a monarchy for bestowal on his brother Louis, was brought under French control. The Italian republic was induced to declare Napoleon king of Italy.

It was now time for him to precipitate matters. His coronation at Milan with the iron crown of Lombardy, the incorporation of the republics of Genoa and Lucca, as well as other northern Italian states, his military celebration on the field of Marengo, were so many insults calculated to excite the anger and the fear of Austria. It was on Austria that the Emperor had resolved to fall first. In August, 1805, that power joined the coalition of England and Russia. To them was added Sweden. Prussia alone, refusing to join them, allowed herself to be led astray by the bait of Hanover which she coveted, and which Napoleon insidiously dangled before her greedy

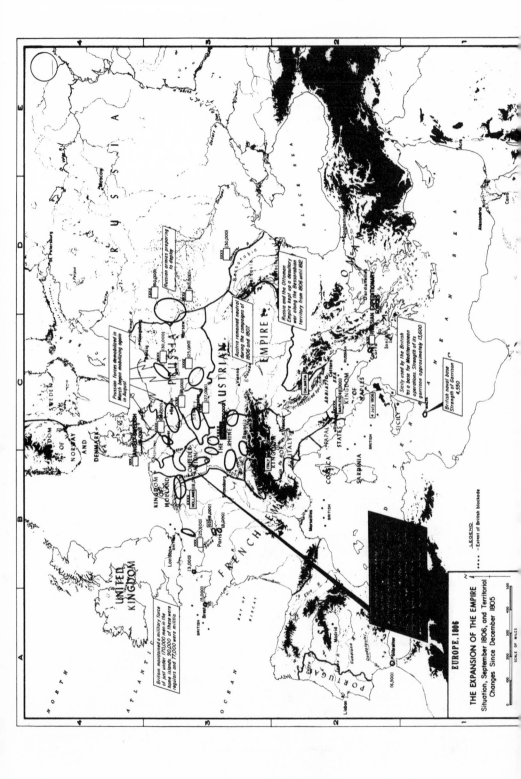

THE EXPANSION OF THE EMPIRE

EUROPE, 1806

Situation, September 1806, and Territorial
Changes Since December 1805

LEGEND
····· Extent of British blockade

Britain maintained a military force
of just under 170,000 men in the
home islands. 90,000 of these were
regulars and 77,000 were militia.

Prussian forces demobilized in
March began mobilizing again
in August.

Russian armies preparing
to deploy

Austria remained neutral
during the campaigns of
1806 and 1807.

Russia and the Ottoman
Empire kept up a desultory
war along the Bessarabian
territory from 1806 until 1812.

Sicily used by the British
as a base for Mediterranean
operations. Strength of its
garrison approximately 13,600.

British naval base
Strength of Garrison
4,550

eyes. He had already occupied it in pursuance of his war with England. On his south-western frontier, his alliance with Spain and Portugal left him free from anxiety.

In the end of July, 1805, Sir R. Calder's naval action convinced Napoleon that all hope of an invasion of England was, for the present, at an end. He had no longer any motive for delaying his meditated attack on Austria.

That power, which had long seen that war was inevitable sooner or later, hoping to steal a march on her wakeful adversary whilst he was occupied with his schemes for the invasion of England, moved, early in September, into Bavaria, a state allied to France. In doing so she, notwithstanding her previous experience of him, underrated Napoleon and, moreover, moved at least two months before she could expect the arrival of the Russian army advancing to her assistance. The Emperor's decision to hurl upon Austria the army of England was taken at once. Every necessary order for the march from Boulogne to the Danube had already been prepared. It was executed with unparalleled rapidity and exactness. On the 20th October, the unhappy Austrian general Mack, surrounded in Ulm by the French, capitulated with 30,000 men, all that remained under his command of the 80,000 with whom he had invaded Bavaria six weeks before. The very next day, Napoleon's power at sea was for ever destroyed by Nelson at Trafalgar. A few days later, the Austrian forces in Italy, under the Archduke Charles, were compelled to retreat before Masséna in the hope of covering Vienna, now threatened by Napoleon's advance. Negotiations for an armistice failed, owing to Napoleon's excessive demands.

Prussia had, at last, come to a sense of the false position she was occupying. She attempted no resistance to the invasion of Hanover, now almost entirely clear of French soldiers, by the allied troops of Russia, Sweden, and England. The Prussian cabinet had taken offence at the violation of Anspach territory, by the march through it of French troops on their way to the Danube. So strong was the feeling against France that Duroc, Napoleon's ambassador, left Berlin whilst the King and the Tsar, who had arrived there, solemnly swore to rearrange Europe on the lines of the treaty of Luneville.

Haugwitz was despatched to inform Napoleon of this intention and, in the event of its non-acceptance by him, to declare
war against him on the part of Prussia. On the 15th December, Prussia had decided on a course which, if she had followed it two months earlier, placed as she was on the flank of
the line of march from Boulogne to the Danube, would have
frustrated the Emperor's whole plan. Whilst she was making
up her mind to an honest course, Napoleon had entered
Vienna, had moved to Brünn, and had finally, on the anniversary of his coronation, inflicted on the Austrians and
their Russian allies the decisive defeat of Austerlitz. Haugwitz, arriving at the French headquarters with the Prussian
ultimatum in his pocket, was put off till after the impending
battle. Its result caused him to take a very different course, to
suppress the ultimatum, the terms of which Napoleon could
guess, to offer Prussia's congratulations on the victory, and
to conclude a disgraceful treaty by which his master bartered
the honour of Prussia for the cession of Hanover.

Austria defeated, not crushed, agreed to the terms of the
treaty of Pressburg, to cede territory to Italy and to Bavaria,
to pay an indemnity, to recognise the recent changes in Italy,
and the elevation of Bavaria and Wurtemberg from elector-
ates to kingdoms.

Everything prospered for Napoleon. The allied invaders
withdrew from Hanover; Naples, attacked by the French,
shortly came under the rule of Joseph Bonaparte.

Having disposed, for the time being, of Austria, the Emperor turned upon Prussia. He had always intended to do so;
her perfidious conduct had rendered him more determined
that ever to destroy her. He could not trust her, even had he
wished to. Prussia had embroiled herself with England by
accepting from Napoleon the cession of Hanover. Under
pretext of defending his new ally against Great Britain, he
heaped insults on her, the last being the creation of the Confederation of the Rhine as a standing threat against her, and
a great base for French operations, whether against Prussia
or against Austria.

After Austerlitz, the Russian troops had retired; but the
Tsar had not been a party to the negotiations at Pressburg,
and his hand was still free. Negotiations between Napoleon

and Russia and England, during the early months of 1806, broke down. Prussia had been lashed to fury by the discovery that Napoleon had attempted to bribe England with Hanover, which he had so recently ceded to Prussia.

Wishing to strike her before succour could reach her from distant Russia, the Emperor anticipated her ultimatum by marching against her towards the Elbe.

The ultimatum reached Napoleon on the 7th October, 1806; seven days later the Prussian army had been destroyed at the fatal double battle of Jena and Auerstädt

"Origins of the War of 1809," from *Napoleon and the Archduke Charles: A History of the Franco-Austrian Campaign in the Valley of the Danube in 1809*

Austria, an aggregate of unrelated lands in Southern and East Central Europe ruled over by the ancient House of Hapsburg, was, after Great Britain, Napoleon's most durable and inveterate enemy. Though repeatedly defeated, Austria always came back ready for a fight, each time stronger than before. In 1805, Napoleon had virtually annihilated Austria's armies in a brilliant, lightning campaign in Southern Germany and Bohemia, forcing on her the humiliating Treaty of Pressburg (December 26, 1805). The following selection illustrates the complex diplomacy of a nation on the edge of war and the general causes of the outbreak of that war.

After Pressburg, Austria had seriously set to work to reorganise her resources and her administration, but her finances were crippled and her army shattered for the time being. She required time before she could venture on a renewal of the struggle with France. Had she been in the least ready, Napoleon's campaigns of 1806-7, in Prussia and Poland, offered her a splendid opportunity for falling on his right flank and rear in Germany. How anxious he was to keep her quiet, even in her weakened condition, has been described in the author's previous volumes on those campaigns. There also will be found an account of the measures which he took in Italy to hold a large portion of the Austrian army on the southern frontier. The risk of a fresh war with France, in 1806 or 1807, was too great; for defeat then could hardly have meant to the Imperial House anything but extinction at the hands of Napoleon. With the victory of Friedland and the Peace of Tilsit, the temptation to risk interference against the victorious Emperor was removed. Austria must now quietly prepare for a 'revanche' at some more favourable opportunity.

For a definite and immediate cause of Austria's attack on the French in April 1809 it is useless to search. Her object was simply a rectification of what she had been compelled to agree to in the end of 1805. Colonel Saski puts the case clearly. "Since 1805 Austria had worked at her military organisation, and her sole thought, encouraged by England, the soul of all the coalitions at that time, was to tear up the Treaty of Pressburg." As regards Austria he is correct, though, seeing that England only concluded formal peace with Austria after her fresh defeat by Napoleon, he seems hardly accurate as regards British encouragement, at least in a substantial sense. As Napoleon began to involve himself in the Spanish affair, Austria perceived that the time was approaching when her great enemy was likely to be hampered by difficulties in his rear which had not existed in any of his previous wars in Italy or Germany.

He first shows in his correspondence that he was anxious on the subject of Austrian armaments in May 1808. Towards the end of that month, he writes to his Minister for Foreign Affairs that he hears, from sources other than his ambassador at Vienna, that Austria is contemplating a fresh levy of 180,000 militia. If the ambassador, Andréossy, found that there was truth in this story, he was to demand that the levy be not made; for, Austria already having 300,000 men enrolled, it was clear that further military preparations must be directed against France. The Emperor threatened, if the levy of 180,000 were persisted in, to raise fresh troops in France, and to mobilise the contingents of the Rhenish Confederation. That would be an expensive operation, of which the cost must fall on Austria herself.

A month later, he was again alarmed by reports of the constitution of magazines in Bohemia, and the collection of horses and supplies of all sorts. He seems to have been particularly badly served by Andréossy at Vienna, for on both occasions the reports came from elsewhere, on the second from the French Minister at Munich.

The Emperor next sent a warning to Bavaria to be in readiness in case Austria should move; for, as in 1805, Bavaria must necessarily bear the first brunt of the attack. He also finds fault with the Austrian observance of the continental blockade at Trieste. On the 11th July he again reverts to the question of the militia levies, and a week later he directs the re-armament of the Silesian fortress of Neisse, which he still held. On the 10th August he jubilantly informs Champagny, his Minister of Foreign Affairs, that he has received from the Tsar an assurance of active alliance in the event of war with Austria. All the information he received from his numerous agents, and especially from Davout, commanding in Germany, confirmed him in his belief that Austria was preparing for war. The Emperor was now back in Paris, and, on the 16th August, at a reception of the 'corps diplomatique,' he conversed at length with Metternich, the Austrian Ambassador, or rather he delivered a long lecture to that diplomat. The substance of the conversation is stated in a despatch from Champagny to Andréossy. If that statement is anything like accurate, it is an extraordinary instance of the arrogance which prompted the use of language to the ambassador of a power with which the Emperor was still at peace, such as, at any other period, must infallibly have led to war. In this report the Emperor is represented, of course with his own sanction, as upbraiding Metternich with Austria's preparations, and rudely waving aside as ridiculous the ambassador's protestations of his master's peaceful intentions. Napoleon scoffs at the idea of the military measures being merely defensive, for Austria had nothing to fear from himself or anyone else. He is full of threats as to how he will reply, by armament, to the action of Austria; he vaunts his friendship with Russia; he even goes so far as to insinuate that that power may justly take umbrage at the Austrian preparations as a danger to herself. His conclusions as to the meaning of Austria's movements were correct enough in fact, but his language is devoid of all diplomatic restraint.

Early in September he writes long letters to Jerome and to the kings of Bavaria, Saxony, and Wurtemberg, in which he

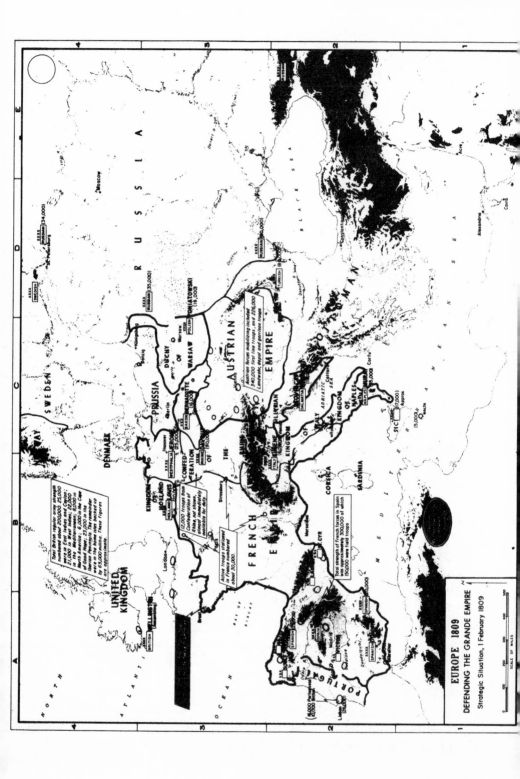

EUROPE 1809

DEFENDING THE GRANDE EMPIRE

Strategic Situation, 1 February 1809

SCALE OF MILES

0   100   200   300   400   500

estimates that, including the troops of the Confederation, he will have 300,000 men available during January in Germany. Again, he boasts of the friendly feeling of the Tsar towards him. This vaunt is so frequently repeated about this period as, by the mere fact of its reiteration, to raise a suspicion that Napoleon is not quite so sure about it as he professes. At the end of his letter to Jerome, he indicates that Austria seems more pacifically inclined, and he hopes by October to be able to send better news of the prospects of peace.

On the 22nd September the Emperor left Paris for Erfurt. To that meeting-place Francis I. had not been invited personally or by deputy. Nevertheless, he sent there Baron Vincent as the bearer of a letter to Napoleon. The letter was humble enough, protesting the writer's devotion to Napoleon, and the peaceful nature of his own measures. On the latter subject Vincent would be able to give further assurances. Doubtless the assurances were left to Vincent's discretion when he should have observed how the wind blew, for he, having been employed in a similar capacity during the campaign in Poland, was well acquainted with the ways of the French court or camp. As the political weather at Erfurt did not favour Austria, the assurances seem to have been conveyed in terms which lulled, to some extent, Napoleon's suspicions. He writes to the Princes of the Confederation that the Austrian militia has been disbanded, and will not be again assembled. The Confederation troops might, therefore, be withdrawn from the camps in which they had been concentrated, and allowed to return to their ordinary cantonments. At the same time, the Princes were to make it clear, through their ministers at Vienna, that any unusual armament on the part of Austria would entail a fresh concentration of their troops.

On the 12th October, the last day of the Erfurt assembly, the "Grand Army" of the Prussian and Polish campaigns was abolished in name, and in its place was constituted the "Army of the Rhine." The Emperor, as a sop to Russia, proposed to withdraw generally behind the Elbe, though he would still keep 10,000 men on the Oder as garrisons of the fortresses of Glogau, Küstrin, and Stettin. A division would remain in Pomerania, 12,500 men at Magdeburg, two small corps in the Hanseatic cities and Hanover, and 23,000 cavalry, of which 10,000 would be cuirassiers. The garrison of Danzig would also remain. That would make altogether an army of 70,000 or 80,000 men. The command of this army was given to Davout.

For the moment the war cloud seemed to have blown aside in Germany, and the Emperor, arriving in Paris on the 25th October, felt secure enough to leave again for Spain three days later.

It is clear, however, from his letter to Davout of the 25th October, that he was not altogether satisfied. In his previous campaigns in Germany he had had nothing to trouble him seriously in his rear beyond the Pyrenees. Now it was very different, for he had the Spanish rising to cope with, and the task of restoring the prestige of his arms, which had suffered so seriously by the capitulation of Baylen, the retirement of Joseph from Madrid to the upper Ebro, the repulse at Saragossa, and Junot's capitulation at Lisbon. He certainly did not want war with Austria for the present, at least not till he had had time to crush all opposition in Spain and Portugal, and to drive the English into the sea. He hoped to stave it off until he had attained these objects, but he was disappointed and compelled to return to France to look after affairs there, and to prepare to meet the Austrians on the Danube, leaving the pursuit of Sir John Moore to Soult, and the attempt to subjugate the Spanish people to Joseph and a team of unruly marshals who could be kept in order by no hand but Napoleon's own.

What was the real position in Austria, the country which was causing Napoleon such anxiety? As in Prussia in 1806, so in Austria in 1808 there were two distinct parties, of peace and of war. The resemblance is intensified by the fact that, as Queen Luise was the centre of the Prussian war party, so the Empress Maria Ludovica, the consort of Francis I., was the chief supporter of that of Austria. Handsome, charming, proud, and energetic, she exercised considerable influence over the Emperor, and was a most useful ally to Count Philip Stadion, the leading statesman of the party. The other principal personages of the party were Metternich, the Austrian ambassador in Paris, Freiherr von Balducci, a member of a

Corsican family settled in Hungary, General von Kutschera, and Count Ferdinand Palfy. The peace party, on the other hand, consisted chiefly of soldiers, at the head of whom was the Archduke Charles, the commander-in-chief. He was followed by his brothers, the Archdukes John, Joseph Palatine of Hungary, and Rainer.

The differences between these parties were based rather on their views of expediency than on any repugnance to war, or any special desire for peace. Stadion believed less in steadfast internal reform and reorganisation than in a bold foreign policy as a means of restoring the fallen fortunes of his country and his sovereign. He was always an advocate of a strong Germany under the joint leadership of Austria and Prussia, and he had strong hopes, destined for years to come to disappointment, of a general rising of Germany against Napoleon. Charles, on the other hand, was no less a patriot than Stadion, but believed his country was not yet ready for a fresh war against the mighty warrior who, less than three years before, had beaten her to the ground. The Archduke felt that he would himself, as the only general who was fit to lead the armies of Austria against a commander such as Napoleon, have to bear the whole burden of military operations. He recognised that there was still much to be done in administrative and financial reform, as well as in army reorganisation. Stadion, however, thought more of the opportunity offered by Napoleon's entanglement in the Peninsula, and of the possibilities of a German uprising similar to that of Spain. He estimated that Napoleon could not, in the beginning of a war in Germany, bring more than 197,000 men on to the field, inclusive of the Rhenish Confederation contingents. Metternich put the French and allied forces at 206,000 men at first, and wrote that, "the forces of Austria, so inferior to those of France before the Spanish rising, will be at least equal to them in the first movements."

Stadion's influence, backed by that of the Empress, was great. Charles' had to some extent waned, and his relations with the Emperor had lost in cordiality. Still he must be gained over, in so far that he might be relied on to carry out his part if war should come.

The differences of these two parties were public property

in Germany, and Napoleon had little difficulty in keeping himself informed as to the progress of the dispute.

Could Austria hope to enter on a fresh campaign with any ally at her back? From England perhaps some financial aid might be got, though even her treasury was at a low ebb just then. She might perhaps make a diversion in Hanover or Holland, but that was not to be relied on, and the unfortunate expedition to Walcheren was actually only undertaken when it was all over with Austria.

Prussia was broken and dismembered by the late war. Her army was ruined, she had no money, and she had lost half her former possessions. The patriots would have thrown in their lot with Austria at all hazards, but Frederick William was not going to risk his own throne, and, when Major v. der Goltz concluded an arrangement under which Prussia was to assist Austria with 80,000 men, the Prussian King would have none of it. As for Russia, the Tsar was formally bound to Napoleon by the treaty signed at Erfurt. He was sounded by Stadion through Prince Schwartzenberg, who was sent to induce Alexander to ally himself with Austria, or at least to promise neutrality in the event of a fresh Franco-Austrian war. Alexander could not well, if he had desired it, get out of his Erfurt promise, and, moreover, he saw that Austria could not make a better bid regarding Turkey than Napoleon. Accordingly, Schwartzenberg returned with nothing better than Alexander's advice to Austria to keep the peace. This was on the 12th February 1809, when war was already decided on. When, finally, finding himself unable to resist the influence of Stadion, the Archduke Charles wrote that, "he washed his hands like Pilate," Austria stood absolutely alone against Napoleon and his allies, threatened by them on all her frontiers. It was on the 8th February 1809 that Austria finally decided on war, though it was not commenced till the 9th April. Metternich, who had returned to Vienna, seems to have given the final push which drove the Emperor to this decision. The grounds of the decision were:—

1. The estimates, already given, of Napoleon's strength at the commencement of war;

2. the disinclination of the French nation for a new war,

which had been impressed on Metternich by expressions of discontent in Paris, notably by Talleyrand;

3. Metternich's belief that under no circumstances would Russia take a decided part against Austria.

Napoleon certainly did not want war at this juncture, for, though he wrote to the King of Bavaria, on the 15th January 1809, that he had "destroyed the Spanish armies and defeated the English army," it is highly improbable that he would have left Spain, as he did on the 16th January, but for the disquieting news from France, and regarding Austria.

II

Organization and Planning

Military history frequently ignores the importance of organization and administration to the success of operations, usually giving these critical aspects of the conduct of war mere passing notice. Petre was among the earliest historians to incorporate such matters in what were essentially operational accounts. This was a considerable breakthrough in the writing of military history, and of particular importance in terms of the period under study, for French organizational and administrative excellence was as much responsible for Napoleon's many victories as was his brilliance as a commander. The following selections illustrate organizational and administrative differences among the various armies at selected periods in the wars, and demonstrate Napoleon's remarkable talents as a planner and military manager.

"Planning the Campaign of 1806," from *Napoleon's Conquest of Prussia, 1806*

By the autumn of 1806 tensions between France and Prussia, which was allied with Russia, had risen enormously. Both France and Prussia began to make serious preparations. This selection shows Napoleon at his best, considering every detail, calculating every angle, observing everything with his enormous capacity for work and his voracious appetite for information, and evolving a logical, bold, yet simple plan of campaign. His performance contrasts sharply with the picture we get of the Prussians and their Russian allies, operating with remarkable inefficiency, considerable carelessness, and incomprehensible confidence.

Holding, as he did in 1806, the lines of the Rhine and the Main with all their passages, Napoleon had the choice of several lines of advance to the invasion of Prussia and Saxony. He might base himself on any part of the Rhine below Mayence for a direct advance eastwards on Berlin. If he marched from Mayence by Frankfort, Hanau, Fulda, Eisenach, and Erfurt, he would have to pass through the hilly country now traversed by the Frankfort-Berlin railway. Though hilly, the country cannot be described as really difficult, for the valleys are open as a rule, and the hills rounded and rarely rugged. Once beyond Erfurt he would find himself on the rolling plateaux, which eventually sink, towards Leipzig and the Elbe, into the level plains of Northern Germany. From any part of the Rhine between Mayence and Wesel the advance would have to cross a more or less hilly country before reaching the Elbe at Magdeburg, and in places—the Harz, for example—the difficulties would be considerable for the movement of a great army. On all these lines the obstructions in the shape of rivers would not be serious till the Elbe was reached. Basing himself on Wesel and the Lower Rhine, the Emperor would find no mountain barrier intersecting his line of advance across the level plains of North Germany; but the river lines, especially those of the Weser and the Elbe, would assume more serious proportions.

Should he, on the other hand, elect to advance northwards from the southern side of his re-entrant rectangular base, across the Main, he would have, before reaching the plains of Northern Germany, to pass through a difficult mountainous country of more or less rugged nature, thickly wooded, and with but few good roads, as roads were understood in Germany in 1806, before the introduction of macadam. From the longitude of Hanau to the western mountain boundary of Bohemia stretches the great Thuringian Forest, barring the way between Southern and Northern Germany, and, everywhere as far east as the longitude of Bamberg, only to be passed by many marches of considerable difficulty. Eastwards of this point, the forest narrows greatly in the Franconian Forest, which forms the connecting link between the main Thuringian Forest and the mountains of Bohemia. In this part the barrier can be traversed in three marches, or less, from the Upper Main to the Saale. Once north of the Saale, the invader would find himself in comparatively open country, where movements of troops are easy and concentration possible. During the two or three days' march through the Franconian Forest close concentration is impossible; but there were, in 1806, three good roads, on which as many columns could march with a front not exceeding forty miles. The lateral communications between them would not be good, and they would be exposed to some risk of defeat in detail should they encounter a great army, concentrated on the plateaux north of the Saale, as they debouched from the Franconian mountains. This danger would, however, be very much greater in the case of an advance from the middle Main northwards, where roads through the Thuringian Forest were much fewer, and lateral communications still worse.

To base himself on the Rhine and advance eastwards or north-eastwards on Berlin would, perhaps, be easier for Napoleon than to move northwards from the Main, but it would offer no strategical advantages; for if he met and defeated the Prussians on any of these west to east lines, he would simply drive them backwards on their supports, first on Saxony and then on the Russians, whose advance from Poland was expected. To turn the Thuringian Forest by an advance from his extreme right, close against the Bohemian frontier of Austria, was no doubt a less safe movement; but, on the other hand, it offered strategical advantages of infinite importance. In the first place, the Emperor might possibly succeed in intruding with his army between the Prussians, if they decided to defend the country west of the Elbe, and the Saxons whom he saw unwillingly drifting into co-operation with Prussia. If he failed in this, he would still threaten the Prussian communications with the Elbe and Berlin, and those of the Saxons with Dresden. Were he to occupy Dresden itself, he would turn the whole defensive line of the Elbe, and, looking to the superior mobility of his own army, might still hope to be in Berlin in rear of the Prussian army, and separating it from the advancing Russians, before it could reach the capital. To thus turn the forest on its eastern extremity, he would require to concentrate to his right, towards the sources of the Main, and push through the mountainous country of the Franconian Forest, forming the watershed between the Main and the Saale, and separating him from the plains of Western Saxony.

The dangers of such an advance appeared to be that, if he drew his supplies from Mayence by the line of the Main, the Prussians, by a rapid advance through the Thuringian Forest against the line of his communications, might sever him from France, and compel him to conform to their initiative. Should they, on the other hand, concentrate on the Upper Saale, there was the risk of his army being defeated in detail as it debouched from the Franconian mountains on the Upper Saale, the same danger which would have threatened a direct advance northwards through the Thuringian Forest. But in moving through the mountains east of the Thuringian Forest the Emperor would find three good roads, instead of the single bad one to which he would practically be restricted in the forest itself.

That Napoleon would advance from the Lower Rhine direct eastward against the Prussian army was never in the least probable. In the first place, as has been already shown, that plan offered no strategical advantages; and in the second place, there were, during the spring and summer of 1806, no less than six French army corps, besides the cavalry reserve, in the space between the Upper Rhine, the Inn, the Main, and the Upper Danube. The Guard alone had been withdrawn to Paris after the Peace of Pressburg. To have placed this great force on the Rhine below Mayence would have involved a gigantic flank march to the left, and would have withdrawn the watch which Napoleon still thought it necessary to keep upon Austria. That country was a constant source of anxiety to him, and he could not feel sure that, if she saw his armies disappear from her frontiers, she would not, forgetting the way in which Prussia had behaved in

1805, seize the opportunity to throw in her lot with the new
coalition, seeking to avenge her defeats of the previous year.
She must be overawed until the march of events, and the
hoped-for destruction of Prussia, should render her intervention too dangerous a move to be undertaken in the
existing state of her army and her finances.

In considering any of Napoleon's schemes for a campaign,
we cannot keep too steadily in mind his own saying, "Je n'ai
jamais eu un plan d'opérations." He never presumed to forecast far ahead the precise course of operations after the first
tactical contact. What he did was to fix his mind on a general
object for attainment, and to carry out his strategical deployment so as to place his army in the best possible position for
effecting that object.[1]

On the present occasion he laid down as his objective two
geographical points, Dresden and Berlin; not that he committed the error of believing that the mere occupation of
geographical points was the object of war, but he saw that
Dresden and Berlin were the best places to aim at in order to
sever the Saxons from the Prussian alliance, to interpose
between the Prussian army and that advancing from Russia,
and to draw towards himself the former, whose defeat and
destruction was his real objective. The shortest road, with
reference to the existing positions of his army, was naturally
to be chosen, and the starting-point of that was the neighbourhood of Bamberg and the Principality of Baireuth.

On the 5th September, fourteen days before he finally
decided on war, we find him indicating this starting-point in
a letter to Berthier. "It is necessary that, in eight days after I
give the order, the whole of my armies—that at Frankfort,
that as Passau, and that at Memmingen—should be assembled at Bamberg, and in the Principality of Baireuth.
Send me the itinerary which each would follow, and the nature of the roads." The letter goes on to order the despatch
of officers in every direction to gather the most complete

[1] "The plan of operations must define what we wish to do, and hope to
achieve, with our available resources. It cannot forecast the individual
movements by which this will be effected. The first important engagement
with the enemy, above all things, exercises a distinctively decisive influence
on them" (Von der Goltz on the Conduct of War, p. 121).

information as to the country, roads, rivers, supplies, fortresses, bridges, &c., between the starting-point and Berlin, and on either side of the direct road.

So long as peace subsisted, the Emperor could draw his supplies in safety from France through Mayence, up the Main, and along the adjacent roads. Once war broke out, that line, a continuation to a flank of the army's front, would be dangerous, and exposed to be cut by an enemy moving southwards against the left of the Grand Army, through the forest. Therefore the Emperor decided to abandon it as soon as war was declared. On the 9th September he writes to Berthier: "If I made war against Prussia, my line of operations would be Strasburg, Mannheim, Mayence, and Würzburg, where I have a fortress; so that my convoys, on the fourth day after their departure from Mannheim, or Mayence, would be in safety at Würzburg." Thus his line of communications with France would be thrown back south of the Main, out of reach of the enemy, until a date when the Emperor could reckon on his own movement northwards, against the Saxon and Prussian communications, forcing the enemy to abandon all idea of operations against those of the French.[1] Napoleon required fortified depôts in the advanced base on the Upper Main, from which he proposed to start. Würzburg was suitable for one; Forchheim had to be taken as the other, though a place farther north—Königshofen, for example—would have been preferred, had it been suitable in other respects.

Napoleon, ever confident of victory, was never careless to provide for retreat in the event of defeat. An ordinary general would perhaps have sought to retreat in that case on the Rhine direct, whatever the danger from a victorious enemy moving against his flank. Not so Napoleon, whose intention was, if defeated, to transfer his base from the Rhine to the Upper Danube, on which he could fall back through the

---

[1] "Therefore he prepared to transfer his communications now to the line Forchheim, Würzburg, Mannheim, which was more in his immediate rear. He was compelled to do this, for in placing his army in the best position for threatening the enemy's communications, he found himself unable to protect, without weakening his concentration, the line Mainz-Bamberg in continuation of his left flank" ("Napoleon as a General," i. 275).

friendly territory of Bavaria, and whence he could, if necessary, reach Strasburg. No clearer or better exposition of the Emperor's schemes can be found than the statement of them contained in a series of notes which he addressed, for his guidance, to his brother Louis, on the 30th September. The first note includes the following passage: "My intention is to concentrate all my forces on the extremity of my right, leaving the whole space between Bamberg and Mayence entirely unoccupied, so as to have nearly 200,000 men united on the same battlefield. If the enemy pushes parties between Bamberg and Mayence, I shall not be disturbed, for my line of communications will be established on the small fortress of Forchheim, and thence on Würzburg. It will be necessary for you, therefore, to direct the most important messengers you have to send me to Mannheim, whence they will go direct to Forchheim, and reach me with the greatest safety. The nature of events which may occur is incalculable, for the enemy, believing me to have my left on the Rhine and my right in Bohemia, thinking, moreover, that my line of operations is parallel to my front, may have a great interest in outflanking my left, in which case I can throw him back upon the Rhine." True to his great principle of concentration on a single object, the Emperor was about to advance with his army in three columns in the smallest area compatible with the nature of the country and the communications in front of him. Thus, if attacked in any direction, he would be able to concentrate for battle in the shortest possible time.

The note proceeds to show how he proposed to deal with the possible advance of a Prussian raid into France, across the Rhine, beyond his own reach. "Employ yourself in putting Wesel in the best possible state of defence, so that you may, should circumstances demand it, be able to pass back your whole army by the bridge at Wesel, and move up the Rhine to restrain raiding forces from passing that barrier. By the 10th or 12th October there will be at Mayence the 8th corps of the Grand Army, 18,000 or 20,000 strong.[1] Its orders will be to avoid being cut from the Rhine, whilst making

---

[1] The Emperor's expectations in this respect were disappointed, for, owing to delay in the arrival of reinforcements, Mortier had but three French infantry regiments on the date named.

incursions as far as Frankfort; but, in case of necessity, it will retire behind the Rhine, leaning its left upon your troops."

The second note goes on: "The observations in my first note above are mere precautions. My first marches will threaten the heart of the Prussian monarchy, and the deployment of my forces will be so rapid and imposing that it is probable that the whole Prussian army will fall back on Magdeburg, seeking by forced marches to defend its capital. It is then, but then only, that you will have to launch an advanced guard to take possession of the Mark, of Munster, of Osnabruck, and of East Friesland, by means of mobile columns which could fall back, if necessary, on a central point. The result would be that the enemy would be able to draw neither recruits nor supplies from the country, whilst you, on the other hand, could derive some advantages from it. You must understand that the bulk of your forces should not go far from Wesel, so that from that point you may be able to defend your kingdom and the coasts of Boulogne, should circumstances so require. For the first period of the war you are merely a corps of observation—that is to say that, until the enemy has been thrown beyond the Elbe, I only count on your corps as a means of diversion to amuse the enemy till the 12th October, the date on which my operations will be fully developed; also to prevent the penetration into France or Holland of any hostile corps which may be cut off with no resource but to throw itself into those countries; or, finally, in the case of a great misfortune, such as a great battle lost, that you should be able to defend Wesel and Mayence with your own army and the 8th corps of the Grand Army (which will remain always near Mayence), whilst I execute my retreat on the Danube, and, at the same time, to prevent the enemy from passing the Rhine to pillage my State."

The third note deals with the possibility of invasion by the English, which Napoleon thinks more probable in the direction of Hanover than on the coasts of France or Holland. Should the English and Swedes attempt a diversion in Hanover, they might muster 25,000 men. In that case there need be no further fear for the French and Dutch coasts, and the central reserve of 8000 men at Paris could in ten days, with the aid of wheeled transport, be carried to the reinforcement of Louis, who would also call up the rest of his own army from Zeist, his central camp near Utrecht. In case of urgent need, the 8th corps could march down the Rhine from Mayence, raising the army of Holland to 40,000 men, a force ample to preclude any possibility of the English and Swedes making their presence felt on the main theatre of war. The fourth note deals with the event of a great French victory, placing at the Emperor's mercy the country west of the Elbe. Then would be the time for the 8th corps and part of the army of the north to occupy Cassel, in the genuine neutrality of whose Elector Napoleon refused to believe. "The Elector wishes to be neutral; but that neutrality does not deceive, though it suits me." The writer's concluding advice is couched in these terms: "Never expose your corps and do not risk your own life, since you command only a corps of observation. The least check suffered by you would disquiet me; my measures might be disconcerted by it, and such an event would leave without direction the whole north of my Empire. On the other hand, whatever may happen to me, I shall act more freely with the knowledge that you are behind the Rhine; even if I experienced a great disaster, I should beat my enemy, had I but 50,000 men left, because, free to manœuvre, independent of any line of operations, and feeling secure as to the most important points in my State, I should always have resources.[1] It is possible that the actual situation is but the commencement of a great coalition against us, the full extent of which will be disclosed by events."

The last sentence points to the possibility of a renewal by Austria of the war in which she had been so heavily defeated. This possibility Napoleon had constantly in mind, up till the

---

[1] Count Yorck remarks on Napoleon's intention to use the Danube as a line on which to retreat if necessary. He quotes Jomini to the effect that if the Prussians had dreamed of an attempt to sever the line to the Danube by Saalfeld, Schleiz and Hof, they would have left open Napoleon's best and most direct line from Saxony to the Rhine, by the Leipzig-Frankfort road, and the others *via* Cassel to Coblentz, Cologne, and Wesel. "On the eve of Jena Napoleon's strategical position, considering his chance of a twofold retreat, seems to have been as carefully secured as is possible in the uncertainty of human affairs" ("Napoleon as a General," i. 300).

date when the victory of Friedland and the Peace of Tilsit finally removed it. From the autumn of 1806 till the summer of 1807, he was constantly striving to chain Austria to neutrality. It is to Eugène Beauharnais, the Viceroy of Italy, that he discloses his plans for forcing on Austria an attitude of neutrality, which he could hardly hope to ensure on other grounds than that of fear. In a letter, dated 18th September 1806, he inculcates on the Viceroy an attitude of watchfulness, tempered by conciliation. Austria's professions were uniformly friendly, but she was busy repairing the losses of her army, and, whilst it was unnecessary and unwise to irritate or alarm her, it was most necessary to have everything ready for the defence of Northern Italy, in case she should take advantage of the Emperor's having his hands occupied elsewhere. The supreme command of the army of Italy was bestowed on Eugène, who, if the worst came to the worst, might be reinforced by 40,000 men from the army of Naples, which was entirely separate from that of North Italy. It had, however, depôts in the north, and the men in these were, for the present, made over to Eugène. He was also given control over seven regiments in Piedmont and the corps in Istria; the latter was to be secretly withdrawn to Friuli. The fortresses of Venice, Mantua, Palmanuova, Osoppo, Legnago, and Peschiera were to be put in a proper state of defence and garrisoned. For the purpose of manœuvring between these fortresses, and of containing the Austrians in the event of war, Eugène would still have 40,000 men, without counting the army of Naples. Marmont, in Dalmatia, was to leave a garrison in Ragusa and collect the rest of the 2nd corps towards Zara, whence he could either threaten Croatia or move into Italy to the Viceroy's assistance. These armies would compel the Austrians, should they declare war, to maintain a large portion of their army on the southern frontier, far from the main theatre of war.

The only remaining point in Napoleon's scheme for the defence of his Empire is the protection of the French coasts against a possible invasion of the English. As has already been said, this danger would cease should England, as was more probable, direct her efforts to the invasion of Hanover; for Napoleon calculated the extreme strength of an English expeditionary force at 25,000 or 30,000 men, too small a force to permit of division.

The scheme for the defence of the French coasts, should they be threatened, is sketched in a letter to Cambacérès of the 30th September. After mentioning that Louis is charged with the defence from the Moselle to the coast, and Kellerman with that between the Moselle and Switzerland, the Emperor points out that he has 8000 infantry at Paris, and 2000 cavalry at Moulins and Amiens. Should the English attempt a landing near Boulogne, they would find there 15,000 men well entrenched. To the assistance of these Louis would march, 6000 National Guards would be available at St. Omer, not to mention the local gendarmerie. Lastly, the 8000 men in Paris and the 2000 cavalry could be promptly moved up, the former being conveyed to the Somme in carts for the purpose of saving time.

The attempt might be directed against Cherbourg. In that case the forts were sufficiently guarded by one regiment stationed there. To support it there would be the National Guards of the neighbourhood, a small force to be brought up from Pontoy, and the 8000 men who could be sent from Paris. At the worst, the enemy could do nothing more than burn Cherbourg, and a frigate which was on the stocks there.

If Brest were the point threatened, it would be held by all the garrisons of the 15th military circle, in addition to 10,000 sailors. The workmen (many of them ex-sailors) could be armed, and the central reserve sent up from Paris, as well as troops from Bordeaux and Nantes.

The difficulties of landing, and the uncertainty of being able to re-embark in the winter storms of the Bay of Biscay, were a sufficient guarantee for the immunity from attack of Bordeaux and Belle Isle. As for Toulon, there were troops enough in the neighbourhood to render it safe against 40,000 men. In conclusion, the Emperor considered that an expedition by sea against the exposed French coast was improbable in the winter.

Here we have the whole scheme, offensive and defensive, explained with Napoleon's usual lucidity and simplicity. Complicated concentric attacks found no place in his strategy, the essence of which was concentration. Like Frederick the Great, Napoleon was hampered by no government imposing conditions and restrictions on his clear apprehension of what was necessary. In other respects he was in a position very different from that of the great Prussian. The latter had sought to build up a strong kingdom of moderate dimensions in face of the jealousy and opposition of the older European powers; Napoleon had already established such a power beyond all probability of molestation, and was now guided in his strategy by his desire to build up an Empire of the West, constructed on the ruins of Europe, to be followed by its extension to the East. Where Frederick merely sought to save his kingdom from destruction, or to wrest a province from Austria, it was sufficient for him to strike a blow which would compel his enemy to sue for peace on reasonable terms. Napoleon, looking for much more, required the entire destruction of his enemy's fighting power. Frederick sought to live and let live, Napoleon to batten on the substance of the existing powers of the whole world. In 1806, his aim was the effacement of Prussia by the capture or destruction of her whole army. That, as we shall see in the later stages of this war, was the goal which he indicated to his commanders in their pursuit of the Prussian army after Jena; that was the one great reason why he could never have rested content with a straightforward advance from the Rhine, or through the Thuringian Forest, which, with his overwhelming force, must probably have ended in victory, though not necessarily in total annihilation of the enemy's army.

Turning now to Prussia, we find her in a position similar to that of Frederick. She neither hoped nor wished to overrun and destroy France; her object would be attained by a victory which should curb the ambition of the Emperor, compelling him to confine his rule to reasonable limits, and to abandon his schemes for the subjugation of central and eastern Europe.

When the Prussian Government first resolved, on the 7th August, that war could not be avoided, they appear to have been ignorant of the position of Napoleon's great army in South Germany, though it is difficult to understand how they could be so. Possibly the arrival of the Imperial Guard at

Paris, which could not have escaped their ambassador's notice, induced the belief that the whole army was following it.

In their ignorance of the distribution of the French army, the Prussian military advisers had to consider its possible advance from any of three directions:—

1. By Hanover, by Cassel, or by Eisenach, on Magdeburg.

2. By Eisenach, by Schmalkalden, or by Baireuth, on Wittenberg.

3. By Baireuth, on Dresden.

In view of this uncertainty as to the direction of attack, the earliest orders for mobilisation contemplated the assembly of troops at the following points:—

1. Blücher, with sixteen battalions and seventeen squadrons, was to concentrate about Paderborn and Osnabrück, and between Leer and Oldenburg, leaving only light troops on the coasts, and watching the French on the Westphalian frontier. Should the latter appear to be endeavouring to turn Blücher by Hesse, his duty would be to concentrate on Hanover.

2. The troops occupying Hanover (twenty battalions, twenty-eight squadrons) would concentrate towards Celle, Hildesheim, and Brunswick, with the exception of a small force watching Lauenburg and the coast, and another detachment at Nordheim. This army, if Napoleon advanced by Hesse, would support Blücher's retirement, or itself fall back on Magdeburg, there to offer, in conjunction with the troops on the spot, a stout resistance.

3. Ten battalions and twenty squadrons, concentrated at Magdeburg, would support the above-named columns.

4. The garrisons of Potsdam, Berlin, and other places in the Mark, would hold themselves in readiness to bring further help to Magdeburg. They numbered seventeen battalions and fifteen squadrons.

5. Kalkreuth, with eighteen battalions and thirty squadrons, assembled about Prenzlau, would be in a position to march, either against the Swedes, who were still hostile, or on Magdeburg, as circumstances might require.

6. In Silesia and South Prussia, thirty-one and a half battalions and seventy squadrons would mobilise as rapidly as

possible between Sagan and Breslau, prepared to march, if necessary, through Saxony, pushing two and a half battalions and five squadrons into the Principality of Baireuth, which, however, they were to evacuate should the enemy appear in force there. It was hoped, in this event, that the Silesian army, joined by the Saxons, would be able to form behind the Elbe at Dresden, thus menacing the right flank of a French advance on Berlin.

7. Eighteen battalions and twenty squadrons in West Prussia, about Küstrin, would be able to bring support to any of the columns requiring it.

These orders failed to provide for the mobilisation of 34,000 men and 198 guns, a failure which is strongly condemned by Hoepfner. It seems impossible to justify it, especially as in 1805 it had been rightly decided to mobilise every available man. Scarcely were the orders issued, when the Prussian headquarters embarked on a series of councils to deliberate on the plan of campaign. At the best a council of war is a poor expedient, the favourite resource of a weak commander. These Charlottenburg councils were peculiarly bad, for every one of any note was encouraged to expound his views; memoranda begat memoranda and plans of operations; worst of all, the course eventually adopted was generally a compromise, which still left each of the advising members in the belief that his pet scheme had not been finally rejected, and might eventually be adopted. Some remarkable schemes were put forward, the most extravagant of which, perhaps, was that of Colonel von Massenbach, an officer with a high scientific reputation, who throughout played the part of the evil genius of Prince Hohenlohe. This extraordinary plan, which Prince Kraft remarks would nowadays be called the utterance of a madman, contemplated an advance with the Silesian army, entirely independent of the rest, through Saxony to Hof, thence to the Danube, and back again by Bohemia to Saxony. How he proposed to effect this *promenade militaire* in the face of Napoleon, the apostle of concentration, is beyond comprehension.

Hohenlohe put forward a scheme scarcely less contrary to all the principles of good strategy. One army was to advance on Fulda, through Gotha, another on Hof, a third through the Thuringian Forest from Erfurt, with yet a fourth in reserve about Naumburg. Three weak armies with a front of ninety miles, and a reserve far behind it! Neither of these plans took any account of the enemy, or allowed for any action on his part.

The plan finally adopted was better, for it gave due consideration to the existence of the enemy, but it was not eventually carried out. Assuming that the French forces were widely scattered over South Germany from Frankfort to the Inn, it was designed to advance with the whole allied army from Erfurt, through the forest, so as to arrive in the French centre and beat its wings in detail.[1] As a matter of fact, it would have struck a blow in the air; for Napoleon had arranged to evacuate the whole tract on which the Prussian army would debouch, to throw back his line of communications south of the Main, and to concentrate to his right. That the Prussian leaders did not know, and their plan had at least the merit of concentration. In condemning the plans of Massenbach and Hohenlohe, we are not committing the common fault of military, and still more of civilian critics, in judging after the event. Both schemes were bad, because they violated one of the first principles of strategy by contemplating a dispersal of forces beyond the possibility of mutual support. The plan for the passage of the forest is not open to that charge, and can only be condemned on the ground of the danger involved in the passage of a difficult country, in which insufficient communications would necessitate the march of the army in a column of inordinate length with a very narrow front, thus exposing it to defeat in detail as it emerged from the forest. Had the assumption of the wide dispersion of Napoleon's army been correct, the risk would have been small, for the head of the column would have found itself exposed only to a small portion of the hostile army. It would have been scarcely more dangerous than the issue of Bonaparte's army from the valley of Aosta in 1800. When the plan was formed, the Prussian leaders were ignorant of Napoleon's preparations for concentration to the

[1] This resolution was formed at Naumburg on the 24th–25th September, and the advance was in progress on the 5th October ("Napoleon as a General," i. 284).

East of the forest. What was fatal in the Prussian plans was that, whilst Napoleon laid down a distinct and decided course from which no deviation was permitted, and no subordinate was allowed to press his own views, his enemies were perpetually hesitating, holding councils of war, and modifying their plans, as one inferior commander or another, for the moment, obtained the ear of the council.

To add to their difficulties, there were two distinct parties at headquarters, The Duke of Brunswick and others were sensible of the inferiority of the numbers which Prussia could expect to oppose to Napoleon's great armies, and, clinging still to the hope of being able to avert war, were anxious to avoid the precipitation of hostilities by a bold and immediate offensive. On the other hand, Hohenlohe, Prince Louis of Prussia, Massenbach, and the enthusiastic military party, believing in the assured victory of Prussia, advocated a prompt advance on a widely extended front. The King himself, perhaps, had a clearer perception of the strategical position and requirements than any of his advisers. Being, however, young and inexperienced in war, he was naturally reluctant to impose his views on men much his seniors, many of whom had served under the great Frederick.

In the last ten days of September, the Prussian army was still spread over a front of 190 miles. Ruchel and Blücher were in Hesse, from Paderborn to Eisenach, Gotha, and Erfurt; the main army was about Naumburg; Hohenlohe was in the country between the Elbe and the Mulde; the Saxons had not yet completed their mobilisation.

In the period from the 5th to the 8th October, the general position was somewhat less widely dispersed. Ruchel, about Eisenach, had outposts towards Hesse and Meiningen.

The main army, in the neighbourhood of Erfurt, pushed its outposts south as far as Hildburghausen.

Hohenlohe was at Jena and Roda, with an advanced guard towards Saalfeld. Tauenzien was away on his left front at Hof, Gefell, and Schleiz.

The whole front still covered 85 miles in a direct line. At the same time Napoleon had seven corps and the cavalry reserve assembled on a front of 38 miles, facing Tauenzien's corps of 7000 or 8000 men, at a distance of three days' march. As Prince Kraft remarks, it was Napoleon rather than the Prussians who was in a position to interpose between the parts of the enemy's army.

At this juncture the interminable Prussian councils of war recommenced at Erfurt. During them, from the 4th to the 7th October, active operations, as usual, practically ceased.

At last Napoleon's real plan had dawned on the Prussian headquarters, as is shown by a letter from the King to Ruchel of the 7th October. It was seen that the Emperor was aiming at the left flank of the widely dispersed allies, and this was placed beyond the possibility of doubt on the 8th, when Müffling reported the advance of the French north-eastwards from Bamberg. Obviously the proper course now was a concentration of the whole army towards its left centre, which would bring it in turn on the left flank of the enemy's advance, forcing him to turn towards it. The time for the offensive had passed; it was no longer possible to carry the war into the enemy's country. The orders issued for the allied armies on the 8th were to the following effect:—

The Duke of Weimar, commanding the advance guard of the main army in the direction of the Thuringian Forest, was ordered to send forward some cavalry, with horse artillery, towards Schweinfurt, whilst his main body advanced as far as Meiningen, leaving a small reserve at Schmalkalden. This was in pursuance of Müffling's suggestion that the enemy's rear should be threatened by cavalry. The bulk of the main army would meanwhile move so as to reach Erfurt on the 9th, and the neighbourhood of Blankenhain and Kranich-feld on the 10th.

Hohenlohe was to draw Tauenzien towards himself, leaving only a small force to observe the enemy towards Hof. The Prince would concentrate his main body on the 9th at Hochdorf, and on the 10th, united with Tauenzien, would be on the left bank of the Saale about Kahla and Rudolstadt.

Ruchel and Blücher, sending out detachments to threaten the enemy's communications in the direction of Fulda, were to concentrate between Gotha and Erfurt, keeping in touch with the main army.

Duke Eugene of Würtemberg, with the reserve, was to move at once from Magdeburg to Halle, where he would stand ready to join the main army either towards Leipzig or towards Naumburg.

The idea of a concentration on the left bank of the Saale was correct; the only fault to be found with the orders was that, by detaching part of Ruchel's and Blücher's forces, as well as the advance guard of Weimar, against Napoleon's communications, they weakened the concentration by about 11,000 men at a time when every available man should have been brought to a central point in order to compensate, as far as possible, for the known inferiority of numbers. Prince Kraft goes so far as to estimate that, allowing for the Prussian army's inferiority in numbers, in organisation, in system of supply, in equipment, and in generalship, it was not worth more than one-third, possibly even one-fourth, of the French.

"The Armies of the Campaign of 1813," from *Napoleon's Last Campaign in Germany, 1813*

The disastrous outcome of Napoleon's invasion of Russia in 1812 signaled the beginning of a general uprising against him in much of Europe. Having lost an enormous army in Russia, Napoleon proceeded to raise another in a remarkable demonstration of his abilities as an organizer. But this army was by no means equal to that which it replaced. Nor did it face opponents as ill-prepared as those of the past. The following selections examine in some detail the general military situation and the quality of the armies in Central Europe on the eve of the Campaign of 1813.

THE NEW GRAND ARMY OF 1813[1]

For his contemplated campaign in Germany Napoleon required practically an entirely new army. It was not a case of a reorganisation of the army of Russia, for that once great force had almost ceased to exist. On the right wing, when Schwarzenberg and his Austrians retired on Cracow, there was nothing left but Reynier's weak corps; for Poniatowski

---

[1] This chapter is based largely on Camille Rousset's *La Grande Armée de 1813*, and *Die Französische Armée*, etc., published in Berlin in 1889.

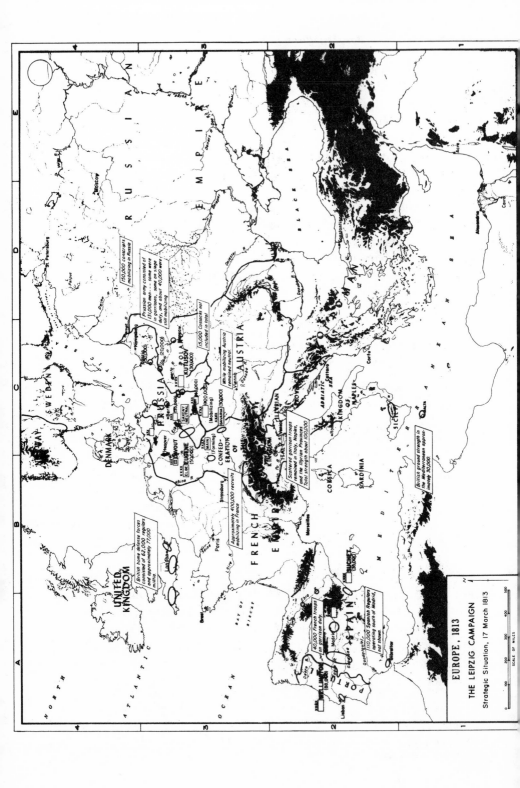

EUROPE, 1813

THE LEIPZIG CAMPAIGN

Strategic Situation, 17 March 1813

SCALE OF MILES

Map labels and annotations:

UNITED KINGDOM

British home defense forces consisted of 62,000 regulars and approximately 75,000 militia

London

PORTUGAL

Lisbon

PORTUGAL 88,000

110,000 Spanish Regulars operating south of Madrid, not shown

40,000 French troops on garrison duty

Madrid

SPAIN

SUCHET 55,000

Gibraltar

NORTH ATLANTIC OCEAN

BAY OF BISCAY

Paris

Strasbourg

FRENCH EMPIRE

Approximately 400,000 recruits mobilizing in France

CONFEDERATION OF

BAVARIA 50,000 (Mobilizing)

EUGENE 50,000

DAVOUT

ELBE

MAIN (Forming)

KINGDOM OF ITALY

ILLYRIAN PROVINCES

Scattered garrison troops remained in Italy, Naples, and the Illyrian Provinces. Total strength about 100,000

British ground strength in the Mediterranean approximately 30,000

KINGDOM OF NAPLES

SICILY

MALTA

SARDINIA

CORSICA

Marseilles

MEDITERRANEAN SEA

DENMARK

SWEDEN

NORWAY

PRUSSIA

KUTUSOV 30,000

100,000

Prussian army consisted of 65,000 men — some were in garrisons, some on siege duties, and about 40,000 were still mobilizing

150,000 conscripts mobilizing in Russia

RUSSIAN EMPIRE

St. Petersburg

Moscow

AUSTRIA

Vienna

While mobilizing Austria remained neutral

15,000 Cossacks not included in total

OTTOMAN EMPIRE

BLACK SEA

ADRIATIC SEA

Corfu

and his Poles were for the present interned in Gallicia. Of the left wing there remained, after the defection of Yorck at Tauroggen, only one weak corps of 7000 or 8000 men.

It was in the centre that the destruction had been most complete. Davout's corps had crossed the Niemen in June 1812 with a strength of 66,345 officers and men; on the 13th January 1813 it counted only 2281. On the 21st December 1812 there remained of the 50,000 men of the Guard only 500 fit for service, and 800 sick and cripples, of whom 200 were permanently disabled by amputations necessitated by frostbite or wounds.

The I., II., III., and IV. corps had, in June 1812, a strength of over 125,000 men; on the 1st February 1813 their united strength was reported as 6400 combatants. There were a certain number of reinforcements in Germany which had never reached Russia, two divisions on the march from Italy, and the garrisons of the German fortresses, but it is hardly an exaggeration to say that the army of 1812 had ceased to exist.

The Emperor's task, looking to the tremendous sacrifices he had already required from France and his allies, was Herculean, but he faced it undauntedly, and his success in conjuring up, as if by magic, a fresh army is perhaps one of his most remarkable achievements.

He had certain elements for his task in France, in Germany, in Spain, and in Italy.

In September 1812, when the calls on the conscription of 1812 had been practically exhausted, Napoleon had obtained a Senatus Consultum decreeing the levy of 120,000 conscripts of 1813, a number which he subsequently raised to 137,000 by assigning an extra 17,000 to complete the so-called "cohorts." The greater part of this levy had reached the depôts when the Emperor got back to Paris in December, but the men were naturally not ready for service.

The force readiest to hand consisted of the "cohorts." This body had been instituted, in March 1812, when Napoleon, about to leave France for the farther end of Europe, desired to leave behind him to protect the country something so nearly akin to the regular army that, in case of need, it might take its place in it.

By a Senatus Consultum of the 13th March 1812, the National Guard was organised in three "bans."

(1) Those men of from 20 to 26 years of age, of the classes of the six years 1807–1812, who had never been called up to active service.

(2) Men of sound physique aged from 26 to 40 years.

(3) Similar men of between 40 and 60.

The decree ended with a demand for 100 "cohorts" (reduced next day to 84) from the six classes of the first ban.

These cohorts, which were not for service beyond the limits of France, were organised by Departments in the different headquarters of military divisions. Each cohort consisted of 6 companies of 140 men, a depôt company, and an artillery company of 100 men. The officers were taken either from retired officers and men of the regular army, or from men of the National Guard who had served with the active army. Each cohort should have had a strength of 1080 officers and men, which would give about 91,000 for the 84. As a matter of fact, the strength was about 78,000.

After the Russian disaster the cohorts were induced, often by the exercise of considerable pressure, to volunteer for foreign service. A Senatus Consultum of the 11th January 1813 finally transferred them bodily from the National Guard to the active army. They were organised in regiments of 4 battalions. The number of cohorts having now been raised to 88, there were 22 regiments. Their strength, at 6 line companies and 1 depot company per battalion, should be 86,240. Once this strength was attained, future recruits would be available for other corps. The artillery companies (1 to each battalion) were reduced to 1 per regiment, the rest being formed into 3 regiments of artillery "à la suite de l'armée."

In addition to disposing of the cohorts, the Senatus Consultum of the 11th January authorised a supplementary levy of 100,000 on the classes of 1809–1812. This was commonly known as the "levy of the four classes." Also a call of 150,000 was made, nearly two years in advance, on the conscription of 1814. The levy of the "four classes" was called up at once; the other 150,000 were not demanded till February, as it would, Napoleon said, be inconvenient to arm too many conscripts at once.

The Emperor, at the same time, induced the Departments and large towns to come forward with an offer of some 15,000 to 20,000 men, mounted and equipped.

The Municipal Guard of Paris had two battalions of a total strength of 1050 men. These were sent to Erfurt to form the nucleus of a new regiment. In the same way, 4000 men raised by contributions from the Municipal Guards of capitals of Departments were amalgamated to form the new 37th light infantry. In the ports there were 12 battalions of marine artillery standing idle owing to British supremacy at sea. These the Emperor split into 24 battalions which, according to him, made up 16,000 men. He raised them to a nominal strength of 20,000 by the addition of 2000 from the levy of the "four classes," and 2000 from the conscription of 1814. The actual strength was, however, only 12,080, of whom the marines were 8000.

Yet another Senatus Consultum, of the 3rd April, authorised the following levies: (1) 80,000 men of 1807–1812 from the 1st ban of the National Guard, that is, from the source which had already supplied the cohorts; (2) 90,000 from the conscription of 1814; these were to be replaced from the Garde Nationale Sédentaire of the South and West; (3) 10,000 mounted Guards of Honour. These last were so-called volunteers, young men of well-to-do families, whose real position was indicated by the soubriquet of "the hostages," given to them in the army.

To sum up, the military elements which the Emperor sought to utilise in the first part of 1813 were:—

(1) Old Soldiers of the Paris and other Municipal
   Guards who had served before 5,000
(2) Artillerymen of the Marines, averaging 23 years of
   age 8,000
(3) The cohorts, aged 20 to 26 years 78,000
(4) Conscripts of the 1st ban of 20 to 26 years 80,000
(5) Conscripts of the "four classes," 20 to 24 years 100,000
(6) Guards of Honour, and horsemen "offered" by
   Departments, 20 to 25 years.................... 25,000
(7) Levy of September 1812, on the conscription of
   1813, 19 to 20 years 120,000
(8) Conscripts of 1814, 18 to 19 years................ 240,000

Total...... 656,000

With the later levies of August 1813 (30,000) and October (240,000) we need not concern ourselves, as they took no part in the campaign in Saxony.

The 5000 at the head of the above list were old soldiers who had seen service; the marine artillery had no experience of land warfare or infantry manœuvres; the rest were conscripts of various degrees of efficiency, but all without experience of war. Of them St Cyr says: "For some time past, and more than formerly, one had noticed that our young men were very delicate and unformed when they attained the age for conscription; those who were two years younger were weak to a degree which was painful to behold." Marmont, on the other hand, speaking of the cohorts, says that, though the officers were often too old, and generally indifferent, the soldiers were admirable. He adds that the four-battalion regiment drawn from the Departments was magnificent, as were the fifteen battalions of marine artillerymen whom he commanded. There was, as might be expected, a great dearth of officers, and various devices had to be resorted to to fill up the vacancies. When the remains of the Grand Army were formed into four weak divisions, the superfluous "cadres" were sent back to help with the new levies. Many young and inexperienced cadets from the military colleges were utilised. These were generally sent to the older regiments, where less leading was required. On the other hand, there was among the officers of the younger battalions a strong leaven of sergeants and corporals promoted to lieutenancies, men of long experience of war, though perhaps not likely to make really good officers. Many officers were drawn from the army in Spain, which was oversupplied in this respect.

The Emperor decided on the following method of reorganising his infantry:—

(1) The 36 regiments which had formed the first four corps in Russia were to be reconstituted with four battalions each. For these more than 100 "cadres de bataillon," over 2000 officers, were required.

(2) There were in France (besides depôt battalions) 100 battalions of regiments serving in Spain, Illyria, etc. These, being merely "cadres," were completed from the recruits of

1813, and were grouped in twos or threes to form "regiments de ligne" or "regiments provisoires," according as the battalions belonged to the same or to different regiments.

(3) The cohorts, as already mentioned, formed 22 regiments.

(4) The marine artillery formed 4 regiments of marine infantry.

(5) The 5000 veterans of the Municipal Guards formed 2 regiments (6 battalions).

(6) Two old regiments in Italy (9 battalions) were transferred for service in Germany.

Of these elements the following corps were provisionally constituted:—

(1) The Corps of Observation of the Elbe (afterwards the V. corps), General Lauriston; 3 divisions (48 battalions). To assemble at Magdeburg between 15th February and 15th March. These were all cohorts.

(2) The 1st Corps of Observation of the Rhine (later the III. corps), Marshal Ney; 4 divisions (60 battalions). To assemble about Mayence during March.

(3) The 2nd Corps of Observation of the Rhine (later the VI. Corps), Marshal Marmont; 4 divisions (50 battalions). Three divisions to assemble about Mayence at the end of March and beginning of April. The fourth was not ready till the end of May.

(4) The Corps of Observation of Italy, General Bertrand; 4 divisions (54 battalions). These later became the IV. and XII. Corps.

(5) The I. Corps; 4 divisions (64 battalions).

(6) The II. Corps; 4 divisions (48 battalions).

(7) Durutte's division of the VII. corps, to which 2 Saxon divisions were to be added.

(8) The Guard. One division of the Old Guard to be formed of what had returned from Russia, added to 3000 old soldiers drawn from Spain. Three divisions of Young Guard to assemble at Mayence. These were conscripts, differing in no respect from those who formed regiments of the line.

(9) Two corps of reserve to be formed at Mayence. They were not ready till the end of August.

The cavalry was still more difficult to constitute than the infantry. About 9000 or 10,000 had wandered back from Russia. For the rest, conscripts had to be taken. As far as possible, men were chosen who had some acquaintance with horses. It was decided

(1) To reconstitute the Guard cavalry entirely.

(2) To reorganise the 52 regiments of the late Grand Army in two corps under Latour-Maubourg and Sebastiani, altogether three heavy and four light divisions. "Cadres" were to be completed from the regiments in Spain.

(3) A third corps, under Arrighi, was to be formed about the nucleus of one squadron supplied by each of the regiments in Spain.

It is not within the scope of this work to enter into all the complicated details of the reorganisation of the French army. Those who are curious on the subject will find full details in the works referred to at the commencement of this chapter.

But something must necessarily be said regarding the military value of the troops with which the great Emperor conducted this his last campaign in Germany.

Colonel Lanrezac, on the whole, passes a more favourable judgment on the army than do Camille Rousset and the author of *Die französische Armée*. He states the numbers of infantry present, according to a return of the 20th April, at 210,000, of whom 175,000 were French and 35,000 Allies. Of the 175,000 French not more than 75,000 were conscripts of 1813; the rest were men of earlier years, for the recruits of the 1814 conscription had not yet joined. Even the 1813 men had four months' service, and averaged 20 years of age. The weaklings and malingerers had dropped out on the way to the front. On the other hand, Camille Rousset tells of one detachment of 600 which had to leave 100 in hospital in Brussels, and another of 950 at La Rochelle, which had 300 in hospital and an excessive mortality. In the west of France it became necessary to hunt up the "réfractaires" with mobile columns, and the commander of one of these reported that he was afraid to use his young recruits for this purpose. He would, he said, rather have 100 old soldiers than 600 conscripts of 1813, such as filled most of his companies. They had never had a musket in their hands before quitting the depôts, and were unfit for the necessary marches. The training seems to have been less than elementary at the depôts. There was an order which required that no conscript be sent forward till he had fired at least six blank and two ball cartridges! Yet commandants of depôts who tried to insist on this very rudimentary fire training often found themselves censured for delaying their conscripts. Camille Rousset gives the following as a common type of report on inspection: "Some of the men are of rather weak appearance. The battalion has no idea of manœuvring; but nine-tenths of the men can manage and load their arms passably."

There was the wildest confusion in the depôts, where it seems to have been tacitly agreed that infantry depôts were equally liable to be drawn on for other arms. In the confusion training was neglected. It often happened that where there were four series of battalions to be reformed the fourth was ready first. There were bitter complaints of the state in which the "détachements de marche" reached the regiments. From Osnabruck General Lambardière writes, on the 15th April: "These battalions arrive very fatigued; every day I supply them with special carriage for the weak and lame. . . . All these battalions are French; I must say that the young soldiers show courage and good-will. Every possible moment is utilised in teaching them to load their arms and bring them to the shoulder."

When the conscripts of 1813 required to complete the 1st battalions began to run short, the Emperor said the deficiency could be supplied from conscripts of 1814, provided only the "big and strong" were picked out. The adjectives could only be applied to the conscripts selected in relation to the weaklings, who were distinctly small and weak. So poor were they in physique that the Minister of Police protests against their being drilled in the Champs Elysées during the hour of promenade, on account of the scoffing and jeering they gave rise to. Besides all this, there was a shortage of muskets, so much so that Napoleon even suggested arming the 1814 levies with foreign ones of the same calibre as the French, though he insisted on ample reserves of French weapons being kept at Strasburg, Mayence, and Wesel for issue to troops on their way to Germany.

Camille Rousset insists on the deficiency of officers, but Colonel Lanrezac shows, on the other hand, that the III. corps, on the 15th April, had the high average of one officer to every 31 men, whilst even less favoured corps had one to every 40. The real difficulty, he says, was that there were no reserves of officers to supply the waste of war. As long as the numbers of the men went on diminishing proportionally the matter was not so important. The rub came when, in the second half of the campaign, reinforcements in men were poured up, without a corresponding number of officers.

Of the whole corps of officers, perhaps, the central portion was the best. The commanders of corps, of divisions, of brigades, of regiments, and, perhaps, even of battalions, were, almost without exception, still the old experienced leaders of many years of war. But the Emperor's system of command, whilst excellent for the training of tacticians, was fatal to the development of strategical initiative. His corps commanders were not encouraged to look upon themselves as responsible in any way for strategy. That, they considered, was the Emperor's province alone, and, with the possible exceptions of Davout and Masséna, they were incapable of exercising an independent command on a large scale. Spain had already laid bare the deficiencies of several of them in this respect. So long as Napoleon had but one army in the field, and that of dimensions which he could manage alone, the strategical deficiencies of his immediate subordinates mattered comparatively little. But when he himself was commanding a vast host in Russia, and at the same time carrying on, through one of his marshals, a deadly struggle in Spain, he had to recognise that his curbing of initiative in his lieutenants must be fatal. As regards his war in Germany in 1813, Eugène's mistakes on the Oder and the Elbe were one instance of the want of good independent commanders, though certainly Eugène was a particularly bad example, and something better might have been expected from Davout, Soult, or Gouvion St Cyr.

When the Emperor once more gathered the reins in Ger-

many into his own hands, in April 1813, he was again operating with a single army of dimensions within his own power of
control, and the marshals slipped back into their old position
of mere instruments of the great leader. In the second half
of the war it was different. The numbers of the army were
too great to be directly commanded by a single man, even by
a Napoleon. Moreover, the strategical position necessitated
something more like the modern system of a war of armies,
each commanded by a subordinate capable of acting independently, without having the great director always at his
elbow.

The marshals, or some of them at least, were aware of
their deficiencies, as is evidenced by Marmont's famous
prophecy, which was realised almost as soon as uttered. In
August 1813, that marshal, criticising the Emperor's plans,[1]
wrote: "I fear much lest, on the day when Your Majesty has
won a victory and believe you have gained a decisive battle,
you may learn that you have lost two." A few days later came
the news of Macdonald's defeat on the Katzbach, and
Oudinot's at Gross Beeren, which had almost coincided in
time with the Emperor's own victory at Dresden. His power,
his throne, everything depended on himself alone. As Count
Yorck von Wartenburg says: "All his actions were connected
with his own personality, and based upon it alone; so, when
this became weak, there was no longer anything in his army
or state that could support or sustain him."[2] Europe freed
herself from the tyranny of the Corsican by the uprising of
her peoples, and at enormous expense in blood and treasure.
All that would have been saved had a stray bullet taken the
charmed life of the conqueror; for his empire must have
collapsed at once with his own disappearance from the scene.

The same causes resulted in an absence of capacity in the
personnel of his headquarters staff. He, like Frederick the
Great, was his own chief of the staff, he managed everything,
and Berthier was but a glorified head-clerk. The organisation of the General Staff was what it had been in the days of

[1] What a change from the old days is evidenced by the mere fact of
Napoleon's inviting his marshals to offer an opinion on his own plan of
campaign!

[2] *Napoleon as a General* (English translation), vol. ii. p. 270.

the Revolution. The Emperor only awoke to its deficiencies as an instrument for the governance of the vast armies he was now leading when, on the 2nd July 1812, he wrote: "The general staff is organised in such a manner that nothing is foreseen." It was good enough for the management of *an* army; but, "the war of armies requires staffs of the first rank, staffs constituted of chosen men, educated in the higher knowledge of war, united by a community of doctrine, and amongst whom initiative has been carefully developed." That description is utterly inapplicable to the staff of which Berthier was the nominal head.

Perhaps the worst part of the army of 1813 was its cavalry. In the first part of the war, up to Lützen, it numbered but 15,000, mostly old soldiers, 11,000 French and 4000 allies. It was opposed to a far more numerous cavalry of generally excellent quality, against which it was almost impotent. Later, it was greatly increased in numbers, but the recruits were of very inferior quality and training. On the other hand, the artillery was very good and numerous, though the draught horses were rather young.

On the whole, we may well accept Lanrezac's estimate of the army of 1813. "Certainly, the new troops were not the equals in value of the bands destroyed in Russia, and, moreover, their constitution exposed them to a rapid exhaustion; nevertheless, they were good. . . . Anyhow, the army with which Napoleon opened the campaign . . . was a good instrument of war; however, it had in itself serious germs of weakness." The estimate is supported not only by the opinion of contemporaries like Odeleben,[1] certainly not prejudiced in favour of the French, but still more by its actual achievements in the victories of Lützen, Bautzen, Dresden, and even the gallant but unsuccessful fighting at Kulm and Leipzig.

---

[1]"The good military bearing which predominated in this new army, sprung, as it were, from the earth, and assembled by the wave of a wand, was truly admirable; and, if one felt horror at the excesses of the French soldiers, the military spirit, the activity in marches, and the bravery of the young troops so rapidly formed and opposed to experienced soldiers, excited no less astonishment."—Odeleben, *Campagne de 1813* (French translation), vol. i. p. 62.

In one department especially, the attack or defence of localities, of woods or villages, the French infantry ever displayed that capacity which, in the French soldier, seems to be an inborn instinct.

Of the Emperor himself what shall we say? Perhaps it will be best to show as we go along the evidences of the decline of his personality, and of his failures to be true to his own principles, which alternated with flashes of the old genius and decision.

As for his marshals and generals, most of them were long since tired of war, by which they had been enriched. Now they looked for a period of peace in which to enjoy their wealth. The prevalence of such a spirit augured ill for success.

THE PRUSSIAN ARMY[1]

By the Treaty of Tilsit in 1807, Prussia's army was limited to 42,000 men of all arms, the proportion of the arms being also fixed. Napoleon had carried 20,000 men, nearly half of the whole army, to Russia with him in 1812, and we already know what had become of that, thanks to Yorck's defection from the cause of the French. Including what Yorck had left, there remained a standing army of about 33,000 men. This "old" army was extremely good, with young and well-instructed officers. So good was it that Von Boyen, writing in 1838, described the infantry as the best he had ever seen. The cavalry was also good, though the horses of some regiments were rather old. It consisted of 2 Guard and 18 line regiments,[2] which, at 600 men per regiment, made 12,000, in 80 squadrons of 150 each.

The artillery comprised three brigades, each of three horse and 12 foot companies. Total 6000 men, in 21 batteries, with 168 guns. There were six companies of engineers (pioneers). In 1813 the strength was raised by calling up reservists, so that there were 36,846 infantry, and the total strength of the army was about 56,000. Moreover, artillery

[1] This section is mainly based on Friederich's *Der Herbstfeldzug 1813*, vol. i, chap. ii.

[2] Seven heavy and thirteen light.

had been collected to such an extent that there were available, even in the spring of 1813, 236 guns. This army was the nucleus round which the new formations were collected.

In 1810 Scharnhorst had started his "Krumper"[1] system, under which each company or squadron, at fixed intervals, discharged a given number of trained soldiers, and took in an equal number of fresh men for training. By thus constantly passing men through the ranks, Napoleon's restrictions were evaded, and it became possible to nearly double the 42,000 by calling up the men who had been trained. So when the king issued his order of the 1st February 1813, calling up the reserves and "Krumpers," 52 reserve battalions could be formed. Several of these took part in the spring campaign; others were only called to the army at a later period. By these means the army received eventually a reinforcement of 42 battalions—33,642 men.

At first these regiments of "Krumpers" and reservists left much to be desired, but, by appointing to them ex-officers of regiments which had been disbanded in 1807, they were worked up to a state of efficiency equal to that of the rest of the army.

It must be noted that the lesson of 1806–7 was taken to heart in Prussia, and the whole military system was radically reformed. It was sought to induce the obedience of the soldier not, as in the old days, by force alone, but chiefly by an appeal to his patriotism. Corporal punishment was abolished, save for dishonourable offences, and the military man, from being the lowest in the social scale, as he was in 1806, was raised to a position of respect, and had come to be looked upon as the eventual saviour of his country from French tyranny.

Though artillery had been collected, there was a great shortage of uniforms. Many of them were of the simplest character. Black or grey cloth jackets with various coloured facings were worn over trousers of the poorest cloth. Some

---

[1] Krumpen = to shrink. According to a memorandum by the king, printed in Von Boyen's *Memoirs* (ii. p. 345), the total effective strength of the army on the 24th July 1810 was only 22,392.

regiments even had old English uniforms. The muskets were of four or five different patterns.[1] To facilitate the supply of ammunition and prevent confusion, advantage was taken of the cessation of hostilities in June–August 1813 to effect exchanges of weapons, so that each regiment might be, as far as possible, armed with muskets of the same calibre.

The next body to be raised consisted of "Volunteer Jägers," young men of independent means, of from 17 to 24 years, equipped and armed at their own expense, or at that of the neighbourhood. They were those who did not already belong to the army, and had no sufficient cause for exemption. As the decree of the 3rd February dealing with them was supplemented by another of the 9th, limiting the causes of exemption and prescribing penalties for failure to join, it seems clear that these were volunteers only in name.[2] Their numbers are uncertain, but they probably never exceeded 5000 infantry, 3000 cavalry, and 500 artillery and engineers. Their moral was probably greater than their military value, though, later, they formed good schools for the training of officers and under-officers, in supplying whom there was considerable difficulty.

A few "free corps" were established as follows:—

Lützow's—3 battalions, 5 squadrons, 8 guns.

Von Reiche's Jäger battalion.

Hellwig's—3 squadrons, one Jäger detachment.

The "Schill" free corps—2 squadrons of hussars.

The Elbe regiment—2 battalions raised from the provinces torn from Prussia in 1807.

These free corps consisted largely of foreigners, were of very varied constitution, not always either well led or well

---

[1] Two Prussian, one Austrian, one English, and, later on, the French muskets captured in the field.

[2] On this subject there is a significant note in Colonel Lanrezac's book, p. 36: "What happened in France in 1792, and in Prussia in 1813, proves that, however great the patriotic feeling of the nation, voluntary enlistment furnishes in time of war but a small number of defenders. Without a law compelling to military service all citizens of a certain age, only insignificant results are obtained."

disciplined, and, altogether, not so important as they might have been.

More was still required for an army which had to struggle for the very existence of the Fatherland.

A decree of the king established the "landwehr," based on the model of that of Austria of 1809. This decree, signed on the 9th February 1813, but only brought into force on the 17th March, required universal service. No preparations for this had been possible during the years succeeding 1807. As the impoverished state of Prussian finances precluded much assistance from the State, the expense of equipment had to fall on the men themselves, or their villages. The consequence was that the men had miserable clothing, which was ruined by the first heavy rain. They had caps which protected them neither against the weather nor against blows; they had shoes which, being unprovided with gaiters, were often drawn off by the mud through which the men had to march—and wretched linen trousers. At first, the front rank was often armed with pikes or scythes, and it was only as French muskets were taken from the battlefields that the men were armed with yet another pattern of firearm. There was a great dearth of officers, as most of the half-pay officers still fit for service were required for the reserve battalions. All sorts of officials, many of them very unsuitable as military officers, joined, and it was only later on that men of some experience were got from the "Volunteer Jägers," etc.

Naturally, the landwehr, as a whole, was at first of no great military value, though their initial worth was in some corps (Yorck's and Bülow's especially) enhanced by long marches and still more by early successes.

The landwehr infantry numbered about 100,000 at their highest strength, and the cavalry about 11,500. The latter were, on the whole, proportionately better than the infantry, but their horses, drawn from the fields and other sources, were a very mixed lot. Friederich says that once a body of this cavalry began to give way no power on earth, saving an insurmountable physical barrier, could stop them. The whole strength of the Prussian army in August 1813, after the armistice, may be summarised thus in round numbers:—

Infantry.

Regular, exclusive of garrison and depot battalions	72,000
Landwehr, garrison and depot battalions, "free" corps, Volunteer Jägers, and Landwehr reserve	156,000
	228,000

Cavalry.

Regular, excluding depot squadrons	12,600
Landwehr, Volunteer Jägers, etc.	18,500
	31,100
Artillery (376 guns) and engineers	13,000

This total of 272,000 later rose to about 300,000, which represents about 6 per cent. on the then population of Prussia.

Of the 272,000 there were actually in the field at the close of the armistice in August about 192,500, inclusive of 30,500 (mostly landwehr) blockading Küstrin, Stettin, Danzig, and Glogau. Prussian writers justly claim that their country supplied the backbone of the uprising which overthrew Napoleon. The greatest actual numbers of troops in 1813 were furnished by Russia, but looking to the general quality of the troops, and the spirit of patriotism and enthusiasm which pervaded them, the slightly smaller Prussian forces were of distinctly greater value. It must always be remembered that they were fighting for hearth and home, whilst the Russians had already saved their own country in 1812, and in 1813 and 1814 were fighting, not so much for their own safety, as for the liberation of Germany and Europe from the yoke of Napoleon.

THE RUSSIAN ARMY

There is a good deal of uncertainty as to the actual numbers of the half-disciplined troops, such as Cossacks and Bashkirs. Though very inferior in quality from a military point of view, these half savages had created such alarm amongst the French that they were far from being a negligible quantity.

The Russian officers were still, as they had been in 1807, very ill-educated and rough, except those drawn from the nobility for the Guard and a few crack cavalry regiments.

The Russian soldier of the regular army was what he was in 1807, and what he still is, a fighter of the utmost bravery and obstinacy, without education or much intelligence.

In the beginning of February 1813 the total strength of the Russian army pursuing the French did not exceed 70,000 infantry, 30,000 cavalry and Cossacks, 10,000 artillery and engineers—110,000 in all. Most of the infantry regiments were reduced to a single battalion of about 350 men; the cavalry regiments had only 4 squadrons (instead of 8) of 100 men each.

A "ukase," of the 5th February 1813, prescribed the formation of a reserve army of 163 battalions, 92 squadrons, 37 batteries, to assemble about Bialystock. Its formation was much retarded by want of "cadres" and material. Between March and August 1813, it furnished to the active army 68,000 infantry, 14,000 cavalry, and 5 batteries. At the close of the armistice the Russian army in Germany and the reserves in Poland numbered about 296,000 men.

The corps, both of infantry and cavalry, were so split and mixed that Lanrezac quotes the saying of an unnamed eyewitness that "the generals did not know what troops to command, and, similarly, the troops knew not which chief to obey."

THE AUSTRIAN ARMY

Austria was neutral till the close of the armistice in August 1813, but it will be convenient to deal here with the army which she then brought into the field. After the campaign of 1809, the strength of the Austrian army was fixed at 150,000 men. The war had brought her almost to the verge of bankruptcy, the strictest economy was required, and it was practised largely at the expense of the army, especially of the Austrian (as distinguished from the Hungarian) portion. It was kept on the lowest peace footing, and the rest of the men received an extremely short annual training. Differences with his brother the Emperor had, unfortunately for Austria, resulted in the disappearance from her councils of her best leader and organiser, the Archduke Charles. Schwarzenberg's auxiliary force in the Russian campaign of 1812 numbered about 29,000 men and 7000 horses. After his return, Austria was quite unable to put a respectable force in the field to join the Russians and Prussians. Therefore, she was compelled to go no further than playing a neutral part, and pretending to serve as mediator between Napoleon and the allies, whilst she was reorganising her army. When, at last, she openly joined the allies, in August 1813, her armed strength was as follows:—

	BATTNS.	SQUADNS.	GUNS.	MEN.
(a) In Bohemia	107	117	290	127,345
(b) Between the Enns and the Traun, opposed to Wrede's Bavarians on the Inn				30,079
(c) In Upper Austria (Hiller)				36,557

Total Field Army, 193,981

In garrison at Prag, Königgratz, and Josefstadt	27,544

Total, 221,525

Besides these, a reserve army, strength not known, was organising at Vienna and elsewhere. There was no corps organisation, the army being divided into 12 infantry divisions, with 3 divisions and 1 brigade of cavalry.

As a consequence of the conditions above mentioned, two-thirds of this army consisted of recruits with scarcely three months' service.

Information regarding the military value of the Austrian army is not so plentiful as in the case of Prussia. The corps of 1812, however, appears to have been excellent, whilst the reserves and recruits were perhaps not far behind the corresponding elements of the Prussian army.

The cavalry was generally good, the artillery less so.

SWEDISH ARMY

Bernadotte, Crown Prince of Sweden, ex-Marshal of France, does not cut an admirable figure in any way in 1813. His political conduct was crooked in the extreme, and as for his Swedish contingent, his main object seems to have been to expose them to as little fighting as possible.[1] The army consisted partly of Swedes, partly of Germans recruited in Pomerania and the island of Rügen. In discipline, equipment, and clothing they left nothing to be desired. They, too, only appeared in the north after the armistice, when their strength was:—

	BATTNS.	SQUADNS.	GUNS.	MEN.
(a) In Brandenburg	33	27	54	23,449
(b) In Mecklenburg with Walmoden	6	5	8	3,814
	39	32	62	27,263

ANGLO-GERMAN TROOPS

Most of these were Germans, or a mixture of all nations. The only really British troops were:—

1 regiment of hussars—5 squadrons.

2 horse artillery batteries with 12 guns, and—

28 rocket apparatus. These Congreve rockets, then a new invention, created much alarm amongst the French at Leipzig.

The strength of this Anglo-German contingent was about 9000 men.

There were also 6 English battalions (3459 men) in garrison at Stralsund.

MECKLENBURG CONTINGENT

Four battalions, 4 squadrons, 2 guns, 6149 men.

Of these only the Guard Grenadier battalions were old troops. The rest were recruits.

---

[1] Friederich refers to an English caricature representing the Crown Prince leading back his army in the guise of a flock of sheep and saying to the old king, "Here am I with the sheep you entrusted to me. Behold! I have not lost one of them."

To sum up the field forces[1] of the allies, about the beginning of the autumn campaign they stood as follows:—

	BATTNS.	SQUADNS.	COSSACK REGTS.	GUNS.	MEN.
Prussian Field Army	185½	174	—	362	161,764
Russian Field Army	212	228	68	639	184,123
Austrian Field Army	107	117	—	290	127,345
Swedish Field Army	39	32	—	62	23,449
Anglo-German Contingent	9	17	—	26	9,283
Mecklenburg Contingent	4	4	—	2	6,149
	556½	572	68	1381	512,113

Adding to these the Russian and Prussian blockading corps, reserves in second line, the garrison of Stralsund, the Austrian armies on the Italian and Bavarian fronts, etc., the allies had some 860,000 troops.

THE ALLIED COMMANDERS

Napoleon's great advantage over the allies, at periods when he began to find himself with inferior numbers, consisted in the absolute unity of his command. The final decision always rested with him alone. The disadvantages of his system in depriving him of men trained to semi-independent command have already been noted.

The allies, on the other hand, had no unity of command whatever. No one could know with whom the final decision lay. Even when the Russians were alone there was some difficulty, so long as Kutusow lived: for he was strongly opposed to embarking on chivalrous adventures for the benefit of the rest of Europe. So great had been his services to Russia that, until his death, even his master, the Tsar, felt bound to defer to some extent to his views.

[1] Exclusive of blockading troops before the fortresses and of the Austrian and Russian reserve armies.

Then Prussia joined in the war against Napoleon, and the difficulties at once increased; for it became necessary to consider the new ally, and the opinions of her generals, amongst whom were men of the highest military capacity, such as Clausewitz,[1] Scharnhorst, Gneisenau, Müffling, and others, like Blücher and Yorck, who, if they were not great commanders, had at least very decided opinions, and still more decided wills. Then came Austria, the views of whose leaders had again to be consulted, and who, on at least one occasion, insisted on changes in the allied plans. Bernadotte introduced a further complication, for he wanted to be commander-in-chief of the allied armies, a position which it was impossible to confer on him.

Of the allied sovereigns, the Tsar generally succeeded in taking the most influential position. He was surrounded by a multitude of advisers, Toll, Barclay de Tolly, Wittgenstein, to whom were added, later, Jomini and Moreau. Knesebeck, Borstell, von Boyen, Scharnhorst, Gneisenau, Clausewitz, Schwarzenberg, Radetzky, and Müffling all had their say in the perpetual councils of war which discussed and tinkered with the allies' plans. To such a pitch did dissensions come that when the Tsar, before Leipzig, was unable to gain over Schwarzenberg to his views, he took the extreme course of telling the Austrian (and allied) commander-in-chief that he might keep his Austrians between the Pleisse and the Elster, but that the Russians and Prussians, being the affair of the Tsar and the King of Prussia, should be brought over to the right bank of the Pleisse. After the battle of Lützen there were dissensions between the Russians and the Prussians, each blaming the other for the defeat.

Then the divergent interests of the Russians, desiring to preserve their direct communication with Poland, and of the Prussians, thinking of directly covering their capital and the Mark, nearly led to a separation which would certainly have been fatal to Prussia.

Even when a commander-in-chief had been appointed to succeed Kutusow, his position became almost intolerable; for

[1] Clausewitz was still in the Russian service which he had entered in 1812, but he had been a Prussian officer and may fairly be classed as such. He returned to the Prussian service in 1815.

Wittgenstein, who was selected, constantly found the Tsar consulting Toll and others without reference to him, and passing important orders over his head.

Many of these difficulties will appear in their proper place in the course of this history. They are only briefly referred to here in order to indicate generally the extremely divided state of the allied command, and the many obstacles to the co-operation of armies with such divergent interests as those of the allies. One expedient adopted was the intermixture of the various forces, so that Bernadotte, Blücher, and Schwarzenberg each commanded troops of two or more nations. By thus mixing them up in separate commands it was hoped to remove the temptation to any one nation to act on its own account.

III

Strategy

Napoleon had no peer as a strategist in his own time. None of his contemporaries ever demonstrated in a sustained fashion the brilliant sort of strategic operations he conducted for over a decade. Basing his strategy upon what were some very simple concepts, he repeatedly proved himself superior to all his opponents practically right to the end, during the Waterloo Campaign. The two selections which follow not only serve to illustrate Napoleon's particular abilities as a strategist, but also show his capacity to control events and act instantly upon critical information. In addition, these selections demonstrate the relative inability of his opponents to develop significant counter-strategies, even when the overall situation tended to favor them.

"Operations Against Prussia, 6 to 13 October, 1806," from *Napoleon's Conquest of Prussia, 1806*

The campaign against Prussia, in 1806, was one of the most perfectly conducted in Napoleon's career. Virtually everything went according to plan as he defeated the much-vaunted Prussian Army in but eight days, and then totally annihilated the Prussian State in the following weeks. Of particular interest in this campaign was Napoleon's use of the "bataillon carré" advancing behind an impenetrable cavalry screen to execute a nearly perfect "manoeuvre sur les derrières," or indirect approach, in order to bring the enemy to battle under circumstances particularly favorable to himself.

In accordance with the orders issued on the 19th September, the French corps were rapidly reaching the line from which their advance was to commence. The Emperor's projects are explained most clearly in his letter to Soult, dated 5th October, 11 A.M., one of those demi-official letters, explanatory of the formal orders issued through Berthier, which Napoleon was in the habit of addressing direct to his marshals. "I have," he writes, "caused to be occupied, armed, and provisioned, Würzburg, Forchheim, and Kronach, and I shall debouch with my whole army by three issues upon Saxony. You are at the head of my right, having behind you Marshal Ney's corps, at a distance of half a day's march. A day's march behind him will be 10,000 Bavarians, making altogether more than 50,000 men. Marshal Bernadotte is at the head of my centre; he has behind him Marshal Davout's corps, the greater part of the Reserve cavalry, and my Guard, making over 70,000 men. He debouches by Kronach, Lobenstein, and Schleiz. The 5th corps is at the head of my left; behind it is the corps of Marshal Augereau. It debouches by Coburg, Gräfenthal, and Saalfeld, and musters over 40,000 men. The day you arrive at Hof all these will be abreast of you."

The strength and composition of the columns may be stated as follows, on the basis of the present states given by Foucart, and further worked out by Lettow-Vorbeck. Seeing, however, that most of these statements are for dates earlier than the 8th October, and that reinforcements were steadily coming in, it is probable that the columns were actually stronger.

Grouchy's cavalry (3004) did not reach the army till the 14th October. On the other hand, we have to add about 9000 for artillerymen, engineers, &c. Napoleon's "battalion square of 200,000 men" would thus come to about 180,000 men and 298 guns, without reckoning reinforcements after the dates of the present states. Including these and departmental troops, &c., the total was probably very close to the round sum given by Napoleon.

Soult was required to be at Baireuth (Prussian territory) on

RIGHT COLUMN—

	Infantry.	Cavalry.	Guns.
IV. Corps—Soult	30,956	1,567	48
VI. Corps—Ney	18,414	1,094	24
Bavarians—Wrede	6,000	1,100	18
	55,370	3,761	90
	59,131		

CENTRE COLUMN—

I. Corps—Bernadotte	19,014	1,580	34
III. Corps—Davout	28,655	1,538	44
Imperial Guard—Lefebvre	4,900	2,400	36
Cavalry Reserve—Murat	—	17,550	30
	52,569	23,068	144
	75,637		

LEFT COLUMN—

V. Corps—Lannes	19,389	1,560	28
VII. Corps—Augereau	15,931	1,175	36
	35,320	2,735	64
	38,055		

the 8th. The country as far as Hof, being hilly and wooded, was unsuitable for cavalry, as was that to be traversed by the centre and left columns until they reached the more open country north of the Saale. It must not be supposed that the right bank of the Saale is a level, open plain. It is, rather, a rolling plateau of well-wooded downs at a considerable elevation above the river, which is generally deeply sunk in a valley of varying width. Through this plateau the tributary streams pass in valleys often broad and open, as is that leading from Pösneck to Saalfeld. Farther north the plateau gradually sinks into the plains towards Leipzig.

On the other hand, the country between the Upper Main and the Saale is one of forest-clad mountains rising to altitudes of 2500 feet or more. It can be traversed only by comparatively few roads leading through the valleys, whilst beyond the Saale roads are numerous—though in 1806 they were not good—and in fine weather it is possible in many parts to march straight across country. The belt of the Franconian and Thuringian forests and mountains stretches from Bohemia to the longitude of Fulda. It is narrowest in Franconia where Napoleon crossed it. It has been shown that, whilst crossing this hill tract, the army would be marching with a front of about thirty-eight miles as the crow flies, and an equal depth. During this period lateral communication between the columns would be difficult, and often circuitous. Closer connection of the columns was, owing to the position of the roads, impossible; it was only when the opener country beyond the Saale was reached that closing up would be practicable. During this preliminary stage Napoleon expressed his intention of accompanying the centre column; for it, therefore, orders could be issued daily by himself. Not so was it with those of the right and left. To them it was necessary to issue precise instructions for the whole period to be spent in the hill tract, and for their action on first debouching from it. Accordingly, the Emperor issues elaborate orders to Soult and Lannes, whilst contenting himself with much more general orders to Bernadotte. Soult was to have with him only his own light cavalry, and he is warned of the risk of pitting it against the Prussian horsemen, whose reputation was of the highest. Rather, he should endeavour to let the latter break itself against his infantry squares. Should the enemy be found in force watching the issue from the mountains, Soult was permitted to attack him, provided, first, that Ney was able to support the attack; secondly, that the opposing force did not exceed 30,000 men; thirdly, that it was not occupying a selected entrenched position. Failing those conditions, the right column would await the advance of the centre. If the enemy were not in force at Hof, Soult must be guided by the intelligence he might gather in coming to a decision to lean, down the Saale valley, towards the centre, or to take a position beyond Hof, preparatory to marching on Plauen.

Napoleon had little fear of serious resistance to this column. "According to all my information to-day," he writes, "it appears that if the enemy makes any movement, he will do so on my left, since the main body of his forces appears to be at Erfurt."

This last quoted sentence is indicated by Prince Kraft[1] as a proof of the imperfection of the Emperor's intelligence as to the enemy's movements, seeing that there were actually three armies, respectively about Eisenach, Erfurt, and Jena, the last with a strong advanced guard towards Schleiz and Hof. Still, his information was correct generally, in so far as it indicated danger to his left rather than to his right or centre.

To return to Soult's instructions, that marshal's first care, on reaching the open country at Hof, should be to seek for direct communication with the centre towards Lobenstein, Ebersdorf, and Schleiz. This duty was equally inculcated on Lannes and Bernadotte; the latter, strong in cavalry, would feel in both directions. In this despatch to Soult the Emperor indicates Dresden, not Berlin, as his objective; he requires full and early reports of all news regarding events on the great road to Dresden. He was most anxious to break up the half-hearted alliance between Saxony and Prussia; possibly he thought there was still time to interpose between the Saxon and Prussian armies. He remarks that it would be a great achievement to place his army in a "battalion square of 200,000 men" about Dresden; but he adds, "however, all that demands some art and some events." It is quite certain that, with the Prussian army standing fast about Erfurt and Weimar, he would never have marched away from it on Dresden. What we would venture to suggest is that he thought it not improbable that the Prussians would commence their retreat to the Elbe as soon as he appeared on the Upper Saale; at Dresden, looking to the superior mobility of his army, he would probably find himself still able to intercept the Prussian communications with Berlin, and to interpose between them and the still distant Russians. At Dresden, too, he would have turned the defensive line of the

[1] "Letters on Strategy," i. 21.

Count Yorck von Wartenburg also says that the Emperor had only an imperfect knowledge of the Prussian dispositions. "On which wing his opponent was massing his main strength he did not know; and, indeed, did not care much. For he was determined to advance in the direction which most threatened the enemy's communications" ("Napoleon as a General," i. 277).

Elbe. Perhaps when he speaks of "some events" he is thinking of an early retreat of the enemy.

Lannes headed the left column, the flank on which the
Emperor anticipated an attack, the one whose direction he
desired to mask as long as possible. He had already expressed his intention of entirely denuding of troops the
whole space between Mayence and Würzburg. He had found
that Königshofen and Schweinfurt were useless to him as
points of support; he intended to leave them in a condition
not to be of any value to the enemy. Würzburg, Kronach,
and Forchheim (south of Bamberg) were his points of support; in them were collected his depôts of food and ammunition. "You must leave nothing at Schweinfurt; you must
assume that, two or three days after your departure, the
enemy will be there," wrote Berthier to Lannes on October 5.
To mask his movement from Schweinfurt to Coburg, Lannes
was to leave cavalry pickets in front of Melrichstadt and
Königshofen, with orders to continue reconnoitring as if
nothing was happening on the 6th and 7th, and to rejoin the
corps at Coburg on the 8th.

The starting-points of these three columns were to be
Coburg, Kronach, and Baireuth; they were to reach the
Saale valley thus—Soult, at Hof, on the 9th October; Bernadotte, at Saalburg, on the same date; Lannes, at Saalfeld,
on the 11th.[1]

The centre was thus the leading column; being the
strongest, it could support, if necessary, the issue of the flank
columns. The left was the exposed column, therefore it was
to be kept well back; though, as a matter of fact, it reached
Saalfeld on the morning of the 10th. Lannes was warned[2]
that at Coburg he might expect the enemy to be moving,
either by the road from Gotha or by that from Saalfeld;
therefore, he was to be fully prepared, and was not to move
on till he had certain news of Augereau's approach to take
his place. In any case his line of retreat would be on Bam-

---

[1] "You will arrive at Gräfenthal on the 10th" (Berthier to Lannes, 5th
October).

[2] Napoleon to Lannes, 7th October (Foucart, i. 366).

berg, by the direct main road, not by that by which he had arrived. Thus, if attacked at Coburg, he would be able to fall back on the support not only of Augereau but of the numerous troops which the Emperor would have at Kronach and Lichtenfels. His zeal in reaching Coburg on the 7th, instead of the 8th, exposed him to Napoleon's censure.

On the 6th the Emperor issued to the army his customary proclamation at the commencement of a campaign:—

"Soldiers! The order for your return to France had already issued; you had drawn nearer to it by several marches. Triumphal fêtes awaited you, and the preparations for your reception had begun in the capital. But, just as we became too confident of security, fresh plots were being woven under the mask of alliance and friendship. Warlike utterances were heard at Berlin. For the last two months we have been subjected to daily increasing provocation. The same faction, the same giddy spirit which, fourteen years ago, favoured then by our internal dissensions, led the Prussians to the midst of the plains of Champagne, still rules their councils. If it is no longer Paris that they seek to burn and destroy, it is to-day their standard which they boast that they will raise in the capitals of our allies; it is Saxony that they seek to compel, by a disgraceful transaction which would range her among their provinces, to renounce her independence; in a word, it is your laurels which they seek to tear from your brows. They wish us to evacuate Germany at the sight of their arms! Madmen! Let them know that it would be a thousand times easier to destroy the great capital than to tarnish the honour of the great people and its allies. In days gone by their schemes were confounded; they found in the plains of Champagne defeat, death, and dishonour. But the lessons of experience fade from memory, whilst there are men with whom the sentiment of hatred and jealousy never dies.

"Soldiers! None of you would wish to return to France by any path other than that of honour. We must re-enter it only under triumphal arches. What! have we braved seasons, the ocean, the deserts, have we conquered Europe, several times united in coalition against us, have we carried our glory to the East and the West only to return to our country to-day as fugitives, abandoning our allies, to hear it said that the Eagle of France has fled terrified by the aspect of the Prussian armies?

"Already they are at our outposts. Forward then, since moderation has failed to calm this astonishing intoxication. Let the Prussian army suffer the fate which met it fourteen years ago! Let them learn that, if it is easy with the friendship of the great people to acquire an increase of power and of territory, that people's enmity, which can be provoked only by abandoning the spirit of wisdom and reason, is more terrible than the ocean's tempests."

The action of the French cavalry at the commencement of the campaign requires careful consideration. Prince Kraft has drawn attention to the great difference between Napoleon's use of his cavalry on this occasion and that of the Germans in 1870. But the circumstances were very different also. In 1870, war having been declared many days previously, the cavalry of either side could, at the end of July, cross the frontier, and push far into the enemy's territory without fear of precipitating war. In 1806 it was Napoleon's design to pass the frontier immediately after the declaration of war, and any cavalry movement before that date would anticipate, as Prince Kraft observes, the outbreak of hostilities, and destroy a great deal of the element of surprise which Napoleon hoped to impart to his advance. Yet there can be little doubt that the Emperor to some extent mistrusted his light cavalry, at any rate, in a contest with that of Prussia. Hence we find him directing Bernadotte, if possible, to have infantry in support of it as it issued from the mountains. His advice to Soult on the same subject has already been noted.

The general scheme for the cavalry action is laid down in Berthier's despatch of the 7th October to Murat. On the morning of the 8th one regiment of Wattier's Light Cavalry Brigade, attached to Bernadotte, was to move as far as possible to the front. Lasalle, also with one regiment, would reconnoitre towards Hof on the right, and Milhaud on the left, with another regiment from Lobenstein, towards Gräfenthal and Saalfeld. In support of them, Murat would hold two of Wattier's regiments and one of Lasalle's. Lannes' Light

Cavalry would push on to Gräfenthal. The objects of reconnaissance were the nature of the lateral communications between Saalfeld, Saalburg, Lobenstein, Gräfenthal, and Hof; also the situation of the enemy towards Saalburg and Hof, and especially on the great road to Leipzig.

The three parties from the centre were to pass the Saale on the 8th. Bernadotte was, if possible, to support them with an infantry brigade between Lobenstein and Ebersdorf; the Saale bridges, if broken, were to be repaired. The Emperor confided the work to Murat in person, as he wished to know, as far as possible, the enemy's position, and to profit by his promptitude in striking a great blow. The dragoons and two divisions of heavy cavalry were in rear; they would be useless at the front during the passage of the hill tract. That country being poor in supplies, the Emperor required his men to carry four days' food on their backs, thus rendering them independent of provision trains, which could be kept back so as to diminish to the utmost the depth of the columns. Once they arrived in the valley of the Saale, provisions would be procurable; for, looking to the Prussian system of magazines, it was safe to calculate on the country not having been exhausted by requisitions. On the 7th October the Emperor announces to Soult the receipt, that morning, of the Prussian ultimatum, which he characterises as the height of folly.

During the 8th the advance progressed, as ordered, without any fighting, beyond a few cavalry skirmishes, the most important of which was at Saalburg. That place was defended by a small force from Tauenzien's advance guard, which had fallen back on it from Gefell, whilst Tauenzien himself retreated from Hof upon Schleiz as Soult advanced. By 3 P.M. Murat was in possession of Saalburg, where the bridge had been left intact. On the evening of the 8th, the leading French corps had reached the following positions:—

Soult was at Munchberg, with light cavalry towards Hof; Bernadotte at Ebersdorf, with four companies of infantry, supporting Murat at Saalburg; Lannes was just beyond Coburg; Napoleon with the Guard reached Kronach.

On the Prussian side, Tauenzien was at Schleiz. Besides his troops there were on the right bank of the Saale 8000 or 9000 Saxons towards Auma, Boguslawski's detachment towards Neustadt, and 600 cavalry under Schimmelpfennig about Pösneck.

On the 9th October occurred the first serious collision between the armies in front of the French centre at Schleiz. When Tauenzien arrived at that place from Gefell on the afternoon of the 8th, and was just starting for Saalburg, he met his detachment falling back and returned with it to Schleiz, intending next morning to continue his retreat on Auma. He waited, however, for orders from Hohenlohe until it was too late to avoid an action with Murat's and Bernadotte's leading troops.

From Saalburg to Schleiz is a distance of about six miles, the road rising gradually along the western slope of the hills separating the Saale from the Elster as it proceeds towards Auma and Naumburg. About half-way, it reaches the large wood of Oschitz lying on the slope on its right and left.

Bernadotte, ordered by the Emperor to attack what was in front of him, directed Werlé, with the four companies in front of Saalburg, to advance on the right of the road clearing the Oschitz wood in that direction, and rejoining Drouet's division on the road beyond as the latter moved on Schleiz. Wattier's cavalry followed Drouet, as the country short of Schleiz was unsuited to its action. About 8 A.M., the Prussian outposts being driven in, the wood was occupied by Werlé. Bila II. had now come up on the enemy's side with an advance guard from Schleiz. The French were still too weak to debouch from the wood, and a desultory fire was maintained on its northern edge for several hours. About 2 P.M., as they appeared in greater strength, Tauenzien decided to continue his retreat, which would be covered by Bila with a battalion and one and a half regiments of cavalry. It was not till 4 P.M. that Drouet's arrival enabled the French to attack Schleiz, which they carried an hour after, partly thanks to a turning movement to their left. Beyond Schleiz, Murat, with the 4th Hussars, was at first driven back by the Prussian cavalry. Reinforced by the 5th Chasseurs, he was enabled to drive the Prussians as far as the wood beyond Oettersdorf, though not without difficulty or without the assistance of the infantry which saved him from being attacked in rear. Bila fell back, pursued by the French cavalry.

There was still on the French left a Prussian force of one battalion, one squadron, and two guns, which Tauenzien had sent towards Krispendorf to guard his right and maintain communication with Schimmelpfennig's cavalry at Pösneck. Hobe, commanding the detachment, finding himself in danger of being cut off as Bila retired, commenced to move back. When he reached the wood about Pornitz he found himself almost on the rear of Murat's cavalry, but with an infantry battalion advancing against his right. Attacked in the marshy wood on all sides, he suffered very heavily; his troops were forced to make the best of their way through, partly towards Tauenzien, partly towards Boguslawski at Neustadt. Many of them were cut down or taken, and one of the guns had to be abandoned.

Bernadotte reports the enemy as 8000 or 9000 strong, and says he only employed 1000 or 1200 infantry and 700 cavalry. As appears from the above account, which is based on Hoepfner's as well as Bernadotte's, all that was engaged on the Prussian side was a weak rearguard which lost about 570 men and one gun.

The French loss was trifling, that of the Prussians occurred chiefly in Hobe's detachment. Tauenzien, reaching Auma about 7 P.M., bivouacked there, his men suffering severely from exhaustion and absence of supplies. The positions of both sides on the night of the 9th were as follows:—

On the French left, Lannes bivouacked about Gräfenthal, with his light cavalry on the road to Saalfeld. Augereau was at and behind Coburg, not far enough advanced to be able to support Lannes in action next day. In the centre, Bernadotte was about Schleiz and Saalburg, the Emperor being at Ebersdorf, after witnessing the action at Schleiz. Davout had reached Lobenstein. Dragoons and heavy cavalry farther to the rear, from Bamberg to Steinwiesen, as well as the Guard cavalry. The Guard infantry was with the Emperor. On the right Soult had occupied Hof without opposition, and reported that Tauenzien had fallen back, partly on Schleiz, partly on Plauen, a few troops still further east. The marshal, deciding to move on Plauen, bivouacked between it and Hoff. Ney was at and behind Munchberg. Bavarians at Baireuth.

The allies were thus disposed:—

Hohenlohe, with his headquarters and main body (about 8000 men) at Orlamunde, had Prince Louis' advanced guard, of 8000 men, at Rudolstadt and Saalfeld. On the right bank of the Saale, Hohenlohe had Tauenzien and Zeschwitz (together 16,400 strong) about Auma and Mittel Pölnitz, Boguslawski (about 3000) at Neustadt. Schimmelpfennig (600 cavalry) towards Pösneck. The main army was about Erfurt. There were detachments at Magdala, Jena, and Lobeda. Weimar's advance guard was between Schmalkalden and Meiningen, with detachments moving southwards towards Schweinfurt.

Ruchel was between Gotha and Eisenach, Blücher at Eisenach, Winning was out to the right at Vach, with a small detachment, under Pletz, still further on the road to Fulda.

From Winning on the right to the Saxons on the left was ninety miles, and the army, besides being thus dispersed, was weakened by the detachment of about 11,000 men under Winning and Weimar. The general reserve, under Eugene of Würtemberg, was completely out of reach near Magdeburg. Napoleon, on the other hand, was still on his front of about thirty-eight miles.

During the night, Napoleon formulated conclusions regarding the enemy's movements and intentions, which he thus expalined to Soult in a letter dated from Ebersdorf at 10 A.M. on the 10th. "This is what appears to me most clear; it seems that the Prussians intended to attack; that their left was intended to debouch by Jena, Saalfeld, and Coburg; that Prince Hohenlohe had his headquarters at Jena, and Prince Louis at Saalfeld; the other column has issued by Meiningen on Fulda, so that I am led to believe you have nothing in front of you, perhaps not 10,000 men as far as Dresden." As he finished this despatch he received Soult's of the previous evening, and added a postscript: "The news which you give me, that 1000 men have retired from Plauen on Gera, leaves me no doubt that Gera is the point of union of the enemy's army. I doubt if they can unite before I arrive there."

Had Hohenlohe commanded the allied army, Napoleon's estimate of his intentions would have been fairly correct; for, influenced by Massenbach, the Prince was anxious to move leftwards across the Saale, to join Tauenzien, and meet the French advance in front. Brunswick's views were different. He proposed to concentrate on the left bank, in the triangle Weimar, Jena, Rudolstadt, in the first instance, and had directed Hohenlohe to unite his forces about Hochdorf. This order had created much excitement at Hohenlohe's headquarters, the Prince having decided to move to the right bank to the rescue of Tauenzien, and having informed Brunswick of his intention. There was a good deal of correspondence between the two headquarters, and it was not till the evening of the 9th that Hohenlohe was informed that the orders to concentrate were peremptory. In one of his despatches during the day, Brunswick had mentioned that he had no intention of awaiting the enemy on the left bank, though it would not be advisable for Hohenlohe to cross to the right until the concentration was complete. The statement was just one of those which left men like Massenbach some excuse for believing that their schemes would, in the end, be accepted. Assuming that Massenbach and Hohenlohe were justified in believing that a passage to the right bank was eventually to be effected, it is easy to understand that they would be reluctant to withdraw the troops beyond the river, with the prospect of their having to retrace their steps within a day or two.

The Emperor, then, had misjudged the intentions of the Prussian headquarters; but, holding the views he did, he naturally, as he explained to Soult, desired a battle with the enemy's army as it concentrated on Gera. Hitherto he had been moving in as close a state of concentration as the nature of the country would permit; but, for battle, he required a much closer union of his corps, and he issued orders accordingly.

Soult was to move on Gera through Weida, Ney to press on to the neighbourhood of Schleiz, Lefebvre with the Guard was to march to Schleiz itself. Lannes, supported by Augereau, hurrying up by forced marches to attack Saalfeld.

Bernadotte and Murat to proceed at once to Auma to intercept the Saalfeld–Gera route.

The heavy cavalry and dragoons (d'Hautpoult, Nansouty,

Klein, Grouchy), and the artillery and engineer parks, were all directed on Schleiz.

Jerome, with the Bavarians, who had blockaded the forts of Culmbach and Plassenburg, and were under orders for Lobenstein, was diverted to Hof, so as to take Ney's place in second line behind Soult. All these orders issued at 8 A.M. on the 10th. As Lannes was only timed to arrive at Saalfeld on the 11th, the concentration could hardly be completed before the evening of the 11th.

During the 10th nothing serious occurred on the line of march of any of the corps except that of Lannes, who fought an action at Saalfeld, the moral effects of which were far more important than might have been expected from the number of troops engaged on either side, for it caused the death of Prince Louis Ferdinand of Prussia, thereby dealing a serious blow to Prussian morale.

The positions of the French army on the night of the 10th October were as follows:—

Soult was at Plauen, with cavalry at Reichenbach on the Dresden road, which appeared to be almost clear of the enemy. On his left, Ney stood between Gefell and Tanna; Bernadotte was about Auma with two divisions, Dupont's being at Posen, Wattier's light cavalry nearly up to Neustadt.[1] Murat, in front of him at Triptis, had Lasalle at Mittel Pölnitz, and Beaumont's dragoons on his left rear. Sahuc's dragoons were at Schleiz, where also were Davout and the Guard infantry. Nansouty's heavy cavalry was at Nordhalben, d'Hautpoult's at Kronach. Klein was at Lichtenfels, the Guard cavalry and artillery still at Bamberg, Grouchy in rear.

The Bavarians were at Culmbach, Lannes at Saalfeld, Augereau at and behind Neustadt on the road from Coburg to Gräfenthal.

At the same time the Allies were thus disposed. Hohenlohe still had part of his force between the Saale and the Elster, but he had received positive orders in the night of the 9th to

---

[1] North of the Saale. There are several places of this name, which must not be confused. The Neustadt mentioned in connection with Augereau is much farther south.

10th to draw them in, and they were now on the march for the Saale. Zeschwitz's Saxons and Tauenzien had reached Roda; Boguslawski was falling back from Neustadt on Kahla, and Schimmelpfennig in the same direction from Pösneck. Hohenlohe's main body was at Jena, Lobeda, Kahla and Orlamunde. The main army was in the neighbourhood of Blankenhain, Gravert's division at Spahl, and detachments at Remda and Stadt Ilm. Ruchel was at Erfurt, with Blücher between Eisenach and Gotha. Winning was still out at, and beyond, Vach. The Duke of Weimar was at Meiningen, with infantry out as far as Königshofen and cavalry close to Schweinfurt.

The necessity for concentration had at last dawned on the Prussian headquarters. At 10 P.M. Hohenlohe received orders to concentrate with his left at Jena, his right towards Weimar. The rest of the army was to assemble at Weimar. This order reached Hohenlohe just after Massenbach had started for headquarters to urge either a general concentration at Erfurt, or a march by the left to anticipate the French on the Elbe.

The news collected on the 11th induced an entire change of Napoleon's views as to the Prussian movements. He learned the defeat of Prince Louis at Saalfeld, and that nothing had been found supporting him as far as Rudolstadt. The Saxon baggage had been captured marching westwards. Mittel Pölnitz, Neustadt, Pösneck had all been evacuated; the enemy's troops were clearly making for the Saale towards Jena. There could be no doubt that there would be no attempt on his part to concentrate towards Gera, or that he contemplated a retreat beyond the Saale. Murat's reports led Napoleon to believe that the Prussians were about to concentrate on Erfurt. Thus he fell into an error opposite to that into which he had fallen with regard to the movement on Gera. He believed that he could not now reach the Allied army east of Erfurt, whereas it was really endeavouring to concentrate east of Weimar. There exists an undated note, entirely in Napoleon's handwriting, containing memoranda of distances and possible positions of his troops on different dates. This note is attributed by the editors of the correspondence of Napoleon to the 10th October, but Foucart shows that probably the first part only was written on the 10th, whilst the second part dates from the night of the 11th to 12th.

The important point is that Napoleon, in the second part, calculates the position he expected his corps to reach on the 14th. The first line would consist of Augereau at Mellingen, Lannes between Jena and Weimar, and Davout at Apolda. The second line would be Ney at Kahla, Soult at Jena, and Bernadotte at Dornburg. Reserve cavalry and the Guard behind Jena. The army would thus be concentrated on a front of about eight miles from Mellingen to Apolda, the depth from Apolda to Dornburg would be about equal to the front, whilst that from Mellingen to Kahla would be about 13 miles. As Lannes is noted to be at Weimar on the 15th, it is clear that a westward march was contemplated. It is also clear that the Emperor did not expect a battle till the 15th or 16th, for it was his invariable practice to concentrate for battle before reaching the battlefield, not on it. On the night of the 11th the army was facing north, with Augereau at Saalfeld, Lannes at Neustadt, Soult about Weida, Bernadotte at Gera, Ney at Schleiz, Davout at Mittel Pölnitz. With the views which he now held as to the Prussian movements the Emperor, seeking a battle, must clearly change front to the west, pivoting on his left. He proposed, in the first instance, to place his army on a front extending from Kahla on the left to Naumburg on the right, a position to be gained on the 12th. On the 13th he would give a general rest to his army, every corps of which had been marching hard, some of them fighting also, since the 7th or earlier. Soult's leading division was at least 30 miles from Naumburg by the shortest route; Ney was still farther. On the other hand, Bernadotte was only about 22 miles from Naumburg, and Davout about 27. Therefore, the centre column (Bernadotte and Davout) could reach Naumburg in one long march, whilst the right (Soult and Ney) could scarcely do so, and it would save time as well as fatigue to the troops to move the original centre to the right, whilst the present right took its place. Notwithstanding the inconvenience of the crossing of the lines of communication, Napoleon decided on this measure. His orders, issued on the evening of the 11th, were thus executed on the 12th.

Bernadotte, marching from Gera by Zeitz, had by evening reached Meineweh, nearly half-way from Zeitz to Naumburg. Davout's leading division, marching from Mittel Pölnitz, reached a point 2½ miles short of Naumburg, his second and third were echeloned along the road from Mittel Pölnitz to a distance of 7½ miles from Naumburg. The light cavalry was in and beyond Naumburg, and down the Saale and Elster, at Weissenfels and Pegau. Sahuc's dragoons were with Davout. Milhaud, on Bernadotte's right, was at Teuchern. The heavy cavalry was behind at Auma and Schleiz. Guard cavalry still at Lobenstein. Headquarters of the Emperor and Guard at Gera. Ney was at Auma, the Bavarians far back at Steinwiesen. None of these corps had found anything in front of them. Before narrating the marches of Lannes and Augereau, it is necessary to give the enemy's positions during the night of 11th to 12th. The main army was at Weimar, on the right bank of the Ilm; Ruchel and Blücher on the left bank. Hohenlohe held Jena and Lobeda. Winning was still at Vach, with Pletz out beyond Fulda. The Duke of Weimar had begun his retreat, moving to his left and reaching Fraunenwald on the 12th. The reserve, under Duke Eugene of Würtemberg, was about Halle. Lannes reached Neustadt from Saalfeld on the 11th, and now received orders to march on Jena, *viâ* Kahla. Augereau's orders, to advance to Kahla from Saalfeld, did not reach him till, in accordance with previous orders, he had arrived within two hours' march of Neustadt. Therefore, instead of proceeding by Rudolstadt direct from Saalfeld, as was apparently intended, he had to go nearly to Neustadt, there doubling back, to recross the river at Kahla behind Lannes. About 2 p.m. on the 12th, Lannes' advance guard came into collision with Prussian outposts at Goeschwitz, rather more than half-way from Kahla to Jena, and drove them in with some loss on their main body at Winzerle. The valley here is more than half a mile wide between the Saale and the foot of the hills on the left bank. Here again there was a sharp fight, ending in the retreat of the Prussian advance guard. The attack appears to have been assisted by one on the bridge of Burgau from the right bank. Lannes, from Kahla, had sent a detachment along the Naumburg road on that bank; apparently it was part of this which attacked the bridge at Burgau. The fifth corps bivouacked behind Winzerle, some three miles short of Jena.

Napoleon's movements on the 12th have been somewhat unfavourably criticised by Prince Kraft. In the first place, he thinks that the interchange of positions, between the centre and right, must have caused great confusion in the crossing of columns. A careful examination of the map appears to show that this idea is mistaken, and that to have maintained Bernadotte, Davout, Soult, and Ney in their original relative positions would, on the contrary, have resulted in the very difficulties expected by the Prince. Taking the orders issued, it appears that Bernadotte, if he started from Gera at the same time as Soult started from Weida and south of it, must have had at least three or four hours to get clear of Gera before the head of Soult's column began to arrive there. As Soult was not to pass Gera without further orders (which the Emperor, himself present at Gera, could issue or withhold as circumstances required), there was clearly no need for him to cross Bernadotte's line at all. Davout's line of march from Mittel Pölnitz would not cross that of any other corps, and would only be crossed by Soult next day in rear of Davout, as the latter marched to his left. Ney, marching on Roda, would equally not cross or be crossed by any other corps. Now take the case if Napoleon had kept the columns in their old relative positions. Soult would still have had to march through Gera, and then towards Naumburg, whilst Bernadotte moved westwards. The case of these two corps would have been much the same as it actually was. Ney, marching on Naumburg, would have had to follow Davout to the crossing of the road from Gera to Roda, and would therefore have been in a somewhat similar position, with reference to Davout's movement, to that occupied by Soult with reference to Bernadotte. Moreover, Bernadotte, marching from Gera to Roda, would have crossed Davout's line, and, as Gera and Mittel Pölnitz are about equidistant from the crossing of the Mittel Pölnitz-Naumburg and Gera-Roda roads, Davout and Bernadotte would have met at the crossing, and there would have been an inextricable confusion at that point of the two corps. Surely Napoleon's arrangement was far better than this!

Again, Prince Kraft blames the exposure of Augereau, unsupported as he marched by the left bank of the Saale through Rudolstadt to Kahla. As a matter of fact Augereau did *not* march by the left bank,[1] though, no doubt, Napoleon intended him to do so, and thereby exposes himself to the Prince's criticism. Nor did Lannes remain on the right bank, as Prince Kraft seems to think. He crossed with the greater part of his corps at Kahla, only sending a detachment along the right bank to feel towards Naumburg. Thus, on the evening of the 12th, Augereau, at Kahla, was on the left bank, with Lannes in front of him, on the same side, at Winzerle. It is impossible to deny that their force, of not more than 39,000 men, was very dangerously exposed to attack and defeat by the Prussian army, as it actually stood. The reason for this has already been implied. Napoleon, as has been shown, believed that the enemy would not be found in force short of the Ilm. Had he realised their actual positions, it is almost impossible to believe he would have exposed his weak left wing to the great risk it undoubtedly incurred, on the 12th and 13th, of being crushed by the greater part of the Prussian army. Even with the belief he held, it would seem that an unnecessary risk was run, seeing the by no means positive character of his information.

During the 12th no very material changes occurred in the position of the allied army. Weimar, at Frauenwald, was still two long marches from the point of concentration, Winning and Pletz were still farther off; otherwise, the army was concentrated at last between Weimar and Jena, with posts on the Saale between Jena and Camburg. Demoralisation had, however, proceeded far in the ranks, and had been aggravated by the disaster of Saalfeld. On the afternoon of the 11th, as the Saxons, retreating from Roda, reached Jena, some one raised the cry, "The French are in the city." The alarm was absolutely groundless, but it produced a most disastrous

---

[1] This is clear from Foucart's book, which had not been published when Prince Kraft wrote.

panic. The troops rushed across the bridge, seeking security from the dreaded foe. Gunners cut the harness of their teams, and fled with the horses, leaving the guns blocking the streets of the suburb on the eastern bank; ammunition and provision waggons, abandoned by their drivers, added to the confusion. Hohenlohe, who had just sat down to dinner, mounted his horse and strove to quiet the tumult, but in vain. The alarm cry was echoed by the inhabitants from all sides, and it was long before this wild terror and panic were discovered to be groundless. There was not a French soldier within many miles; had there been but a handful of cavalry they would have gathered a rich harvest of prisoners, guns, and supplies. Even in the main army discouragement and insubordination had made headway. Confusion reigned in all quarters, food was not always forthcoming; the Saxons especially had already known the pangs of hunger.

It was on the 12th that Napoleon at last deigned to send an answer to the Prussian king's ultimatum. The terms of the Emperor's letter were overbearing, and expressive in the plainest terms of his assurance of victory. No king with any self-respect, or any chance of escape, could have accepted its offer of peace on Napoleon's terms. That Napoleon believed or hoped that it would procure the Prussian submission without a battle is certainly not the case. He would not even send it by one of his own aides-de-camp; he gave it to Rapp first, but recalled him, saying that that was making too much of it, and made it over to de Montesquiou, an orderly officer and aide-de-camp of Davout. The bearer, whether purposely delaying or not, only reached Dornburg on the evening of the 13th, and the letter was placed in the King's hands, when his armies at Jena and Auerstädt were already half defeated, next day. On the morning of the 13th Napoleon had received reports from all his marshals except Lannes. Davout had announced the capture of Naumburg, with immense magazines collected for the Prussian army. It being the Emperor's intention to give his army a rest on this day, the only movements at first ordered were, Ney from Auma to Roda, Bernadotte to join Davout at Naumburg. Orders were despatched for the collection of a great central magazine at Auma, by moving up the supplies on the road from

Kronach. The day was to be employed, by the corps not moving, in filling up stores of provisions and ammunition. The Emperor still, at 7 A.M. on the 13th, expected battle only on the 16th beyond Weimar; at 9 all was changed; "At last the veil is rent asunder; the enemy is commencing his retreat on Magdeburg." Murat and Bernadotte were ordered from Naumburg to Dornburg to fill the space between Davout and Lannes, and to be able to succour the latter should he be attacked. Soult was ordered to move one division and his cavalry to Roda, the other two to Kostritz. Nansouty and d'Hautpoult were called up to Roda.

By the time the Emperor was within five or six miles of Jena, in the early afternoon, he fully expected to be attacked the same evening, or, at any rate, next day. The Guard infantry were ordered to advance with all haste on Jena, Soult and Ney receiving similar orders. Napoleon now knew that Lannes was faced by 40,000 or 50,000 Prussians. If Davout and Bernadotte heard an attack on Lannes that evening, they were to manœuvre to their left to his assistance. In all the orders after 9 A.M. there is breathless haste. The Emperor had calculated the final concentration of his army for a battle on the 16th; he now found he would have to fight two days sooner, and he was not concentrated as he would wish to be.

We must return to the doings of Lannes and the 5th Corps, whom we left bivouacking about Winzerle, after driving in the enemy's advance guard. At daybreak on the 13th the marshal, in the midst of a thick mist, picked his way cautiously along the valley to Jena and the road from Weimar, which reaches the Saale at that town.

When Lannes' men reached Jena on the morning of the 13th October, they found the town scarcely held by the enemy, and had no difficulty in establishing themselves in it. The skirmishers of Suchet's division, which led the advance, at once began to push up the steep wooded slopes of the Landgrafenberg. Presently the rattle of musketry showed that they were in contact with the enemy. Instantly Reille with the 40th of the line was sent to their assistance. The height was gained, and a precarious foothold was obtained on the angle of the plateau as Tauenzien's advance guard, which had feebly defended the steep slope, fell back to the line between Lutzeroda and Closewitz. Lannes, standing on the Windknolle, as the mists were dissipated by the increasing heat of the sun, gazed upon a grand though alarming scene. Before him lay an army, which he rightly estimated at about 40,000 men, ranged in three lines between him and Weimar. As he watched the sun sparkling on the long lines of bayonets, sabres, and cuirasses he must have realised to the full the peril of his situation. Tauenzien's force, about Lutzeroda and Closewitz, was alone more than sufficient to sweep back, down the precipitous hill by which they had ascended, the handful of infantry Lannes had. For hours he could not hope to be more than one-fourth of the strength of the great army which appeared to be on the point of surging forward to overwhelm him. But Lannes' personal courage was equalled by his confidence in command; he had no thought of retirement. Suchet's men were hurrying up, and, even without artillery, he hoped to be able to hold on. Fortune indeed favoured him. He was right in believing that the enemy contemplated sweeping him in ruin into the Saale, and had the attack, as Hohenlohe was preparing to make it, been delivered, the result was almost a foregone conclusion. Just at this juncture, however, Hohenlohe's evil genius once more misled him. Massenbach had, after the vicious practice of the Prussian staff, been summoned to headquarters to receive an explanation of the plans which had now been decided on.

Clausewitz, discussing the strategical situation of the Prussian army on the 13th October, looks upon it as by no means a hopeless one. It stood on the left flank of the French line of advance to Berlin. If Napoleon continued his march on the capital, the Prussians would be able to operate against his communications. This case may be dismissed at once, for Napoleon was the last commander in the world to neglect the enemy's army merely for the sake of occupying territory which, with victory over the main army, must necessarily fall into his hands, and without victory would be useless and dangerous. There were two other alternatives. The Prussian army might await Napoleon's attack across the Saale. In that case the strong line of the river, if properly defended, would be an obvious advantage. The other alternative was to make a flank march towards Leipzig, seeking to head off the French about that city. Even in this case the Saale would be of great advantage in covering the right of the flank march, provided the passages at Dornburg, Camburg, and Koesen were firmly held; for the Saale is "a river deeply sunk, and offering few points of passage," at least in this part of its course. This last alternative was the one accepted.

Clausewitz says all three plans were discussed, grimly adding that even if the best were chosen, it was safe to be ruined in execution in the confusion and irresolution prevailing at the Prussian headquarters. Whatever might be thought of the flank position in the abstract, the same author says that it was not a desirable one to be held, against a very superior foe like Napoleon, by an army which was not very sure about what it was doing or intended to do. It had been decided then that the main army should march on the 13th by the left bank of the Ilm, making for the passage of the Unstrut, at Freiburg; beyond that river it would be joined by the reserve under Duke Eugene of Würtemberg, moving from Halle. The right flank of the march was to be protected by seizure of the defile of Koesen on the 13th.

Ruchel (without Blücher, who led the cavalry of the main army) was to wait at Weimar till joined by the Duke of Weimar, who could only reach Ilmenau on the evening of the 13th, and would then still be 28 miles from Weimar. The united forces would then follow the main army. To Hohenlohe the part assigned was the covering of the whole of this movement, by means of his 38,000 men, in the triangle of which Weimar, Jena, and the mouth of the Ilm indicated the angles. He was to play a purely defensive rôle.

On the rebellious Massenbach the defensive nature of Hohenlohe's part seems, as Prince Kraft surmises, to have been impressed with such force as, at last, to reduce even him to passive and blind obedience to the letter of his orders. He failed to see that the observance of the strategical defensive by no means excluded a tactical offensive. Thus, when he found Hohenlohe about noon bent on attacking Lannes and driving him into the Saale, as he could so easily have done, Massenbach related his orders, and maintained that the contemplated attack would be a violation of them. Hohenlohe, whilst vehemently asserting that it would be the right course, as it undoubtedly was, allowed himself to be overpersuaded by his quartermaster-general. The movement being abandoned, Hohenlohe's army quietly returned to camp, in the space between Isserstadt and Capellendorf, leaving Lannes and Napoleon, who reached the Landgrafenberg in person about 4 P.M., to fix themselves firmly in their dangerous position.

The Emperor, whilst rightly accepting Lannes' estimate of 40,000 or 50,000 as the strength of the army before him, wrongly thought—and he continued so to think till the morning of the 15th—that he had before him the whole of the Prussian army. He was entirely ignorant of the march of the King, with Brunswick and the main army, beyond the Ilm.

The whole of Lannes' corps, except the artillery, reached the plateau in the afternoon; the Guard infantry arrived in the evening. These were all the troops the Emperor had on the plateau as night fell.

"Champaubert, Montmirail, Vauchamps," from *Napoleon at Bay, 1814*

Napoleon's disaster in Russia in 1812 was followed by the brilliantly conducted, but ultimately equally disastrous Campaign in Germany in 1813. Napoleon retreated to France, where in the winter of 1813–1814 he conducted one of his most impressive campaigns. Greatly outnumbered, suffering enormous shortages of men and equipment, Napoleon nevertheless managed to stave off defeat by repeated spectacular operations. His successes were due largely to the cautious, frequently inept leadership of his enemies. Ultimately he could not win, for the forces ranged against him were overwhelmingly superior. Momentary triumphs were possible, but a secure victory was no longer within his grasp. Napoleon's ambitions would not permit him to see the simple realities of the situation. In the end, he went down to crushing defeat, still striving for the one victory which would set everything aright. Nevertheless, his conduct of the campaign was brilliant, and perhaps no more so than during the period February 10–14, 1814. On February 1 Napoleon had suffered a defeat at the hands of a combined Allied force at La Rothière. But his enemies had then split up, destroying their concentration. After a bit of maneuvering, he inflicted three separate defeats upon greatly superior Prussian and Russian armies, all at minimal cost to himself, through superb use of the strategy of the central position.

Napoleon, as we have seen, had already on the 2nd February foreseen the probable separation of Blücher and Schwarzenberg after La Rothière, and begun to meditate a blow against the former. He was now in a position analogous to that he had hoped to hold at Châlons on the 26th January. The question was whether he should strike first at Blücher or at Schwarzenberg. Clausewitz holds that he rightly chose Blücher, the more dangerous and determined enemy, who might take the opportunity of an attack on Schwarzenberg to advance direct on Paris. Blücher was, too, the weaker in numbers, whilst Schwarzenberg would, with his known indecision, be more easily contained by a force left for the purpose.

Before starting, the Emperor reorganized his army. The cavalry, under the general command of Grouchy, was formed into four corps[1] and the separate division of Defrance.

He created a new VII corps under Oudinot, composed of the two divisions of Leval and P. Boyer just arriving from Soult's army. To contain the Bohemian army, he left the VII corps, Victor with the II corps, Gérard's Reserve of Paris, and the 5th cavalry corps. Pajol and Allix were on the Yonne. Mortier, with two divisions of Old Guard at Nogent, was to mask the Emperor's movement and be ready to follow it. No supreme command was created over the containing troops.

Under this scheme, Victor in the centre would defend the heights of Pont-sur-Seine and the passage at Nogent, retiring to the right bank and blowing up the bridges if the enemy advanced in great strength. Oudinot would form the right, and would be reinforced by Rottembourg, at present guard-

---

[1] 1st (Bordesoulle), 2nd (St. Germain), 5th (Milhaud), and 6th (Kellermann). Defrance had four regiments of Guards of Honour and the 10th Hussars.

ing the parks at Provins. He would also have under his orders Pajol's cavalry at Montereau, Allix at Sens, and a
brigade (600) of cavalry shortly due at Bray. If Schwarzenberg marched on Sens and Pont-sur-Yonne, or if Victor was
forced on to the right bank of the Seine, Oudinot would
concentrate with Victor towards Montereau. The total force
left to contain the army of Bohemia was about 39,000 strong.

The left group of the army was the striking force which
Napoleon took against Blücher, consisting of Mortier (tem-
porarily left behind), Marmont, Ney's two divisions of Young
Guard, part of the cavalry of the Guard, the 1st cavalry
corps, and Defrance's cavalry division, in all about 20,000
infantry and 10,000 cavalry.

Here we must summarize the movements, since La
Rothière, of Blücher, Yorck, and Macdonald.

Blücher, by the 4th February, was marching on Somme-
sous, after capturing a large convoy on the Châlons-Arcis
road; Yorck, meanwhile, had driven Macdonald back to and
out of Châlons on the 5th February. On this day Blücher,
convinced that Napoleon was not endeavouring to draw
Macdonald to himself, decided on joining Yorck in an attempt to destroy that marshal. In the evening Blücher received Schwarzenberg's letter explaining his southward
move. Inferring from that letter that Napoleon was likely to
be drawn well away from himself, Blücher decided on a
manœuvre which would certainly be very risky if Napoleon
was likely to be able to interfere with it. Yorck was to pursue
Macdonald directly by the great Paris road along the left
bank of the Marne to Château-Thierry, and thence by the
right bank to La Ferté-sous-Jouarre. There Blücher,
marching by the chord of the arc by the "little" Paris road,
through Champaubert and Montmirail, might hope to anticipate Macdonald, and either to crush him between Yorck
and the rest of the Silesian army, or else to compel him to
seek by difficult crossroads to gain the Soissons-Paris road.
But Blücher wanted to combine two incompatible objects. In
addition to the attack on Macdonald westwards, he wanted to
wait for Kleist and Kapzewitch, expected shortly from the
east. He decided to keep Olsufiew's weak corps with himself,
as a link connecting Kleist and Kapzewitch with Sacken, who

was to move on La Ferté-sous-Jouarre. By the 8th the position was this: Macdonald, fully alive to his danger, had passed the Marne at Château-Thierry, and sent on cavalry to secure the next crossing at La Ferté-sous-Jouarre. Yorck's advanced guard (Katzeler) was pressing Macdonald, but the main body was still far behind.

Sacken's main body was at Montmirail, with cavalry at Viels Maisons. Twelve miles behind him, at Etoges, was Olsufiew with about 4000 men. Blücher's headquarters were at Vertus, nine miles behind Olsufiew, and Kleist and Kapzewitch were yet another sixteen miles behind, at Châlons. Thus, on the evening of the 8th, Blücher's main column was scattered over a length of some forty-four miles, whilst Yorck was some twelve or fourteen miles north, separated from Sacken by almost impassable roads. Had Napoleon really been where Blücher believed, there was no serious risk in this dispersion, for Macdonald had only some 10,000 men. Blücher, being unaware that Seslawin no longer watched the space between his left and Wittgenstein, the right-hand corps of the army of Bohemia beyond the Aube, naturally expected that any French movement in that space would be reported to him by the cossacks. So little anxiety was there in the Silesian army that when, in the evening of the 8th, Karpow's cossacks were driven back from Sézanne on Montmirail, Sacken considered it of no importance, and did not report it. Yet, that same evening, Marmont had his leading division in Sézanne, and Ney was behind him, between Villenauxe and Sézanne.

During the 9th Macdonald got safely across the Marne again at La Ferté-sous-Jouarre, where he with difficulty repelled an attack of Wassiltchikow with Sacken's cavalry. Yorck had abandoned the pursuit of Macdonald as hopeless at Dormans; the French marshal had gained too long a start.

On the evening of the 9th Blücher's position was as scattered as ever; for, though he had sent Olsufiew on to Champaubert, and had been joined at Vertus and Bergères by Kleist and Kapzewitch, Sacken's advance towards La Ferté-sous-Jouarre had equally lengthened the line at the western end.

During the day (9th) Marmont's cavalry, advancing northwards, had shown themselves as far forward as St. Prix on the Petit Morin, and even towards Champaubert. Even this created no alarm at Blücher's headquarters; for the very fact that this cavalry subsequently retired tended to allay the suspicion, which Müffling says he expressed, that it was the advanced guard of a large force. Blücher was still enjoying his fancied security without any suspicion of the storm gathering on his left. Gneisenau, according to Müffling, would have nothing to do with the latter's inferences from the appearance of French cavalry, or his proposal to recall Sacken. The most Gneisenau would agree to was that Sacken should be told to remain at Montmirail, whence, if there was any serious movement of the enemy, he could either return to Blücher or join Yorck and pass the Marne at Château-Thierry, with a view to joining Winzingerode, who was now approaching from the north. In the former case there would be 39,000 men (Sacken, Olsufiew, Kleist, and Kapzewitch) towards Etoges, and 18,000 (Yorck) at Château-Thierry. In the other case there would be 38,000 (Sacken and Yorck) at Château-Thierry, and 19,000 about Etoges.[1]

At this juncture there arrived a letter from Schwarzenberg requesting Blücher to send Kleist to reinforce Wittgenstein on the right of the army of Bohemia. Consequently, Kleist and Kapzewitch were ordered to march, on the 10th, on Sézanne, whither also Olsufiew would go from Champaubert.

Napoleon reached Sézanne late in the night of the 9th with the Guard. There had been immense difficulty in getting the guns over the terrible roads and marshes of the forest of Traconnes. The weather, which throughout this campaign was alternately freezing and thawing, was just now in the latter stage. But for the assistance of the peasants and their horses, the task would have been almost insuperable.

During the night of the 9th–10th Blücher at last learnt that Napoleon himself was with the troops at Sézanne. What was the Emperor going to do? Would he attack Olsufiew; or would he, disregarding this small Russian corps, make

---

[1] The figures are Müffling's. He puts Sacken at 20,000, though Janson says he had only 16,000 at Montmirail.

straight for Sacken by Montmirail? Was he only seeking to join Macdonald at La Ferté-sous-Jouarre? Blücher knew not. Sacken had been left some discretion as to what he would do. Müffling, according to his own account, sent one of his staff officers to try and persuade Sacken to exercise his discretion by marching on Champaubert. Gneisenau, however, stopped this officer, and changed his message to one telling Sacken that, if he still thought the repulse of Karpow's cossacks on the 8th was unimportant, he should continue his pursuit of Macdonald. When the news of Napoleon's presence arrived it was too late to countermand this order.

Blücher now set off from Champaubert to join Kleist and Kapzewitch in their march to Sézanne. As they marched, in the morning of the 10th, they heard the roar of guns on their right, in the direction of Champaubert, but it was only in the afternoon that Blücher heard of the disaster which they heralded.

The "little" Paris road, along which Blücher's main column was spread, runs from Bergères westwards along the southern edge of the undulating plateau which extends between the Marne on the north and the great marsh of St. Gond and the Petit Morin stream on the south. The road runs far enough from the edge to pass round the heads of the lateral valleys, which, especially about Champaubert and Montmirail, cut back into the plateau. On the Sézanne-Epernay road, on which Napoleon stood, the Petit Morin is crossed, just west of the St. Gond marsh, by a bridge at St. Prix. Over that bridge Olsufiew would have to pass on his march to Sézanne; therefore, he had not destroyed it. But he had also taken no measures to guard it, so that, when Napoleon sent forward his cavalry in the early morning of the 10th, it seized the passage unopposed.

Olsufiew had about 4000[1] infantry and 24 guns, but no cavalry. He was, therefore, not in a position to fight Napoleon, and he should clearly have retreated towards Etoges. But he was smarting under censures for his mistake in letting the French capture the château at Brienne on the 29th Jan-

---

[1] Poltoratzki told Napoleon he had only 3690. Danilewski, p. 106 (English translation).

uary, and for his management of his troops at La Rothière. Sacken had even threatened him with a court-martial. Therefore, he resolved to stand when he heard of the French advance. He sent Udom with four regiments of infantry and six guns to hold Baye, about half-way between St. Prix and Champaubert.

Napoleon's cavalry was followed by Marmont and Ney. About 11 a.m. Ricard attacked Udom and drove him into Baye and the neighbouring woods, whilst Lagrange bore to the left towards Bannay. Olsufiew had now sent another brigade to support Udom, but Ney was soon up and firing with his artillery on Bannay, from which Lagrange's first attack had been repulsed.

By 3 p.m., after a stubborn resistance, both Baye and Bannay had been cleared of Russians. On the French right Bordessoulle's cavalry, on the left Doumerc's were pushing forward to cut off the Russian retreat.

Olsufiew, who had hitherto obstinately refused to retreat, though he had sent news to Blücher of what was happening, now attempted to fall back. Poltoratzki, with two regiments and nine guns, was left to hold Champaubert to the last, whilst Olsufiew, who had already sent off some of his guns, endeavoured to follow them to Etoges.

Poltoratzki, now surrounded by infantry, was charged on all sides by French cavalry. He made a brave resistance, and only surrendered, with 1000 men and nine guns, when his ammunition gave out.

Olsufiew, unable to get along the main road, took a side track through the woods towards Epernay; but, in the terrible weather on a wretched road, only about 1600 or 1700 men and 15 guns succeeded in escaping through the woods. Olsufiew himself was captured.

Napoleon's victory was as complete as might have been expected from his great superiority of numbers.

The Emperor now stood in the midst of Blücher's widely separated corps. To the east were Kleist and Kapzewitch, now, on the receipt of news of Olsufiew's disaster, making a night march back to Vertus. They had already got nearly to Fère Champenoise when Blücher turned them back. Due west of Napoleon was Sacken, who had made matters worse

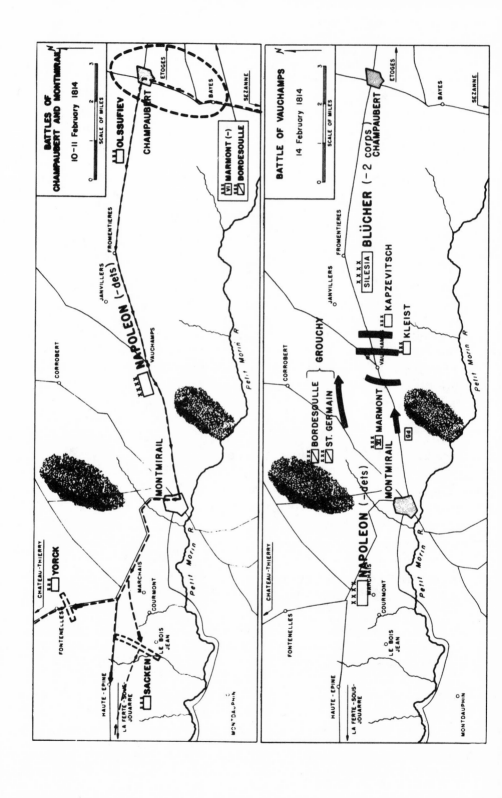

BATTLES OF CHAMPAUBERT AND MONTMIRAIL

10–11 February 1814

SCALE OF MILES

0   1   2   3

CHATEAU-THIERRY

YORCK

FONTENELLES

HAUTE-EPINE

LA FERTE-SOUS-JOUARRE

SACKEN

MARCHAIS

COURMONT

LE BOIS JEAN

MONTMIRAIL

MON'DAUPHIN

Petit Morin R.

NAPOLEON (-dets)

CORROBERT

JANVILLERS

FROMENTIERES

VAUCHAMPS

Petit Morin R.

OLSSUFIEV

CHAMPAUBERT

ETOGES

BAYES

SEZANNE

MARMONT (-)

BORDESOULLE

BATTLE OF VAUCHAMPS

14 February 1814

SCALE OF MILES

0   1   2   3

CHATEAU-THIERRY

FONTENELLES

HAUTE-EPINE

LA FERTE-SOUS-JOUARRE

MONTDAUPHIN

LE BOIS JEAN

COURMONT

MARCHAIS

NAPOLEON (-dets)

MONTMIRAIL

Petit Morin R.

MARMONT

Gd

ST. GERMAIN

BORDESOULLE

GROUCHY

CORROBERT

JANVILLERS

FROMENTIERES

VAUCHAMPS

KLEIST

KAPZEVITSCH

SILESIA   BLÜCHER (-2 corps)

CHAMPAUBERT

ETOGES

BAYES

SEZANNE

Petit Morin R.

by continuing his march on Trilport. Yorck was north-west at Château-Thierry and Viffort.

There could be little doubt as to the direction Napoleon would take. A movement against Blücher could only result in his retreat on Châlons or Epernay, whilst Yorck and Sacken escaped over the Marne at Château-Thierry.

If, however, the Emperor marched westwards against Sacken's rear, whilst Macdonald again advanced from Trilport, there was every possibility of annihilating Sacken, though Yorck might get away over the Marne. That, therefore, was the direction Napoleon chose.

Blücher, meanwhile, had written to Yorck to advance on Montmirail. The bridge at Château-Thierry, if restored, was to be kept open, "in order that, if unfortunately the enemy should cut your corps and Sacken's from my army, you may be able to escape to the right bank of the Marne." These orders only reached Yorck at night on the 10th.

To Sacken Blücher wrote merely that, concentrating with Yorck at Montmirail, he should be able to open the road to Vertus, if the enemy were between him and Blücher. Nothing was said to him about an escape over the Marne.

Napoleon had written, at 3 p.m., to Macdonald announcing his victory over Olsufiew, and telling him to move eastwards. At 7 p.m. he ordered Nansouty, with two divisions of cavalry, supported by two of Marmont's brigades, to seize Montmirail and reconnoitre towards Viels Maisons. Mortier, now at Sézanne, was to march at daybreak for Montmirail, leaving a rear-guard at Sézanne and sending Defrance to get into touch with Leval's division which Oudinot had been ordered to send towards La Ferté Gaucher.[1] Leval, on reaching La Ferté Gaucher, was to march to the sound of the guns, which he would probably hear between Viels Maisons and Montmirail. Ney was to march, at 6 a.m., on Montmirail. Marmont to send Ricard at 3 a.m. to support Nansouty. He was himself to remain at Etoges, with Lagrange's division and the 1st cavalry corps, watching Blücher, and endeavouring to ascertain whether he was retreating on Châlons or

---

[1] Oudinot was also to send Rottembourg's division if he was not hard pressed. He was unable to do so.

Epernay, or contemplated the offensive westwards on Napoleon's rear.[1]

Of Napoleon's two prospective opponents, Yorck replied to Blücher's order of 7 a.m., saying that, if Napoleon's offensive movement continued, his own junction with Sacken seemed impossible. He had no information as to Sacken's intentions, and, as his own troops were too exhausted to move that night, he proposed to concentrate them next day at Viffort, with cavalry out towards Montmirail. Sacken, on the other hand, started on his return journey to Montmirail at 9 p.m. on the 10th, after again breaking the bridge at La Ferté-sous-Jouarre. It took him twelve hours to get to Viels Maisons, his advanced guard being in contact with the French farther east. Yorck was, at the same hour (9 a.m. on the 11th), at Viffort. His cavalry had encountered French cavalry at Rozoy and Fontenelle. Knowing that Karpow's cossacks had been driven from Montmirail in the early morning, and that Sacken had lost one possible line of retreat by destroying the bridge at La Ferté-sous-Jouarre, Yorck realized more clearly than Sacken the latter's danger. He sent to urge Sacken's immediate retreat on Château-Thierry. His staff officer found the Russian preparing for battle with what he persisted in calling only a weak detachment. He was unaffected by the information that Yorck could not reach the field till late, and even then without his heavy artillery, which the badness of the roads compelled him to leave at

[1] Having issued his orders, Napoleon wrote to Joseph a ridiculously exaggerated account of his victory. A great deal of nonsense has been written about Napoleon's bulletins. He made no pretence that they were true, and, as in the case of this letter (Corr. 21,217), they were often deliberately exaggerated for political or military purposes. He has very frankly stated his views on this subject in another letter to Joseph (Corr. 21,360, dated 24th February, 1814). "Newspapers are no more history than bulletins are history. One ought always to make the enemy believe one has immense forces." Unless report lies, the Bulgarians of to-day have gone one better than Napoleon in encouraging the spread of reports of pursuits and actions which never took place at all. The author, for one, does not see that they or Napoleon can be blamed if exaggerated, or even false statements thus published were calculated to deceive the actual or possible enemy. In such matters, commanders can hardly be expected to adhere to a very severe standard of truth.

Château-Thierry with a brigade of infantry. When Napoleon reached Montmirail, in the night of the 10th-11th, he was ignorant of the fact that Macdonald, by destroying the Trilport bridge, had put out of his own power that advance on Sacken's rear which Napoleon fully expected. The Emperor was satisfied, by an early reconnaissance, that Sacken and Yorck were still separated. Nansouty had already driven Russian outposts from Les Chouteaux farm, half-way to Viels Maisons. In order to prevent the union of Sacken and Yorck, the Emperor decided to take post at the junction of the road from Château-Thierry with the main road. In those days it was between Le Tremblay and Montmirail, where a bye-road now comes in. Nansouty was across the Château-Thierry road short of le Plénois farm, with his artillery on his left, extending to the La Ferté road; Friant's Old Guard stood at the junction of the roads, with Defrance on his right. Mortier had not yet reached Montmirail.[1] This disposition shows that Napoleon expected an attack north of the La Ferté road, which, indeed, Sacken's staff urged on the ground of proximity to Yorck. But Sacken seems to have thought he could break a way past the "weak detachment" by the valley of the Petit Morin.

Tscherbatow's corps was sent against Marchais, with Liewen's corps between it and the road. The cavalry alone was north of the road. Most the heavy artillery was in the centre.

Sacken had about 16,300 men and 90 guns.[1] Napoleon, according to Houssaye had only 12,800. The highest accounts give him 20,000.

It was about 11 a.m. when Ricard was driven from Marchais. An hour later, more French artillery having come up in the interval, Napoleon sent him to retake the village, Friant moving up to Tremblay where Ricard had been. Mortier now replaced Friant at the cross roads.

[1] He marched by the cross road direct from Sézanne to Montmirail.

[1] The number is given by Janson, but Müffling says Sacken had 20,000. He had 26,500 in the beginning of January: he had lost perhaps 5500 at Brienne and La Rothière. Sacken had 13,679 men left on the 16th February, and, as his losses on the 11th and 12th were about 4300, he should have had 18,000 at Montmirail.

At Marchais a furious combat raged till 2 p.m., the original 2300 Russians who had taken it being constantly reinforced. The French failed to retake it finally by this hour. Napoleon now sent Ney forward, covered on his right by Nansouty, on La Haute Epine north of the road.

This attack fell upon Sacken's left which he had weakened in order to strengthen the force towards Marchais. Ney broke through the first line and the fight was only restored by the use of Russian reserves. Nansouty, meanwhile, had been brought to a standstill by Wassiltchikow's cavalry, now in touch on its left with that of Yorck. Then Guyot charged with four squadrons of the Emperor's personal Guard. Charging past La Haute Epine, simultaneously occupied by Friant, Guyot broke up some Russian infantry trying to cross the road northwards.

Sacken's centre was now seriously shaken, his left, still in Marchais, in great danger.

We must now see what Yorck had been doing. Finding that Sacken was determined to fight, he first safeguarded his own retreat by sending back another brigade to Château-Thierry. He feared an attack by Macdonald on his right and rear. His two remaining brigades (Horn and Pirch) could only reach Fontenelle over the sodden road at 3:30 p.m. Katzeler's cavalry had already joined Wassiltchikow against Nansouty. The Prussian reserve cavalry now deployed between Fontenelle and Les Tournaux, as did the infantry. As they advanced on Plénois and Bailly they were met by Mortier with Michel's division, who, after a stubborn fight, drove them back on Fontenelle where night brought the fighting to an end. Sacken was in great danger of being completely surrounded; for Napoleon, reinforcing the attack on Marchais, at last took the village. Its defenders, charged by Defrance as they left it, were nearly all killed or taken.

Nevertheless, Yorck's timely intervention had gained time for the débris of Sacken's corps to get away by their left to join him on the Château-Thierry road.

In their short combat with Michel the Prussians had lost about 900 men. Sacken naturally lost more heavily, altogether about 2000 killed and wounded, 800 prisoners, 6 standards, and 13 guns. The French loss was about 2000 killed and wounded. They were too exhausted to pursue that night.

Blücher, with Kleist and Kapzewitch, had got back to Bergères on the morning of the 11th. As he had no cavalry for the moment, he proposed retreating through the wooded country towards Epernay, rather than over the open plain to Châlons.

Receiving Yorck's message of the previous night, he at once despatched orders to him and Sacken to cross the Marne and make for Reims, where the army would re-assemble. When Yorck received this, he had just heard Sacken was moving by his right instead of his left. He felt bound to try and rescue the Russians.

Macdonald, receiving at Meaux the order to advance, found himself unable, owing to his own destruction of the Trilport bridge, to do more than send St. Germain's cavalry round by Lagny and Coulommiers, promising to follow by the same road next day. St. Germain reached Napoleon after the battle; Sebastiani, who had tried to get over by La Ferté-sous-Jouarre, was held up by the broken bridge.

The French pursuit of Sacken and Yorck only started again at 9 a.m. on the 12th, Mortier by the direct road, the Emperor through Haute Epine and Rozoy.

The Prussians covering Sacken's retreat made some stand at Les Caquerets and again in front of Château-Thierry, but on each occasion they were forced back, and at the last place Ney, defeating the cavalry on their left, arrived on the heights overlooking the Marne. The Prussian infantry with difficulty escaped, and Heidenreich, on their right, was compelled to surrender with two Russian regiments. Finally, the passage of the Marne was only effected in safety thanks to the fire of a heavy battery from beyond the river.

This day cost the Prussians about 1250 men, 6 guns, and part of their baggage, whilst Sacken lost 1500 men, 3 guns, and nearly all his wheeled transport. The French loss did not exceed 600. Mortier was detailed for the pursuit of Sacken and Yorck with Christiani's Old Guard division and the cavalry of Colbert and Defrance. It was only on the afternoon of the 13th that the bridge could be restored for his passage. By that time, Yorck and Sacken were far away at Fismes.

Napoleon spent the night of the 12th–13th at Château-Thierry. Believing that Oudinot and Victor were still holding Schwarzenberg at Nogent, and that Blücher had retreated either on Châlons or Epernay, he ordered, (1) Ricard to march from Montmirail to rejoin Marmont, (2) Macdonald to amalgamate his own (XI) corps and Sebastiani's (V) into one (XI), and to be ready to march with it, reinforced by a National Guard division just arrived at Meaux from Paris.

At 2 p.m. news of the advance of Schwarzenberg decided the Emperor to leave the Silesian army and return to the Seine. Macdonald was to march for Montereau, where Napoleon hoped to have 27,000 infantry and 10,000 cavalry by the 15th. But news presently arrived from Marmont which showed that a blow must be struck at Blücher first. The Prussian Field Marshal had not retreated; for Marmont, with only 2500 infantry and 1800 cavalry, had not dared to molest him. His inactivity at last induced Blücher to believe that Napoleon was off to the Seine, with Marmont covering his march to Sézanne. On the evening of the 12th, Blücher decided to attack Marmont next day, hoping then to descend on Napoleon's rear as the Emperor marched for the Seine. He had now got some 800 cavalry.

Marmont, at Etoges, at once recognized that he could not make head even against Ziethen's advanced guard of 5000 infantry and 700 cavalry. By night on the 13th, Blücher's headquarters were at Champaubert, with Ziethen in front of him, and Kleist and Kapzewitch behind. Marmont had retired in good order to Fromentières.

It was 3 a.m. on the 14th when Napoleon heard of Blücher's advance. He at once ordered to advance east of Montmirail Ney, St. Germain, Friant, Curial, and Leval, the last named having only reached Viels Maisons the previous evening. The Emperor said he hoped to be at Montmirail in person by 7 a.m. and to give Blücher a lesson by noon. A good position was to be chosen east of Montmirail.

At 4:30 a.m. Marmont had begun to fall back. Blücher only moved two hours later. There was a little skirmishing

with Ziethen before Marmont got through Vauchamps, behind which village he drew up the 5000 men he had since
Ricard had rejoined. His left was thrown forward into a small
wood. At 10 a.m. Ziethen attacked with his Prussian infantry
on the right, the cavalry on their left, and 3000 Russian
infantry on the left rear of it.

Blücher, starting three hours after Ziethen, was only at
Fromentières when he learnt that there was French infantry
in the wood of Beaumont and cavalry north of the road,
threatening to push in between Ziethen and himself. Marmont, with the Emperor's reinforcements now coming up,
sent Ricard forward with the 800 men who were all that now
remained of his division. Ziethen at first repulsed him, but
then, as he pursued, was attacked by Lagrange in front and
by cavalry on his right. The latter was Grouchy's which the
Emperor had sent round by Sarrechamps. Ziethen was disastrously defeated, only 532 men out of four Prussian battalions escaping to Janvilliers. The Russian infantry retreated
in squares in good order. Kleist and Kapzewitch, meanwhile,
had only reached Fromentières at noon, where they heard
the sound of Ziethen's fight. Hacke's 2000 cavalry, which had
reached Blücher on the 13th, was sent forward, whilst the
infantry deployed across the road a mile east of Vauchamps.
Blücher now saw Grouchy's cavalry moving in great strength
round his right. His inference that Napoleon was present
was confirmed by a French prisoner. With his line of retreat
threatened by Grouchy, he decided to fall back on Etoges.
The road was reserved for guns and wagons, whilst the infantry, with only a few guns, marched over the sodden fields,
Kleist north, Kapzewitch south of the road. Udom, with the
remains of Olsufiew's corps, had been left at Champaubert,
and was now ordered to hold the great wood of La Grande
Laye, between that place and Etoges.

At first the retreat progressed in good order, though harassed by constant attacks by Grouchy's cavalry on the north,
and the Guard cavalry on the south.

Müffling, marching with Kleist, was hurrying the retreat
of the right in order to seize the defile between La Grande
Laye and the large pond. Kleist was thus some way ahead of
Kapzewitch, who was more harassed by the French infantry

in front, and by cavalry charges. Blücher, who was with Kapzewitch, now ordered Kleist to wait for him. By this time
Grouchy was up to La Grande Laye which, under orders
from Kapzewitch, Udom had evacuated in order to retreat
on Etoges. At 4.30 Grouchy advanced southwestwards in
four long lines between La Grande Laye and the Cham-
paubert-Epernay road. Carrying away Hacke's cavalry, he
fell upon Kleist's infantry, which was simultaneously charged
by Laferrière's Guard cavalry on its left. Assailed in front,
flank, and rear, with many of his squares broken, Kleist's
plight seemed desperate. It was only by immense personal
exertions on the part of Blücher, Müffling, Kleist, and others
that the men were rallied and a way was forced through
Grouchy's cavalry to Etoges. Had Grouchy's horse artillery
not been kept back by the clayey soil, Kleist could hardly
have escaped at all. Blücher again narrowly escaped capture.

Night having now fallen, Ney rallied his cavalry and sent
only a portion of it after the enemy as they retreated.
Blücher's remaining troops were utterly exhausted. Nevertheless, the old marshal decided to continue his retreat on
Châlons at once, leaving only Ouroussow's division in Etoges
to cover the retreat. Fighting seemed over for the day.
Ouroussow's men were dispersed in Etoges, hunting for
food and fuel, and keeping no look-out, when once more the
French fell on them. Napoleon, already on his way back to
Montmirail with Ney, the Guard, and Leval, had sent orders
to Marmont to follow on Blücher's heels. It was between 8
amd 9 p.m. when Marmont's troops surprised Ouroussow.
The attack was made with the bayonet on men who had
mostly laid aside their arms in the search for food. All but a
very few were killed, wounded, or taken, Ouroussow
amongst the latter. This day (14th February) had been almost more disastrous than its predecessors for Blücher's
army. The Prussians lost about 4000 men and 7 guns, nearly
half Kleist's strength. Kapzewitch lost over 2000 men and 9
guns. The French loss was again insignificant, being estimated at only 600. In the four days' fighting at Champaubert, Montmirail, Château-Thierry, and Vauchamps,
Blücher's army of about 56,000 men had lost over 16,000

men and 47 guns. Napoleon's loss had been only about 4000.

This is a convenient place for reviewing generally Napoleon's manœuvre against Blücher, which is considered, rightly probably, to be the finest he made in 1814. His conduct has been praised to the sky, whilst Blücher has been blamed equally. Both praise and blame seem to be excessive. To begin with Napoleon, the idea of an attack on Blücher whilst Schwarzenberg was contained on the Seine was exactly what might have been expected from the great master of operations on interior lines, from the commander of the French army in Italy in 1796. The way in which he masked his march from Schwarzenberg, the rapidity of its execution in the face of fearful difficulties of roads, were worthy of Napoleon's best days, and of the pluck and tenacity of his soldiers. Neither Blücher nor Schwarzenberg realized what was happening till the Emperor fell like a thunderbolt on the hapless Olsufiew. Yet Napoleon owed much, in his escape from the notice of Blücher, to luck, or rather to the mistakes of his opponents. Blücher still believed, up to the 9th February, that Seslawin was watching the country between his left and the Aube. Had that been so, Seslawin should have been able to report Napoleon's march. Blücher must certainly be blamed in part for his ignorance of Seslawin's departure. Of course he ought to have been informed of it, but, on the other hand, he would have done better to keep himself in touch with Seslawin through a staff officer deputed to the latter's headquarters. This want of intercommunication between commandants of corps was one of the marked defects of the allied command.

When Napoleon fell upon Olsufiew, the army of Silesia was scattered in isolated corps over an immense distance. This was due to Blücher's endeavour to compass two separate and incompatible objects, (1) the destruction of Macdonald, and (2) the rallying to himself of Kleist and Kapzewitch. For the dispersion of his army Blücher has been greatly blamed. But it must be remembered in his favour that he had good reason to believe himself safe from any movement of Napoleon against himself. That belief was based on his assumption that Seslawin was still watching between himself and the Aube, and on Schwarzenberg's statements as to Napoleon's supposed intention of moving farther south. In that case, the Emperor would have been far out of reach of Blücher, and there would have been no risk in the separation of the corps, with only such a weak opponent as Macdonald before them. Either Yorck or Sacken alone was more than a match for him. On the other hand, critics after the event seem to have considered that Napoleon knew before he started that he would find Blücher's army scattered as it was. He knew nothing of the sort, and it was probably only at Champaubert that he realized how wonderfully lucky he had been in coming on the centre of a long line, instead of finding his 30,000 men opposed to a concentrated army of over 50,000.

Blücher's march with Kleist and Kapzewitch on Fère Champenoise on the 10th, a march which still continued to the accompaniment of the guns at Champaubert, is condemned even by Clausewitz, who is little inclined to find fault with Blücher. Perhaps Blücher believed that the movement towards his right rear would stop Napoleon; but more weight may probably be given to his habitual loyalty and his desire to move Kleist as ordered by Schwarzenberg. Olsufiew certainly made a grievous mistake in deciding to fight a hopeless battle at Champaubert, and in refusing to retreat, though urged to do so by Blücher's aide-de-camp, Nostitz, and his own generals, until it was too late. We have already alluded to the fear of censure which influenced a general of little capacity.

Napoleon, after Champaubert, was in a thoroughly congenial position. Little credit need be given him for marching against Sacken whilst Marmont watched Blücher. It was a course obviously right even to smaller men than the Emperor. Sacken sinned, like Blücher and Olsufiew, in obstinately refusing to attribute its true importance to Napoleon's advance on Montmirail till it was too late. He insisted on advancing towads his right, instead of bearing to his left towards Yorck. Gneisenau, however, should have warned him, as he did warn Yorck, of the possibility of a retreat across the Marne being necessary. As it was, his movement to the right played into the hands of Napoleon, whose design was to cut him from Yorck. Sacken had much to be thankful for that he effected an almost miraculous escape in the end. Müffling says he had only a forest road by which to reach Yorck, and that he only got his artillery along by hitching on cavalry horses. He owed the possibility of escape mainly to Yorck's timely intervention on Napoleon's right. On the other hand, Yorck might perhaps have done more towards helping Sacken. Had they united in time to meet Napoleon they would have had a great advantage in numbers. Blücher did nothing against Marmont on the 11th or 12th February, which seems difficult to explain, except on the ground of his want of cavalry, of which he only got 800 on the 12th and 2000 more on the 13th. His advance on the latter date was due to his belief that Marmont was merely the rearguard of Napoleon's march by Sézanne to the Seine. He, too, was very fortunate in escaping at Vauchamps, an escape which was probably due mainly to Grouchy's being unable to bring up his artillery, and perhaps to some slackness in the French infantry pressure on his front. Kapzewitch certainly made matters worse by his unwarranted order to Udom to retreat from La Grande Laye on Etoges. Had Grouchy found Udom's 1500 men in the wood, instead of only a few skirmishers on its edge, he would have been greatly hampered in his attack on Kleist.

Napoleon's movement against Blücher was a brilliant success, but by no means so complete as he hoped for. He started with the hope of annihilating the army of Silesia before returning to the Seine. He had inflicted losses on it amounting to between one-fourth and one-third of its strength, but he had certainly not annihilated it. When it had been two days (16th–18th February) at Châlons, and been reinforced by 6000 Russian infantry, 2000 of Korff's cavalry and other bodies, it was ready to march again, 53,000 strong, as if it had never been defeated at all.

Blücher was always hopeful and plucky. On the 13th, before Vauchamps, he wrote to his wife, in a letter full of misspellings, "I have had a bitter three days. Napoleon has attacked me three times in the three days with his whole strength and all his Guard, but has not gained his object, and to-day he is in retreat on Paris. Tomorrow I follow him, then our army will unite, and in front of Paris a great battle will decide all. Don't be afraid that we shall be beaten; unless some unheard-of mistake occurs, that is not possible."

IV

Battle

Napoleon's brilliance as a strategist only served to bring the enemy to the battlefield. Battle was always the ultimate object of all of Napoleon's planning and thought. Indeed, he conducted more battles than most great commanders before or since and managed to win most of them. Many of these successes were due to his personal brilliance as a commander, but certainly French tactical excellence must receive some of the credit. The selections which follow all illustrate various battles conducted by Napoleon or his army, and serve to demonstrate the numerous different operational and tactical techniques which were used with such effectiveness.

"Auerstädt," from *Napoleon's Conquest of Prussia, 1806*

Napoleon was by no means the only able commander France possessed. On October 14, 1806, during the conquest of Prussia, Marshal Louis Nicolas Davout inflicted a defeat upon the Prussians at Auerstädt which was as brilliantly conducted a battle as anything Napoleon himself could do, and indeed far more spectacular than that which Napoleon was simultaneously inflicting upon the enemy nearby at Jena. Auerstädt was a remarkable demonstration of the Napoleonic battle of maneuver, as Davout executed a perfect double envelopment of a greatly superior enemy force, and also is a fine illustration of French tactical flexibility, as shown by the operations of Morand's division.

The main Prussian army had started from Weimar on the 13th, as ordered, to march for the Lower Unstrut, expecting to meet the reserve, under Duke Eugene of Würtemberg, advancing from Halle. But the prevailing confusion resulted in so many delays that the army bivouacked for the night about Auerstädt, some distance short of the defile of Koesen, the seizure of which was absolutely essential as a protection for the right flank against the French, who were known to have occupied Naumburg in force. No attempt seems to have been made to seize this all important defile and passage of the Saale, which, on the contrary, was occupied by Davout on the night of the 13th–14th. The outposts of the leading division (Schmettau's) extended no farther than Gernstadt. Behind Schmettau were the divisions of Wartensleben and the Prince of Orange, the former with outposts watching the Ilm and the Saale about Sulza. It was not till midnight that Kalkreuth's reserve encamped behind the division of Orange, whilst Blücher's light troops were not up before 2 A.M.

The strength of the army thus assembled is given by Lettow-Vorbeck and Hoepfner as 52 battalions, 80 squadrons, and 16 batteries, numbering 39,000 infantry, 9200 cavalry, and 1600 artillerymen. Altogether there were 49,800 men, with 230 guns, of which 136 belonged to the artillery and 94 were attached to the infantry.

The French force, which was destined to meet in mortal combat this army, consisted of the single corps of Davout, who gives his own numbers as 26,000, of whom not more than 1300 or 1400 were cavalry, and whose artillery numbered but 44 guns.

Instead of this inferiority of 1 to 2 the French would have had a slight superiority but for the action of Bernadotte in not only refusing himself to support Davout, but also in dissuading such of the reserve cavalry as were available from doing so.[1] It will be more convenient to deal with the case of

[1] Sahuc's dragoon division had been placed at the disposal of Davout (Napoleon to Berthier, 12th October—Foucart, i. 515), but that marshal notes that it was withdrawn from him by Murat on the 13th (Davout to Napoleon, 14th October—Foucart, i. 672). Savary (ii. 287) says Bernadotte stopped the cavalry from joining Davout.

Bernadotte presently, after Davout's battle has been described.

The latter marshal, it will be remembered, had received orders on the afternoon of the 13th to manœuvre to his left should he hear an attack on Lannes in progress; if there were no such attack on the 13th he was promised further orders during the night. The original of those orders is not forthcoming, but their substance has been preserved in Davout's history of the operations of his corps. They reached him at 3 A.M. on the 14th, being dated 10 P.M. on the 13th, from the Emperor's bivouac on the heights of Jena. They clearly indicate the writer's ignorance of the movement of the enemy's main army on the left bank of the Ilm; for they require Davout to march on Apolda, where he would come upon the rear of the Prussian army. Provided only that he took part in the battle, which Napoleon intended to fight on the 14th, Davout was left a free hand in the choice of his road to Apolda. The Emperor only knew the country from the map, and wisely left details to the man on the spot. The orders, in so far as they concerned Bernadotte, will be dealt with later. Here it suffices to say that Bernadotte took no material part either in Napoleon's or in Davout's battle.

Davout's shortest way to Apolda from his position at and south of Naumburg lay over the bridge at Koesen. Thence the road rises steeply, by a zigzag in one place, along the face of the hill leading to the plateau on the left bank of the Saale, a plateau corresponding to that of Jena, but separated from it by the Ilm, and not so high above the Saale as is the Landgrafenberg. Just before the top of the hill is reached, the Napoleonsberg (Windknolle) can be clearly seen, twelve or thirteen miles to the south, making a distinct feature in the landscape. Arrived at the plateau the road turns from south to due west, and falls by the gentlest of slopes for nearly two miles to the substantial village of Hassenhausen. The plain over which it passes is almost absolutely flat and featureless. There is no village on it, no fence, no wood until, away to the left, the woods are seen which clothe the steep bank of the Saale and, farther on, of the Ilm. The junction of the two rivers is at the railway station of Gr. Heringen, about two miles south of Hassenhausen. Like that of Jena the battlefield of Auerstädt is to-day, save for the metalling of a few roads and the plum-trees now lining them, exactly as it was in 1806. No railway crosses it, and even Hassenhausen appears to have expanded only by two or three houses on the south side of the road.

From the west side of Hassenhausen the whole battlefield can be seen and understood. The road thence goes on, sunk for the first 300 yards, due west down the gentle slope of an open valley. At the bottom of the slope, about a mile from Hassenhausen, lies the village of Taugwitz, and just beyond it, on the farther side of the brook which drains the valley, is Poppel, about 100 feet lower than Hassenhausen. A mile north-east of Poppel, Spielberg marks the head of this valley. Below Poppel the brook flows south by east to Rehausen, a mile off; then it doubles back south-westwards for rather more than a mile, and finally turns again to the east round the end of the Sonnenberg to join the Ilm. Thus Hassenhausen is in the centre of a rough crescent of heights, of which the horns project on the right past Spielberg, on the left to the Sonnenberg. Straight on beyond Poppel from Hassenhausen are Lisdorf and Eckardsberga. To the left, on the road to Apolda and Weimar, which turns south-west at Poppel, are Gernstadt and Auerstädt, the latter hidden from view by the downs over which the road passes above the former.

Hassenhausen has orchards and fences on its west side, and the road, as it passes along its southern edge, is sunk some ten or twelve feet, forming a ready-made entrenchment.

On the north-west, beyond Spielberg, the battlefield is bounded by wooded heights. A small brook, the Liesbach, flows eastward through Lisdorf into the main valley at Poppel, or perhaps it should be considered as the main brook and the branch leading down from Spielberg as a tributary of it.

On the evening of the 13th some of Davout's chasseurs, reconnoitring the Weimar road some three or four miles from Koesen, had been repulsed by Prussian cavalry, and the marshal had then occupied Koesen with a battalion of infantry.

FIRST PERIOD OF THE BATTLE—UP TO 9 A.M.

Before daybreak on the 14th both forces were in motion. On the French side the 25th Light Infantry, preceded by a squadron of chasseurs, passed the Koesen bridge, followed half-an-hour later by the rest of Gudin's division. The same thick morning mist which pervaded the battlefield of Jena had descended on that of Auerstädt. Davout, accompanying his advance guard, sent out his A.D.C., Colonel Burke (or Bourke), with a small detachment of chasseurs, to endeavour, by the capture of prisoners, to obtain definite news of the enemy. That officer, pushing on through Hassenhausen, encountered no vedettes or advanced body, until he suddenly stumbled in the mist, near Poppel, on the whole of the Prussian advance guard of 600 cavalry led by Blücher. The latter promptly charged, and, though the French were of course compelled to a rapid retreat, they succeeded in capturing a few of the enemy. The French cavalry fell back on the 25th Light Infantry which was now approaching Hassenhausen. That infantry regiment was on the right of the road, with the 85th of the line on its left. Behind the 25th was the 21st of the line, and behind the 85th the 12th.

Blücher, after driving back Burke, following him through Hassenhausen with the leading squadrons of his cavalry and some infantry, at once found himself under artillery fire from a battery about 700 paces to his left front. He was now reinforced by more cavalry and a horse artillery battery, which at once engaged the French guns. Unable, however, to match the French artillery, the Prussian battery soon endeavoured to withdraw. Attacked in the operation by French skirmishers, against whom its escort was unable to defend it, it lost five out of its eight guns, and the French 25th Light Infantry pushed its victorious advance into and to the right of Hassenhausen, which village was strongly occupied by skirmishers, the main body of the regiment taking post on the right of it. On the left of the village the 85th was drawn up.

Blücher, after his ejectment from Hassenhausen, had moved off to his left, seeking to outflank the French right, and sending back to the Duke of Brunswick for more

cavalry. Schmettau's division was now being arrayed in front
of Poppel for an advance on Hassenhausen; the French skirmishers were already in the pastures of the intervening valley. These skirmishers were driven back on Hassenhausen,
on which village it was of supreme importance to Davout to
maintain his hold. Between it and the edge of the plateau
there was no point of support should he be driven back
before the arrival of his 2nd and 1st divisions. He had already marked Blücher's movement threatening his right
flank, and had, to support the 25th Light Infantry, moved to
the right the 21st, followed by the 12th. About 8 A.M. the
storm broke upon the squares of the 25th and 21st. Blücher,
leading in person ten squadrons, which he now commanded,
charged furiously from the direction of Spielberg, hoping by
the violence of his onslaught to break the French defence.
He had six squadrons of cuirassiers and four of dragoons
and hussars, some 1150 men in all. For the moment he
seemed to be succeeding. The squadron of chasseurs, whom
he first encountered, gave way before him, and it looked as if
the infantry squares too must go down before the weight of
the cuirassiers. But now came a great change. The French
squares steadily poured their fire into the charging cavalry,
which was also fired upon by a 10-gun battery which Davout
had moved up. General Reitzenstein of the cuirassiers was
severely wounded, and his misfortune produced a panic
amongst his men. Nevertheless, the attack was renewed more
than once, only, however, to meet with the same stubborn
resistance. In the last attack the right of the Prussian cavalry
rode into the fire of their own horse artillery battery, and, to
add to their difficulties, they now perceived in the distance
the advance of the 108th French infantry, the leading regiment of Friant's division, which, as it arrived, Davout
promptly hurried to the support of his hard pressed right.
Blücher's horse was shot under him, and his temporary disappearance was, no doubt, a further discouragement to the
already badly shaken cavalry. By 8.30 A.M. that cavalry had
reached the point at which they could no longer hold firm,
and they soon broke into a wild confused flight towards the
woods beyond Spielberg. Blücher, now remounted on a bu-
gler's horse, and the other Prussian officers, shouting to the

men that no one was pursuing them, in vain endeavoured to stay the panic and reform the regiments. Utterly broken, the cuirassiers and dragoons continued their mad flight.

If Blücher had performed prodigies of valour and exerted himself to the utmost in his attack on the French right, Davout had done no less in encouraging the defence. Moving from square to square, encouraging and exhorting the men, he was rewarded by witnessing Blücher's complete repulse; but he, nevertheless, realised that Gudin's division was in imminent danger. Whilst its right flank had been attacked by Blücher, its front had been approached by Schmettau's infantry, which, however, was waiting, before making a general advance, for the support of Wartensleben's and Orange's divisions. The former had at the start got into confusion in Auerstädt, where several roads converged on a single bridge, and it was, in consequence, much delayed.

SECOND PERIOD—9 TO 10 A.M.

It was about 9 A.M. when Schmettau was reinforced by the arrival of Wartensleben on his right. Davout, too, had now got up the whole of Friant's division, which he moved to Gudin's right. Two battalions of the 111th and one of the 108th, joining the right of the 21st, captured the horse artillery battery left behind by Blücher's fleeing cavalry. The rest of Friant's division (five battalions) moved on Spielberg.

Schmettau's men had already suffered heavily from artillery and infantry fire during Blücher's cavalry fight, and as they moved forward with their right on the main road the loss continued and increased. The French skirmishers, ensconced in the houses and orchards of Hassenhausen, in the hollow roads about it, and behind the hedges on their right of it, were able to do much more damage than they suffered. In front of Schmettau the fight went badly for the Prussians. Friant with his infantry, towards and beyond Spielberg, captured that village after a severe fight, whilst his victory was completed by a charge of the three regiments of Vialannes' light cavalry—all that Davout had. Schmettau again and again attacked Hassenhausen, and Gudin's right beyond it. Each time he was repulsed by the steadiness of the French

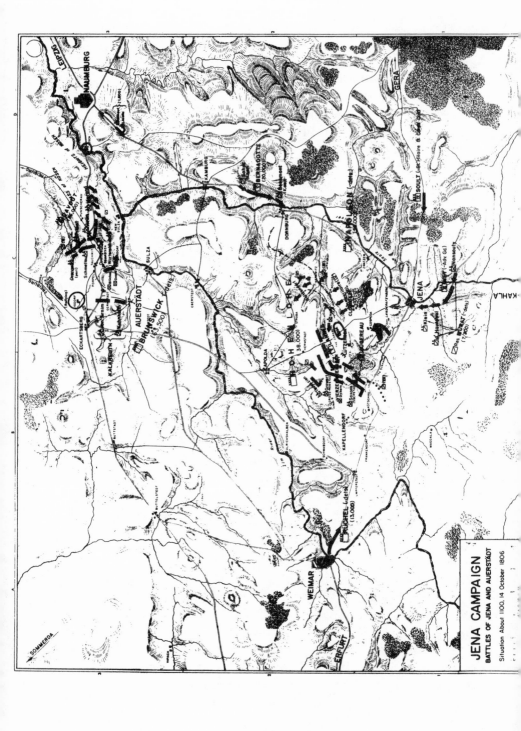

JENA CAMPAIGN

BATTLES OF JENA AND AUERSTÄDT

Situation About 1100, 14 October 1806

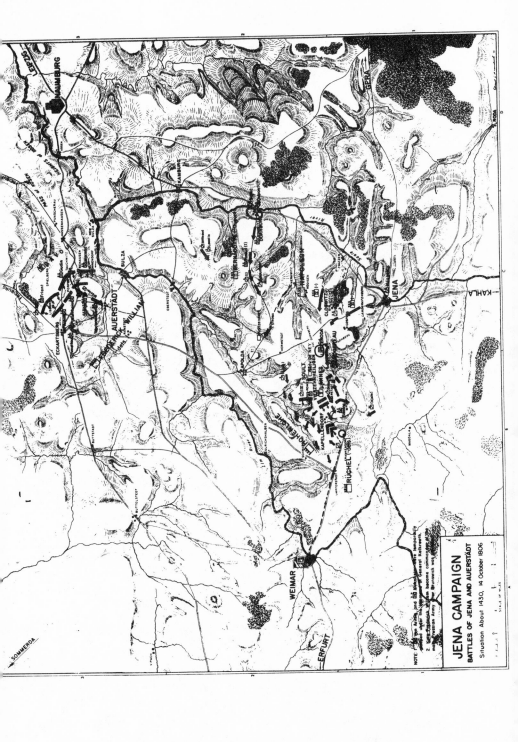

JENA CAMPAIGN
BATTLES OF JENA AND AUERSTÄDT

Situation About 1430, 14 October 1806

infantry, and he now saw his left flank exposed by the steady advance of Friant from Spielberg towards Poppel.

The French left, south of Hassenhausen, was, during this period, very hard beset. As his right was strengthened by Friant, Davout again moved back the 12th to support the 85th, which stood alone south of the village, at the same time sending the 21st to relieve the exhausted defenders of the village itself. The 12th was almost too late; for, as it reached the hollow road behind the village, it found the 85th being forced to a position on the edge of Hassenhausen along the road.

At this time the Prussian main line was in the shape of a hockey stick, the handle pointing east by south across the plain in the direction of the Ilm, the curve close up to the south-west corner of Hassenhausen, and the toe reaching a point almost north of the village. The 12th occupied the road just east of the village in continuation of the line of the 85th. The pressure of the overwhelming superiority of Wartensleben's numbers was more than these two regiments could stand against in the open. When, however, they found themselves able to utilise the support of the houses and of the hollow road, they were able at last to bring Wartensleben's triumphant advance to a standstill.

At ten o'clock Gudin's position was one of extreme peril. He had, it is true, repulsed all Schmettau's attacks on his right wing; Schmettau had been mortally wounded, and the king himself had had a horse killed under him. The Duke of Brunswick too had been carried off the field mortally wounded by a bullet passing through both his eyes. Of his wound he died on the 10th November near Altona. The spot where he fell is marked by a monument 100 yards south of the Hassenhausen-Taugwitz road, and about midway between the two villages.

On the other hand the French regiments on the right had, at times, been almost driven back into the village, his resolute hold on which alone saved Gudin from destruction. His left wing had been forced back to the line of the road, and Wartensleben was swinging his right round, so that his front now lay in the line from Hassenhausen to Saaleck. The gap between his left and Schmettau's right had been filled by Lützow's brigade of the division Orange, the other brigade (Prince Henry of Prussia) moving to support Schmettau's left against Friant's turning movement.

On the open plateau, on Wartensleben's right and front, had been collected nearly the whole available cavalry under Prince William of Prussia, including such of Blücher's advance guard as that general had been able to rally after their defeat north of Hassenhausen.

THIRD PERIOD—10 A.M.

Again, in the nick of time, Davout received his last reinforcements, by the arrival of Morand's division, which was now marching in column by the road to Hassenhausen. There was no time to be lost, and as the head of the fresh division nearly reached Gudin's extreme left on the road, the whole began to move by regiments to the left of the road against Wartensleben and the cavalry. The division was short of one battalion of the 17th, left to guard the bridge at Koesen. Davout and Morand now led the 13th Light Infantry and two light guns against the Prussians, already close up to the south side of the village with a battery and numerous infantry. These the 13th charged, driving them back towards the slope running south from Hassenhausen. Pursuing too hotly, the French found themselves almost surrounded, and compelled to fall back again to the left of the village. The rest of the French column was simultaneously advancing across the plain south of the road. In first line came the 51st and 61st, under General de Billy, who here lost his life. In second line was the 30th; the first battalion of the 17th moved on the left rear, along the edge of the Ilm valley. On these advancing lines there descended the Prussian cavalry, led by Prince William. Had there been the same unity in command of that cavalry as existed in the great charge led by Murat at Eylau, it might have fared ill with Morand's men as they moved forwards. But no one on the Prussian side seemed to know who commanded; every cavalry leader acted as seemed to him best. Some regiments were in column, others in line, and instead of the whole body sweeping forward in a succession of waves, each regiment attacked separately, without any common direction or object. With admirable promptitude the French battalions, forming square, poured a steady fire into their assailants. The latter, unsupported by the infantry, could do nothing against the squares, and their isolated attacks soon died out, leaving Morand at liberty to move on to the destruction of the Prussian infantry south of Hassenhausen.

The 51st reached the top of the slope leading up from Rehausen, suffering fearful losses at short range from the Prussians defending it. At last they succeeded in driving back the enemy, who abandoned their guns. Simultaneously the 61st, on the left of the 51st, as it pressed on through a heavy artillery fire, charged by cavalry supported by infantry, was only saved by the timely arrival of a battalion of the 30th. Yet another desperate attempt to outflank Morand's left was made by a strong Prussian force from Sonnendorf. The greater part of it, including four battalions of Royal Guards from the reserve, advanced along the Sonnenberg, whilst three companies moved above the Ilm. This attack was met and repulsed by the 30th, and the one battalion of the 17th led by Morand himself. As the Prussians fell back through Sonnendorf, Morand gained possession of the whole projecting horn of the crescent-shaped heights on the left bank of the brook, and found himself on the right flank of the Prussians fighting in front of Hassenhausen. On the opposite flank, Friant had meanwhile been making steady progress. He had, after a long and bitter fight, gained the village of Spielberg. Thence he had sent forward the 108th against Poppel, and he now found himself opposed by Prince Henry's brigade of Orange's division, which had gone to Schmettau's left when the other division (Lützow's) joined the right. Poppel was occupied, but recaptured by the Prussians. Again attacked and turned, it was a second time taken by the French. Friant's 48th was moving still farther to the right, towards Lisdorf. Thus by noon, whilst Gudin was still at Hassenhausen, Morand and Friant were enfilading with their artillery fire and threatening the retreat of Schmettau, Orange, and Wartensleben. Gudin now pressed on against the Prussian centre, which had fallen back 700 or 800 yards from Hassenhausen. Taugwitz was stormed, and by 12.30

the Prussians began to retreat. Before the retreat had degenerated, as at Jena, into a panic, succour was brought by Kalkreuth with his two reserve divisions, less the four battalions of Guards defeated on the Sonnenberg. That general drew up his forces on the heights of the right bank of the Liesbach. His left comprised two infantry regiments and a battalion of grenadiers; on their right was Blücher's now rallied cavalry. Even this position was enfiladed by Morand and Friant, but Kalkreuth was able to show a bold front sufficiently long to cover, to some extent, the retreat of the three beaten divisions. Then he fell back to the line of heights running south-east from Eckardsberga behind Gernstadt, his left occupying an advanced position on the wooded height (Puck Holz) between Eckardsberga and Lisdorf. Here his left was exposed to the attack of Friant from Lisdorf, whilst Gudin moved against his centre and right. Davout now ordered Petit, with 400 men of the 12th and 21st, to storm the (French) left of the wooded height between Eckardsberga and Lisdorf, whilst Friant attacked it in front. As Petit's men, holding their fire, moved with fixed bayonets up the slope, the whole of Friant's division attacked the Prussian left. Kalkreuth's men once more gave way, abandoning twenty guns.

The whole army was now in more or less disordered retreat, though the disorganisation was by no means so complete as that of Hohenlohe's army. It would soon have become so had Davout possessed the means of following up his victory in a great body of cavalry; but his sole force of this arm consisted of only three regiments of Chasseurs, who had already had hard fighting and had lost heavily. The infantry was exhausted by a long day of marching and fighting, and by 4.30 P.M., when it had occupied Eckardsberga, it could carry the pursuit no farther. The light cavalry on the right did what it could, following the Prussians in front of it as far as Buttstadt, which Vialannes entered on the heels of the enemy.

If Davout failed to rout the main army so completely as did Napoleon that of Hohenlohe, he nevertheless gained a very notable victory against almost double his numbers. According to his own account, he took 115 guns and 3000 prisoners, besides inflicting a loss of 15,000 killed and wounded. Hoepfner admits the capture of 57 guns, not including those of the infantry, so that there seems no reason to doubt Davout's statement, which is accepted by Lettow-Vorbeck as regards the guns. As at Jena, it is hopeless to estimate the losses in killed and wounded on the side of the vanquished. Davout's losses were proportionately enormous, being stated by him at over one-fourth of his entire force—over 7000 out of 26,000.

"Friedland," from *Napoleon's Campaign in Poland, 1806–1807*

Napoleon's defeat of Prussia in 1806 did not end the war despite his virtual annihilation of the Prussian state. Some Prussian forces survived the debacle of Jena and Auerstädt, and strong Russian forces intervened. A winter campaign in East Prussia and Poland resulted in an inconclusive French victory at Eylau on February 8, 1807. Both sides then entered winter quarters, while striving to build up their forces. In June, the Russians resumed the offensive, and on June 14, Napoleon brought them to battle in front of the town of Friedland. The battle of Friedland not only is interesting as an example of Napoleon's favored battle of maneuver, but also illustrates the relative lack of ability of many of his enemies. In addition, it was one of those actions which Napoleon particularly desired, for his victory led almost immediately to a general peace with Russia which would last nearly five years.

During the last four miles of the route from Domnau to Friedland, the general slope of the country is downwards towards the Alle, on the left bank of which stands the little town of Friedland.[1] Two miles before it is reached, a slight elevation, in rear of Posthenen, affords a clear and uninterrupted view over the whole battlefield, and down to Friedland, lying directly to the spectator's front. On the right front, some 500 paces from the village of Posthenen, is the

---

[1] The chief materials for this account of the battle of Friedland are the narratives of Dumas, Hœpfner, Savary, Victor *(Arch. Hist.)*, Jomini, Wilson, Marbot, Kausler (atlas and text), etc.

great wood of Sortlack, extending down to the village of the same name, at the head of a re-entrant angle of the Alle, which here flows between high and steep banks. A mile and a quarter to the left (north) of Posthenen is the village of Heinrichsdorf. Two-thirds of the distance, in a direction but slightly north of east, from Heinrichsdorf to the Alle, is the small wood of Damerau. Behind the line joining Posthenen and Heinrichsdorf are large woods.

The whole space, between the left bank of the river and the points which have just been denoted, is a gently undulating, open plain, with no gradients sufficient to impede the free movement of troops of all arms.

On the 14th June, the whole of this plain was one sheet of crops, rye and wheat.

Open as the plain generally was, there was one feature in it the supreme importance of which was at once recognised by Napoleon. Rising west of Posthenen, a small stream, known as the Millstream, flowing through the village, thence takes a course direct for Friedland. It divides the plain into two portions, the greater extending northwards to the Damerau wood, the lesser southwards to that of Sortlack. In its passage from in front of Posthenen till it reaches the outskirts of Friedland, the brook flows between steep banks, and, though narrow, is a serious military obstacle, entirely obstructing the free passage of troops. At Friedland, it expands into a semicircular pond, covering the greater part of the north side of the town. On the south side is the Alle, flowing at this point from west to east, and then turning north after passing the town. Friedland is thus built at the end of a peninsula, of which the north and south sides, respectively, are closed by the Millstream and by the Alle.

On the opposite bank of the Alle there is a plain similar to that on the left bank, backed by a great wood on the Allenburg road. The large village of Allenau stands back from the river, opposite Sortlack; a smaller village, Kloschenen, is on the brink of the high right bank, 2000 paces below Friedland.

It was 6 p.m. on the 13th June when the head of Bennigsen's army, under Gallitzin, began to reach the neighbourhood of Friedland. Lannes' cavalry had already ejected from the town the few Russian troops guarding the magazines there. A French patrol was surrounded and captured on the right bank of the river. Passing into Friedland, Gallitzin captured 60 cavalry in it; beyond the town, on the west, he found the French 9th Hussars, which he forced back on Lannes' corps at Domnau, taking post with his cavalry at Posthenen.

Kologribow detached small bodies to Wohnsdorf, Allenburg, and Wehlau, to watch the lower passages of the Alle, and to gain communication with Lestocq. There then remained at Friedland, 28 squadrons, and 17 guns.

Towards 8 p.m., Bennigsen himself reached Friedland. Informed of the proximity of Lannes' corps, he ordered the first troops which arrived to cross the river in support of the cavalry, and directed the construction of three pontoon bridges, one above and two below the permanent bridge. It was not till 11 p.m. that the head of the Guard infantry column arrived at Friedland. One battalion was sent over at once to the support of the cavalry, and three more regiments as day dawned (about 3.30), and the French began to appear in force. It was 5 a.m. before the first battalions of the main Russian body came up.

As soon as Lannes had heard, from his retiring cavalry, of the Russian passage at Friedland, he despatched Ruffin's brigade, and part of Oudinot's grenadier division, towards that point. Scarcely had they started, when a despatch from Napoleon warned Lannes that Bennigsen appeared to intend crossing at Friedland, and marching direct on Königsberg.[1] The Emperor had promptly ordered Grouchy, from Eylau, with his own dragoon division and Nansouty's cuirassiers, to join Lannes as quickly as possible. Lannes followed shortly, with the rest of Oudinot's and Verdier's divisions.

It was still night when Oudinot, between 2 and 3 a.m., debouched on the Friedland plain, to find Ruffin in front of him, advancing against the Russian cavalry. He pushed for-

---

[1] *Corr.* 12,573. To Lannes, dated Eylau, 13th June, 9 p.m. The Emperor is, he says, uncertain whether it is the whole Russian army or only a detachment that is at Friedland. He promises to send on Ney at 1 a.m., and to have Victor at Domnau by 10 a.m., in case he is required. He presumes Lannes will seize Friedland, if the enemy is not in force there.

ward two battalions into the Sortlack wood, and held his main body in front of Posthenen, on the near bank of a small brook, which issues from the wood towards the Millstream. In front, he placed 2 batteries, and behind them were 5 or 6 battalions, and 1 gun, somewhat to the left, with their backs to the Bothkeim wood. From the Russian side also, skirmishers were sent into the Sortlack wood, where they met the French. Musketry and artillery fire broke out all along the line. The Russian skirmishers were from the Guard infantry, which had been sent over to the left of the cavalry. They were exhausted by a long march without rest, and they were ignorant of the ground.

At 3 a.m., Grouchy arrived with French and Saxon dragoons. At this hour Lannes had on the ground 9000 infantry, and 3000 cavalry.[1] The next to arrive were Oudinot's dragoons, who took post behind his right, on the south bank of the Millstream.

This cavalry moved out, between 5 and 6 a.m., across the

---

[1] The numbers engaged at Friedland are, as in the case of every other action in this campaign, most variously stated, thus—

Thiers gives 75,000 Russians and 80,000 French.

Alison takes the French at 80,000 and the Russians at 55,000, including the detachments to Allenburg, etc.

Dumas puts the Russians at 61,000.

Hœpfner gives Bennigsen 46,000 on the left bank of the Alle, besides the 14th division and other troops on the right bank, and the detachments to Allenburg, etc.

Plotho (pp. 162–165), guessing the French force at 70,000 or 80,000, says that, after Heilsberg, Bennigsen still had 76,000. Of these he detached 9000 under Kamenskoi, and 6000 to Allenburg, which would give him 61,000 on both banks of the Alle at Friedland, or, say, 55,000 actually engaged on the left bank. Considerable deductions must, however, be made for stragglers in the long march from Heilsberg.

The text of Kausler's *Atlas des Plus Memorables Batailles*, etc., gives 75,000 Russians and 85,000 French.

Marbot allows Napoleon 80,000.

There is a close agreement as to the French numbers, and it will not be far wide of the mark to call them 80,000. As for Bennigsen, considering all the authorities, it seems doubtful if his numbers were higher than these:—

On the left bank of the Alle............ 46,000
On right bank........................ 6,000
Detachments to Allenburg, etc.......... 6,000
                                        58,000

little brook in front of the guns, against the Russian cavalry.
They were not as yet strong enough to beat Kologribow's
horsemen. As they were being driven back, they received
timely succour by the arrival, at 6 o'clock, of Fresia's Dutch
cavalry (of Mortier's corps), who made a fresh addition to the
strength of the French right, and forced Kologribow to retire. Whilst these cavalry combats were in progress, Grouchy
had observed that the Russians, who were now rapidly crossing the river, were advancing in force on Heinrichsdorf by
the road to Königsberg. From the village they would be in a
position to gain the French rear through the Georgenau
wood.

Sending Nansouty forward from the Domnau road,
Grouchy followed towards Heinrichsdorf, direct from Posthenen. Nansouty, passing through the Georgenau wood,
drove out of it, through Heinrichsdorf, the advanced troops
of the Russians, until he was stopped by infantry and artillery. Ordering Nansouty to form front towards the enemy at
the village, Grouchy himself charged their guns as they entered it; whilst Nansouty, aided by Albert's dragoons, now
sent up by Lannes, attacked in front. Disordered by a successful onslaught, the French were, in turn, charged by Russian cavalry, who, however, only succeeded in facilitating the
withdrawal of most of their own guns before they were
beaten off. Grouchy then drew up his men on either side of
Heinrichsdorf at its eastern entrance.

All this time a desultory combat, without any decisive result on either side, had been in progress along Lannes' whole
front. That marshal found himself in a position in some ways
similar to that which he had held at Pultusk. As at Pultusk, he
was facing a very superior force, for the Russians were now
hurrying across the Friedland bridges, Bennigsen hoping
and believing that only Lannes was at hand. But there was
this great difference between the two cases, that, at Pultusk,
Lannes felt he had nothing to fall back on, whilst, at Friedland, he knew that the Emperor was hurrying up an overwhelming force to his aid.

It was now 9 a.m., and there were on the field 9000 French
infantry and 8000 cavalry. Lannes had made the most of his
small force. He covered the whole of his front with an unusu-

ally dense line of skirmishers; the troops behind them were able to give the impression of larger numbers, owing to the detached groups of trees, the inequalities of the ground, and the high crops. Lannes also, by moving them about and deploying them in different positions, conveyed the impression of the arrival of more troops. Their business was to fight a delaying action, to keep Bennigsen occupied, and to induce him to bring across the river his whole army, very inferior in numbers to the corps which Napoleon, in a few hours, would be able to collect against it. By 9 o'clock, Bennigsen had passed across the river 46,000 men, a force amply sufficient to overwhelm Lannes, with whom alone he still believed he would have to deal.[1] Six divisions of infantry, and most of the cavalry, had crossed. As his troops arrived, the Russian commander drew them up on the plain between Sortlack and the Damerau wood. On the northern half of this space, between Damerau and the Millstream, the 8th, 7th, 6th, and 3rd divisions, under Gortchakow, stood, whilst the smaller southern portion, from the Millstream to Sortlack, was occupied by the 1st and 2nd divisions, the advance guard, and part of the cavalry under Kologribow. The greater part of the cavalry was in the northern portion, under Uwarow and Gallitzin. The infantry were drawn up in two lines; in the first the regiments stood with their first and third battalions deployed, the 2nd battalion in column behind. The second line consisted of entire regiments in columns of battalions, behind the 3rd battalions of the front line. The greater part of the cossacks were about the Damerau wood. In the Sortlack wood were about 3000 picked jägers, who had been driven back into it, and were fighting there. In support of them, at Sortlack, stood two battalions, five squadrons, and four guns.

To obliterate, as far as possible, the separation of the left from his centre and right, Bennigsen threw four small bridges across the Millstream. On the right bank of the Alle remained the 14th division and 20 squadrons, on the Schippenbeil road, as well as Platow's flying column, and a large part of the artillery. The detachments which Kologribow had

---

[1] At 9 a.m. all the divisions had passed except one. The 6000 men detached towards Allenburg were sent back from the left bank.

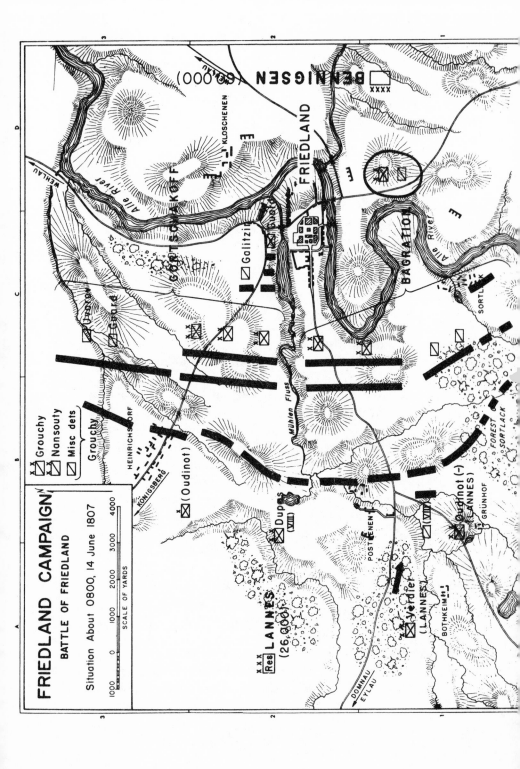

FRIEDLAND CAMPAIGN

BATTLE OF FRIEDLAND

Situation About 0800, 14 June 1807

Grouchy
Nansouty
Misc dets

SCALE OF YARDS

1000 0 1000 2000 3000 4000

Grouchy

KÖNIGSBERG

HEINRICHSDORF

(Oudinot)

Dupas

Grünhof

Oudinot (-) (LANNES)

FOREST OF SORTLACK

SORTLACK

POSTHENEN

Mühlen Fluss

Verdier (LANNES)

BOTHKEIM

DOMNAU EYLAU

LANNES (26,000)

Res

BAGRATION

FRIEDLAND

Golitzin

Alle River

GORTSCHAKOFF

KLOSCHENEN

WEHLAU

Alle River

BENNIGSEN (60,000)

made to Wohnsdorf and Allenburg, were reinforced by a
Guard infantry regiment, 3 cavalry regiments, some cossacks, and a part of the Guard artillery.[1] Some of the guns
covered the pontoon bridges, a battery at Kloschenen supported the right wing across the river, another fired on the
French issuing, from Sortlack wood, against the left flank.

The fight in that wood had oscillated backwards and forwards: at one moment the Russian jägers had driven the
French out of it; a few moments later the latter had returned, and again made their way deep into the covert, only
once more to be driven back to its edge. So the fight swayed
backwards and forwards.

About 9 o'clock, the whole Russian army moved forward,
bringing its left into line with the front then held by the
jägers in Sortlack wood, whilst the right wing stood 500 or
600 paces short of Heinrichsdorf.

The cossacks, pushing into and through that village, arrived on the rear of the French line towards Schwonau, as
the Russian cavalry of the right wing attacked it in front.
Beaumont and Colbert, with 2500 cavalry of the 1st and 6th
corps, quickly drove off the cossacks, and then, joining in the
severe cavalry fight which was in progress, they turned the
balance in favour of the French.

Mortier's corps[2] was now beginning to appear on the
scene, Dupas' division of it reaching Heinrichsdorf just in
time to arrest the progress of the Russian infantry. Dupas
then took his stand on the right of the village, which was still
occupied by 3 battalions of grenadiers. The remainder of the
grenadiers returned to their own division, on the right,
whilst 3 Polish regiments, of Dombrowski's division, placed
themselves behind the battery in front of Posthenen. The
French now had 23,000 infantry and 10,500 cavalry present
when, at 10 a.m., Verdier's division, the rear of Lannes'

[1] Wilson says Bennigsen detached 6000 men to guard the lower passages
of the Alle at Allenburg. This number may perhaps fairly represent the
detachments made and thus reinforced.

[2] The return for the 15th June *(Arch. Hist.)* shows this corps as comprising only one weak French division of 3976 men, besides cavalry and artillery. The other two divisions, the numbers of which are not stated, were
Poles.

corps, at last put in an appearance, raising the French to 40,000 against 46,000 Russians. Bennigsen at last began to see that he was likely to have more on his hands than he could manage. He could only hope that Napoleon would not be able to overwhelm him before night should afford him an opportunity of retrieving the error which he had committed in crossing the river. Meanwhile, officer after officer had been despatched to inform Napoleon of the position of affairs.

He reached the field about noon, and, from the height in rear of Posthenen, scanned the battlefield. A very different sight was before him on this bright summer morning from that which he had witnessed under the wintry sky of Eylau, and he was in very different spirits. To his staff he had remarked at Domnau, "The enemy appears to wish to give battle to-day; so much the better, it is the anniversary of Marengo." His wonderful power of grasping the points of a battlefield at once showed him the faultiness of Bennigsen's position, split in two by the Millstream, with his left wing across the opening of the triangular peninsula ending at Friedland, bounded on one side by the Millstream, on the other by the Alle. He saw that this wing was cut off from the support of the rest of the army by the stream, and that the four bridges, by which Bennigsen had attempted to remedy this fatal defect, were almost useless. He saw that, as the left wing was forced back, it would be driven closer and closer together, until it was enclosed in Friedland, where its defeat, with the capture of the town, must infallibly bring disaster upon the centre and right, if they attempted to maintain their position, with the river, unfordable as he believed it to be, close behind them. He felt that Bennigsen had lost his only chance of escape by neglecting to fall upon Lannes with far greater vigour, and to destroy him before the rest of the army could arrive.

By this time, Napoleon had sufficient strength to hold back the wearied Russians until the arrival of Ney, Victor, and the Guard. Till then, he was not anxious to press the fight, in which a lull now occurred. By 2 p.m. the orders for the battle were dictated and issued. They were as follows:

"Marshal Ney will take the right from Posthenen towards Sortlack, and will rest on the present position of General

Oudinot. Marshal Lannes will form the centre, which will commence at the left of Marshal Ney, from Heinrichsdorf, up to about opposite the village of Posthenen; the grenadiers of Oudinot, at present forming the right of Marshal Lannes, will lean insensibly to the left, in order to draw upon themselves the attention of the enemy.

"Marshal Lannes will close in his divisions as much as possible, by this closure enabling himself to form two lines.

"The left will be formed by Marshal Mortier, holding Heinrichsdorf and the Königsberg road, and thence extending opposite the Russian right wing. Marshal Mortier will never advance, as the movement will be by our right, pivoting on the left.

"The cavalry of General Espagne, and General Grouchy's dragoons, united to the cavalry of the left wing, will manoeuvre so as to cause as much harm as possible to the enemy when he, pressed by the vigorous attack of our right, shall feel the necessity of retreat.

"General Victor and the Imperial Guard, horse and foot, will form the reserve, and will be placed at Grünhof, Bothkeim, and behind Posthenen.

"Lahoussaye's division of dragoons will be under the orders of General Victor; that of General Latour-Maubourg will obey Marshal Ney. Nansouty's division of heavy cavalry will be at the disposal of Marshal Lannes, and will fight alongside the cavalry of the reserve, in the centre.

"I shall be with the reserve in the centre.

"The advance must be always from the right, and the initiative of the movement must be left to Marshal Ney, who will await my orders to begin.

"As soon as the right advances against the enemy, all the artillery of the line will redouble its fire in the direction most useful for the protection of the attack on the right."

But the Emperor was still in some doubt as to what force was in front of him. On the previous evening, his cavalry had not been able to give him any precise information as to the enemy's movements.[1] Murat, according to Savary, had informed him, on the morning of the 13th, that the bulk of the Russian army was marching direct on Königsberg. The

[1] *Savary*, iii. 84: "Our cavalry could give no precise account of the enemy's march."

cavalry had, apparently, over-estimated Kamenskoi's 9000 men. The fact of his detaching two entire corps and three cavalry divisions to deal with the enemy at Königsberg shows that Napoleon believed the Russians to be in much greater strength in that direction than they really were. When he reached the front, at Posthenen, Oudinot had told him there were 80,000 men in front of him. Savary, sent out to see if the enemy were, as Napoleon could hardly believe possible, determined to fight a great battle with the river close behind them, reported that they were still crossing the bridges in great numbers. The Emperor's doubts are clearly exhibited by a despatch dated, "Before Friedland, 3 p.m., June 14th," which is worth quoting in full.

"The cannonade has been in progress since 3 a.m.; the enemy appears to be here in order of battle *with his army;* at first he wished to debouch towards Königsberg; now he appears to be seriously meditating the battle which is about to commence. His Majesty hopes that you are already in Königsberg (a division of dragoons and Marshal Soult are sufficient to enter that town), and that, with two cuirassier divisions and Marshal Davout, you will have marched for Friedland; for *it is possible the battle may last over to-morrow.* Endeavour, therefore, to arrive by 1 a.m. We have not, as yet, any news of you to-day. Should the Emperor be led to suppose that the enemy is in very great force, *it is possible he may rest satisfied to-day with bombarding him, and wait for you.* Communicate part of this letter to Marshals Soult and Davout."

From noon till 5 p.m. the action was maintained in a desultory fashion, chiefly by the artillery of both sides. The Russians who had been marching all night, and most of the previous day, were exhausted. At 4 p.m., Victor's corps and the French Guard arrived.

As Bennigsen saw column upon column arriving on the edge of the woods behind Posthenen, moving into line, and forming a "deep girdle of glittering steel," on the horizon, he bitterly repented his passage of the river, and had already given orders to attempt a retreat. They had scarcely been issued when they had to be cancelled.

At 5 o'clock, the comparative silence was broken by three salvoes of 20 guns, the signal for the advance. The echo of the last had not died away before, from the whole line of French artillery, there burst forth a furious fire. At the same moment, Ney's corps, already collected in the clearings of the nearer portion of the Sortlack wood[1] dashed forward with loud cheers, driving the jägers slowly back. By 6 o'clock the wood was cleared, and Ney's columns began to debouch on the farther side. The supporting Russian troops, at Sortlack, were powerless to stop their movement, but a battery on the farther bank of the Alle caused them some annoyance.

In mass of divisions, Marchand leading on the right, Bisson on the left, Latour-Maubourg behind, Ney pushed on. Marchand, overwhelming the retiring Russians at Sortlack, drove them in wild confusion into the Alle below the village. To accomplish this he had to diverge to his right, into the eastward bend of the river, thus leaving an open space between himself and Bisson. Into this space dashed Kologribow at the head of his cavalry; but he was promptly met by Latour-Maubourg, moving up to fill the gap. Charged by this force in front, fired into by Marchand and Bisson on his flanks, Kologribow's attempt to split Ney's infantry failed. Marchand, as the Russians retired again, moving westwards along the river, effected, once more, his union with Bisson, and the two ranged themselves across the neck of the Friedland peninsula, from the re-entrant angle of the Alle to the Millstream. The Russians in the peninsula, now bent back at an obtuse angle from the line north of the brook, were gradually being compressed by the narrowing space into compact masses on which the French artillery wrought fearful havoc.

As Ney advanced, Napoleon had moved up Victor's corps, on the right of the Eylau road, in two lines, with Lahoussaye's dragoons in 3rd line. Durosnel's cavalry followed. Ney's

---

[1] Ney formed his columns in the wood. Only the artillery were on the roads through it; but, fortunately, there were three broad clearings, each sufficiently wide to allow of a column of infantry and one of cavalry, as well as the artillery, standing in them (*Savary*, iii. 87–88).

corps, with a cloud of skirmishers in front, again moved forward towards Friedland, Latour-Maubourg following some way behind. Marchand, on the ground sloping towards Friedland and the Alle, was suffering heavily by case from the Russian batteries beyond it, to silence which Ney moved his corps artillery to the bank. Bisson, protected by the slope towards the Millstream, was less exposed.

Both divisions, however, lost heavily from this artillery fire, as well as from the infantry and artillery fire, against their front. They were already wavering when Bennigsen's reserve cavalry, standing beyond the brook, crossed it and fell upon their left flank. It wanted but this blow to complete the repulse of Ney. His troops were retreating in considerable disorder when help reached them. Dupont, with his division of Victor's corps, had pushed forward his guns, which had barely time to fire a round of case before the Russian cavalry was upon them. Dupont, with great promptitude, for which he earned the special approval of Napoleon, changing direction to the right, hurried up his infantry at the double into the gap, on Ney's left, cut by the cavalry. This division was specially enthusiastic in its attack, for, up to the surrender of Ulm, it had belonged to Ney's command. The men felt, therefore, that on them depended the safety of old friends and comrades in the glorious fields of 1805. Latour-Maubourg and Durosnel also galloped forward against the Russian cavalry, which was now carried back on the infantry across the neck of the peninsula, spreading disorder in its ranks. The confusion was still further increased by the fire of 38 guns, which Senarmont, holding 6 more in reserve and escorted by Lahoussaye's cavalry and a battalion of infantry, moved steadily forward, opening fire first at 600 paces, then at 300, at 150, and, finally, at 60. The Russian cavalry made a desperate effort against this battery, but the French gunners, calmly awaiting their approach, mowed them down with a volley of grape.

The Russian left, in the peninsula, was now, in hopeless confusion, making the best of its way into Friedland, pursued hotly by Ney's rallied troops, as well as by Dupont and the fire of Senarmont's guns.

Dupont, having restored the fight here and completed the Russian disaster, wheeled to his left, across the Millstream, a movement which brought him upon the left flank and rear of the Russian centre, still maintaining its forward position.

Ney, pressing on into Friedland, and engaging in a fierce fight in the streets, was in possession of the town by 8 p.m. The Russian cavalry and infantry in front of him streamed towards the now burning bridges. At 7.30, the Russian artillery, beyond the river, had set fire to the houses nearest the bridges, and the flames had spread to the bridges themselves. The river was too deep to ford with safety; great numbers of the Russians, failing to reach the bridges whilst they were still passable, were drowned in the attempt to cross by swimming. Their heavy accoutrements dragged down the infantry.

The battle, as designed by Napoleon, was as good as won when Friedland was captured.

Lannes and Mortier had intelligently carried out their orders by fighting a waiting action, merely detaining Gortchakow north of the Millstream, though harassing him with a terrible artillery fire, to which he could but feebly respond. It was only when he saw the thick smoke rising from the houses and the bridges of Friedland, that he realised that his retreat in that direction was cut off. He had already fallen back to the position of the early morning before the overwhelming fire of the artillery of the 1st and 6th corps. Dupont was north of the pond, at Friedland, on his left flank.

Leaving his cavalry to hold in check, as far as possible, the corps of Lannes and Mortier, he sent his two nearest divisions of infantry to the recapture of Friedland. These brave men, charging with the bayonet Dupont's and Ney's troops, carried them back into the town, and re-occupied the part of it nearest the lower pontoon bridge, only to find the bridge burning and impossible to cross. Some sought to cross to the right bank there, the majority wended their way, still fighting, down the river to Kloschenen, where, fortunately for Bennigsen, late in the evening, there had been discovered a deep ford, the existence of which had previously been unknown. Bad, and deep, as it was, it proved the salvation of the Russian army; for it not only gave a chance of crossing to its infantry and cavalry, but also enabled Bennigsen, with infinite difficulty, to get back many of his guns. These he managed to get up the steep right bank, and range there as a cover to the retreat, though it was for long impossible for them to fire on the confused throng of friends and foes. Much of the ammunition was rendered useless by water in the deep ford.

Instant retreat was now the only course open to Gortchakow, with his remaining two divisions of infantry, his artillery, and his cavalry. The last he still left, to cover him against Mortier and Lannes. First he withdrew his guns, then his infantry. The latter slowly retired in great masses, through which the French artillery tore wide lanes, marking every halting-place with heaps and lines of dead and wounded.

It was now the moment for Napoleon to slip the leash in which he had, so far, held his centre and left. Rejoicing to be at last allowed to take an active part, the infantry of Lannes and Mortier poured over the plain towards the Alle, to complete the destruction which the artillery had begun. They found their enemy in no mood for surrender; the brave Russian infantry preferred death by the bayonets of their opponents, or to take their chance of drowning in the river, to yielding themselves prisoners; few were taken. Part of the cavalry crossed with the broken infantry near Kloschenen; the majority retreated down the left bank, to Allenburg. Had Napoleon's cavalry, beyond Heinrichsdorf, shown the energy which might have been expected from them, this retreat by the left should have been impossible. There were 40 French squadrons in this direction, opposed to but 22 Russian. Even Savary, no friend of Murat, deplores his absence. He would have seen the opportunity and have rolled up the Russian right, so that scarcely a man could have escaped. As it was, the French squadrons remained dismounted during the greater part of the renewed battle, content with what they had accomplished in the morning, doing nothing. The reason given, forsooth, was that they had no orders.[1] Murat at least would not have waited for orders with such a chance before him.

The defeated Russians who succeeded in crossing the river, united with the reserve in the Gnatten wood. Thence, in two columns, they marched for Wehlau, their rear covered by Platow's flying column, which, during the day, had made a futile attempt to cross the river behind Ney's right, but had been easily beaten off.

At Allenburg, the retreat was joined by the cavalry, which had followed the left bank. At noon, on the 15th, Bennigsen had got together, at Wehlau, his broken army. Pursuit, there was none worth mentioning. A French general is said to have remarked that Friedland was "a battle gained and a victory lost."

During the night, the French corps occupied the following positions when the battle at last, about 11 p.m., ceased. Lannes on the Königsberg road, between Friedland and Heinrichsdorf. Mortier beyond Friedland, on both banks of the river. Victor at Posthenen. Ney in and behind Friedland. The Guard, surrounding their victorious Emperor, slept on the plain where had stood the Russian centre.

"Wagram," from *Napoleon and the Archduke Charles: A History of the Franco-Austrian Campaign in the Valley of the Danube in 1809*

The Campaign of 1809 was the first in which Napoleon suffered a serious setback in the field, and was ultimately to prove his last success. It opened brilliantly, despite the absence of many of Napoleon's finest troops in Spain. A rapid offensive swiftly cleared the

---

[1] This was not even correct, for Napoleon's orders had directed Grouchy, Espagne, and the cavalry of the left wing, to "manœuvre so as to cause as much harm as possible to the enemy when he, pressed by the vigorous attack of our right, shall feel the necessity of retreat." Their inaction was certainly no compliance with this order.

The cavalry reserve engaged at Friedland, according to Murat *(Arch. Hist.)*, consisted of the 1st, 2nd, and 3rd heavy divisions, the 1st, 2nd, and 4th dragoon divisions. The last-named was with Victor.

Austrians out of Bavaria and Napoleon captured Vienna within a month of the opening of the campaign. But the Austrian Army was strongly positioned across the Danube near the city. The Battle of Aspern-Essling, May 21–22, proved a bloody and unsuccessful affair, demonstrating a significant decline in the quality of the French Army and a simultaneous increase in that of Austria. It was also the first decisive tactical defeat in the field in Napoleon's career. Over the next six weeks both sides concentrated on a renewal of the struggle. And on the night of July 4–5 the French armies again crossed the Danube, opening the Battle of Wagram. Wagram proved a tough fight. In order to win, Napoleon had to abandon all pretense of tactical finesse and had to resort to the use of a massive assault column, and the achievement of that victory was far costlier than any ever before.

Before describing the progress of this, the greatest battle, in point of numbers engaged, that Napoleon had yet fought, let us get an idea of the numbers of the two armies. It seems safe for this purpose to accept the figures of Binder v. Krieglstein, which are worked out with great care, and are probably as near the truth as can be got. The French corps were the following:—

	INFANTRY.	CAVALRY.	GUNS.
Imperial Guard	7,300	3,700	60
2nd corps (Oudinot) and Colbert's light cavalry.................	18,000	1,200	92
3rd corps (Davout), Montbrun's light cavalry, and the dragoon divisions Grouchy and Pully....	30,000	4,800	98
4th corps (Masséna) and Lasalle's light cavalry.................	24,000	3,200	90
9th corps (Bernadotte's Saxons and Dupas' division)	15,700	2,200	42
7th corps (Wrede's division)	4,800	1,000	36
Army of Italy (Eugène).........	22,000	1,200	100
11th corps (Marmont)..........	9,000	...	12
Cavalry Reserve (Bessières)	...	6,000	24
	130,800	23,300	554
	154,100		

All of these were up on the 5th July, except Marmont and Wrede. Besides them, there were Reynier's troops in the Lobau, numbering some 6000 infantry, with 129 guns of position. When we add in artillerymen and engineers, it may be taken that Napoleon did not much exaggerate when he said he intended attacking with 180,000 men.

The Austrian forces were altogether:—

	INFANTRY.	CAVALRY.	GUNS.
Advance guard (Nordmann)	11,950	2,500	48
I. corps (Bellegarde)	20,900	800	68
II. corps (Hohenzollern).	25,800	560	68
III. corps (Kolowrat)	17,000	740	58
IV. corps (Rosenberg)	17,900	800	60
V. corps (Reuss)[1]	7,550	800	32
VI. corps (Klenau)	16,200	1,400	64
Reserve corps (Liechtenstein)	11,200	8,800	48
Archduke John (Army of Italy). . .	11,000	2,200	34
	193,500	18,600	480

158,100

But of these the V. corps, the Archduke John, and 1800 men of the III. corps detached on the Bisamberg never came into the battle. Thus Charles' army which actually fought at Wagram numbered 119,150 infantry, 15,600 cavalry, 414 guns, or, including artillery and engineers, say 142,000. A great many of these were landwehr who had been collected during the seven weeks between Essling and Wagram. There were 31 such battalions out of a total of 175.

As Masséna reached the left bank, he posted his troops at right angles to it, with Boudet next the river, then Molitor and Carra St Cyr, to whom was added, about 4 P.M., Legrand. The latter was withdrawn from the Mühlau, his place being taken by Reynier's troops, when the passage had been established on the east of the Lobau. Lasalle and Marulaz were on the right of the infantry. Masséna gradually pushed forward, and, by 5 A.M., had driven the Austrians into Enzersdorf.

---

[1] Exclusive of Schustekh's detachment at Krems.

Davout had also moved forward towards Wittau, and, as his cavalry was not yet over, Lasalle and Marulaz had helped in clearing out the Austrian detachments, until they were stopped at Rutzendorf by the infantry fire of a battalion from the IV. corps holding the village. By 8 A.M., Masséna was master of Enzersdorf, the pivot on which the Emperor meant to wheel his army to the left. The place was held by two battalions, but it was overwhelmed by artillery fire, and Masséna's aide-de-camp, St Croix, with the 46th, after a sharp fight in the streets and houses, captured the greater part of the garrison. About the same hour, Oudinot moved up into his place between Masséna and Davout, and the latter, having now got his own cavalry, sent it to his right flank to look out for the possible arrival of the Archduke John.

Masséna's advance had cut off the retreat of the Austrian detachment in the Ile Pouzet and it had to surrender. This island being in Napoleon's possession, he now ordered the construction of two more bridges, one at a point between the Iles Alexandre and Lannes, and one connecting the Ile Pouzet to the Lobau on the one side, and to the left bank near Enzersdorf on the other. The former was ready by 2 P.M., the latter not till 9 P.M.

We must now see what the Archduke Charles had been doing. It was only at 5 A.M. that he received news of the French crossing, though he had heard the cannonade during the night. Then he received a report from Nordmann that strong French columns were marching against his left flank, and the Bisamberg observatory announced a constant stream of troops from the right bank into the Lobau.

Then, at last, orders were issued for the fortification of the Russbach position, so as to enable it to be held by a comparatively small force, whilst the rest of the army resumed the offensive. Charles still seemed to believe that there would be no serious battle on the 5th, but that the French would be satisfied with strengthening the position they had acquired on the left bank. Nordmann was told that probably the French sought to pass below Enzersdorf and establish themselves so as to be able, later, to advance against the village. At 5.30 A.M., Charles wrote to John that he had no intention of fighting near the Danube, where the French would have every advantage with their heavy artillery in a well-established position. John was ordered, after a three hours' rest at Marchegg, to join the left of his brother's army at Markgrafneusiedl. Liechtenstein, when Enzersdorf was taken, sent his seven light cavalry regiments to Pysdorf, two cuirassier regiments to the Neu-Wirtshaus, and four in reserve to Raasdorf.

Nordmann, though his prescribed line of retreat was seriously threatened by the advance of the French right, hoped to be able to attack their left from Essling as they advanced from Enzersdorf. He therefore posted an infantry brigade and a regiment of hussars there. He was, however, compelled by artillery fire, about 9 A.M., to abandon his work No. VIII. to the east of Essling.

There now ensued a long pause in the battle; for the passage of a great army, even with the numerous bridges available, was necessarily a slow matter. It was not till 2 P.M. that Bernadotte reached his place in line, and the Guard was not up till 4 P.M. Eugène arrived at noon. Between 10 and 11 A.M., the first line had occupied a great arc extending from the Stadlau arm south-west of Enzersdorf to Kimmerleindorf. On the extreme left, next the Stadlau arm, was the cavalry of Lasalle and Marulaz, with Boudet on Marulaz's right, all facing north-west. The rest of Masséna's corps faced north, as did Oudinot's, and both were now in line. Davout, in columns of divisions between Rutzendorf and Kimmerleindorf, faced north-east, whilst Grouchy's and Pully's dragoon divisions were massed in front of the last-named village.

As they came up, Bernadotte formed the 2nd line behind Masséna's centre and right, Eugène behind Oudinot, the Guard and the cavalary Reserve in the interval between them.

A letter from Charles to the Austrian Emperor, dated 9.30 A.M., shows that by that time he had again changed his views, and expected a general attack that day.

At 11 he betook himself to the left flank, but passed no orders, pending the return of Wimpffen who had ridden to Nordmann at Essling.

At noon, Napoleon sent the light cavalry forward towards Raasdorf, Pysdorf, and Glinzendorf, covered by a heavy artillery fire, and Davout seized Rutzendorf with an infantry detachment. The cavalry manœuvred towards Liechtenstein's left flank, whilst overwhelming him with the fire of their horse artillery. Charles seems to have contemplated a half-hearted measure, by pushing forward Liechtenstein, supported by Rosenberg if necessary, to relieve the pressure on Nordmann's left. It came to nothing, as Liechtenstein was already retreating when he got the order at 4 P.M.

It was 2 A.M. when Napoleon began his general advance with the first line, Eugène and Bernadotte, the Guard, and the cuirassiers being still on the march. Davout took the direction of Glinzendorf and Markgrafneusiedl, followed by Eugène; Oudinot marched towards Parbasdorf (Baumersdorf), followed by Bernadotte (less the 1st Saxon division, left to guard the bridges till Marmont was up); Masséna leant to his left, keeping Boudet touching the Stadlau arm and compelling the Austrians to evacuate the Aspern-Essling line. The next division on the right was Molitor's, directed on the space between Hirschstetten and Breitenlee. In touch with Molitor's right was Carra St Cyr, and on his right again was Legrand moving on Süssenbrünn. The direction of march of Oudinot and Masséna necessarily resulted in a great gap between them, and this was filled by Eugène on the right and Bernadotte on the left moving into first line. The Guard on arrival took post in rear of Eugène. The general order of advance was artillery in 1st, cavalry in 2nd line, and infantry in rear.

Masséna wheeled to his left on Boudet, who stood still in the line of Austrian works between redoubts VIII. and IX., until the operation was completed, about 5 P.M.

Meanwhile, the commencement of the French advance threatened the retreat of Nordmann from Essling to Grosshofen. He had lost heavily and had scarcely a serviceable gun left. He commenced his retreat at once, passing back to the Russbach position without any serious fighting.

Klenau, though he had reported at 2 P.M. that he would soon be forced to retreat, did not commence his retirement till 5, when he fell back before Boudet on to the slopes of the Bisamberg, having the III. corps on his left and the grenadiers beyond that, at Gerasdorf.

Boudet halted north-west of Aspern, with detachments in front at Kagran and Leopoldau. The rest of Masséna's corps was at and beyond Breitenlee, with a strong detachment at Süssenbrünn. Part of St Cyr's division, however, had reinforced Boudet, so that St Cyr had only 5 Hessian battalions at Breitenlee. On the French right Davout had stormed Glinzendorf by 5 P.M., and the line to his left passed through Raasdorf.

Thus, at 5 P.M., when Masséna was facing west, the corps of Davout, Oudinot, and Eugène were facing the Russbach position, and Bernadotte was moving into the gap south of Aderklaa, between Eugène's left and Masséna's right. Behind the Russbach the Austrians stood thus:—I. corps with its right in Deutsch-Wagram; II. on both sides of Parbasdorf (Baumersdorf); IV. with its left flank at Markgrafneusiedl; Reserve cavalry and Nordmann in rear of IV. corps; Fröhlich's hussars, which had retired from Rutzendorf, at Ober-Siebenbrünn.

Charles now once more changed his plans and gave up Wimpffen's "pair of pincers" idea. He proposed to assemble his whole army on the position Wagram-Markgrafneusiedl. The order was drafted, but, the rapid march of events rendering its issue impossible, it was torn up. It was too late to carry out the idea, and Charles had no course left now but acceptance of Wimpffen's scheme.

As Bernadotte was advancing on Aderklaa, he found his left flank threatened by Roussel's[1] cuirassier brigade, retiring from Neu-Wirtshaus. Against it he sent his Saxon light cavalry. The cuirassiers committed the fatal mistake of standing still to receive the charge, with the natural result that they were defeated, and only escaped pursuit owing to the opportune support of Lederer's cuirassiers.

The Russbach position, which Charles was now holding with some 90,000 men, was an extremely strong one; it might have been made much stronger had it been properly fortified. As it was, the works, ordered to be begun only at 5 A.M., had not made much progress. On the left bank of the stream, the plateau had a considerable command over the

[1] A French "émigré" in the Austrian service.

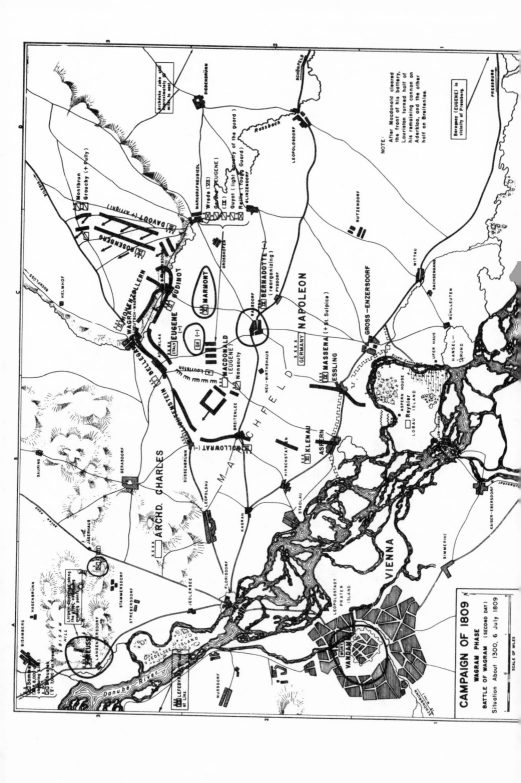

CAMPAIGN OF 1809

WAGRAM PHASE

BATTLE OF WAGRAM (SECOND DAY)

Situation About 1300, 6 July 1809

SCALE OF MILES

NOTE:

After Macdonald cleared the front of his battery, Lauriston turned remaining half of his remaining cannon on Aderklaa, and the other half on Breitenlee.

Beriadey (EUGENE) in vicinity of Pressburg

plain on the south. As the bank was turned back at right angles at Wagram on one side and Markgrafneusiedl on the other, the whole plateau formed as it were a sort of fortress with a good command on three sides of a square, the fourth resting on the hills about Bockflüss. The front and right flank were further protected by the stream in front of them. It was but a small obstacle, 3 yards wide and 2½ feet deep, easily passable by infantry, but its fringe of osier beds and willows made it almost proof against cavalry and artillery, except at the bridges, of which there were eight.

The Austrian right and left rested respectively on Wagram and Markgrafneusiedl, a front of nearly four miles. Almost in the centre of this front, the Austrians held the village of Parbasdorf (Baumersdorf), forming a great bastion projecting into the plain, and flanking attacks on either side of it against the front.

The Austrians were thus in two great groups, the left wing on the line Markgrafneusiedl-Wagram nearly 90,000[1] strong, the right wing, of over 50,000,[2] having its left (the grenadiers) at Gerasdorf, thus leaving a gap of three miles between it and the I. corps at Wagram.

Napoleon had succeeded in passing to the left bank of the Danube with his whole army, except Marmont and Wrede, not yet up, and in deploying it with something like 110,000 men facing the Austrian left, whilst another 27,000 faced westwards. He had gained some successes, but had done nothing decisive. The Austrian cannonade from beyond the Russbach had informed him that that position was to be held determinedly, and he was aware of the general position of Charles' right. If he could carry the Russbach position on the 5th, he would prevent the junction, during the night, of the separated Austrian wings. That he resolved to attempt, though the day was now fast declining. Though he rode far to the front, the trees bordering the Russbach, and the bank

---

[1] Strength at commencement of battle: I. corps, 21,700; II., 26,360; IV. corps, 18,700; Nordmann's advance guard, 14,450; Reserve cavalry, 8800. Total, 90,010 with 256 guns.

[2] Inclusive of the V. corps—Initial strengths: III. corps, 17,740; V. corps, 8350; VI. corps, 17,600; Grenadiers (Reserve), 11,200. Total, 54,890 with 190 guns.

beyond, prevented him from ascertaining the enemy's dispositions or strength with accuracy.

It was between 6 and 7 P.M., when he began to send out orders for a general attack, almost too late, even on a July night, to hope for decisive results. Besides, the various French corps were by no means at equal distances from their objective, a fact which caused the attack to be disjointed and piecemeal; for there was not enough of daylight left to defer it till Davout on the right and Bernadotte on the left had brought themselves on a level with the centre.

It was about 6 P.M. when Oudinot received his orders. A furious cannonade now broke out along the whole line, which soon set Baumersdorf in flames. Frère's (late Claparède's) division was sent against Baumersdorf, which was strongly occupied by Hardegg with 10 Austrian battalions. Notwithstanding the support of Tharreau's division, Frère was unable to take the village. At 8 P.M., Oudinot sent in the "Terrible" 57th and the 10th light infantry, both of Grandjean's (late St Hilaire's) division. The 57th, breaking into the village, engaged in a desperate combat in the streets and houses. But it never succeeded in driving out Hardegg, or in getting possession of the two bridges which were so essential for the passage of cavalry and artillery. The 10th light infantry, meanwhile, passed the stream and forced its way on to the heights beyond. There, however, it was attacked on all sides by Austrian infantry, and, finally was charged by hussars led by Hohenzollern himself. Unsupported by either cavalry or artillery, or by other infantry, the regiment was driven back across the Russbach. Austrian reinforcements poured into Baumersdorf; the French were forced to evacuate such portion of it as they held, and to retire half-way to Raasdorf. Oudinot was thus driven off with heavy loss.

Eugène, meanwhile, advanced with Macdonald leading Lamarque's division, supported by the divisions of Serras and Durutte, and by Sahuc's light cavalry. On the way, however, Dupas' division, of Bernadotte's corps, joined the column and took the lead in it. Then he turned to his left up the Russbach towards Wagram, driving in the Austrian skirmishers as he passed, and seeking a crossing. On his right,

Macdonald advanced direct against the heights, at first with 7, then with 11 battalions. As the French charged up the bank, panic seized the opposing Austrian infantry of the first line. Ranks were broken and the men streamed to the rear, many prisoners and some standards falling into the hands of the victorious French. But the second line held fast, and the regiments of the first line on either side of Macdonald's column formed against his flanks. Suffering from a heavy fire on both flanks and in front, the French were compelled to fall back, losing many of the prisoners just taken. Now reinforced by part of Durutte's division and some of Sahuc's squadrons, which had succeeded in crossing the stream, they once more advanced to the attack. Three squadrons charging an Austrian battalion captured its standard. The Austrian line was in serious danger of being broken when Charles himself arrived on the spot, and, with his usual intrepidity, rallied his regiments and led the counter-attack. Hohenzollern also appeared on the French right with his hussars, fresh from their success against Oudinot, and charged the flank of Macdonald's column. Before the superior forces now opposing them, Macdonald's men yielded, gradually at first until, overcome by panic, they fled in disorder across the Russbach, never stopping their flight till they were brought up by the Guard standing in reserve.

Whilst Macdonald was fighting on his right, Dupas had crossed the Russbach and pushed even into the easternmost houses of Wagram. But it was clear that he could not hold out on the left bank, especially as the two Saxon battalions attached to his division appear to have been fired on by mistake by their French comrades. One of them disappeared altogether, and only 43 men of the other were to be found.

The disorderly flight of the defeated troops of Eugène's command is notable evidence of the deterioration of many of Napoleon's young soldiers. No such panic is conceivable, under similar circumstances, in the armies of Austerlitz or Jena. It was well for the French that darkness prevented the Austrians from following up, or even appreciating their success. Bernadotte received his orders at 7 P.M., and it was only as the columns on his right were defeated that he led his troops forward by Aderklaa against Wagram. He was very weak, for he had not Dupas with him, and he had had to leave detachments behind for the protection of the bridges. He had but 10 battalions when he attacked Wagram, and it was already dark. The scene was lighted only by the burning houses of the village, and the confusion in the fighting was such that friends constantly fired on friends, this being due no doubt also partially to the fact that the combatants on both sides were mainly German-speaking. The Austrians had six battalions, of which two were in reserve on the flanks of the village, but joined in the defence from the commencement. The Saxons were thus attacked on both flanks, as well as in front. Bernadotte's attack was not more successful than those of the centre, and by 11 P.M., he had been forced back from Wagram on to Aderklaa.

There remains Davout's attack on the right. His orders also were late in arriving. His cavalry advanced first against the hussars in Ober-Siebenbrünn and the left of the Austrian cavalry reserve below the bank which runs north from Markgrafneusiedl. The divisions of Morand and Friant crossed at Glinzendorf, behind the cavalry, and then moved against the eastern side of Markgrafneusiedl. Simultaneously, Gudin and Puthod attacked in front across the Russbach from Grosshofen. Nothing, however, came of the attack. The cavalry were unable to make way against the four regiments of Nostitz, and the other attacks never got beyond an artillery duel. Looking to the darkness and the gradual subsidence of the sound of the attacks in the centre, Davout withdrew his corps to Glinzendorf for the night. Thus Napoleon's attack on the Russbach position was everywhere repulsed, in parts disastrously. That accounts for the fact that the whole affair is slurred over, in the 25th bulletin, in a few words regarding the attack on Wagram. The Emperor occupied practically the same positions as he held before the attack on the Russbach.

Towards midnight Charles issued his orders for the continuation of the battle on the 6th July.

He now determined to make an early attack with his right wing on the corps of Masséna, and his orders were to the following effect.

III. corps (less one brigade left on the heights of Stammersdorf) to advance by Leopoldau on Breitenlee against the left flank of the French marching against Wagram. Klenau would be on its right, towards the Danube.

Grenadiers to move with the same object on Süssenbrünn.

Cavalry Reserve between Aderklaa and Süssenbrünn, linking the III. corps to the I.

I. corps to advance against Aderklaa, with its left on the Russbach at Wagram.

II. to hold on to the Russbach position to the last, and, as the III. gained ground, to cross the stream. A heavy artillery fire was to be maintained against the French.

IV. corps to attack the French right.

V. corps to hold Am-Spitz and other posts on the Danube opposite Vienna. Great silence was enjoined, in order to conceal the movements, the earliest of which was to be Kolowrat's (III. corps) at 1 A.M., whilst the advance of the I. corps was to begin at 4 A.M. The Archduke himself would be with the I. corps. Rosenberg's attack on Davout was also to begin at 4 A.M.

Of the Archduke John nothing was known at headquarters, though he was presumably nearing Marchegg. As a matter of fact, the first orders, of 7 P.M. on the 4th, had only reached him, owing to the terrible weather during the night, at 5 A.M. on the 5th at Pressburg. He had, on the 4th, acted on orders of the 2nd, requiring him to make a diversion from the Pressburg bridge-head. Consequently, when the new orders reached him, many of his troops were on the south bank of the Danube. He had also numerous posts out towards the Schütt island, etc. This was some excuse for John's failure to at once march on Marchegg, but it was not enough, even taken with the confusion which may have arisen owing to the constantly varying orders of the last day or two. He did not even reply to the first order, and it was only on receipt of the second (of 5.30 A.M. on 5th) at 6 P.M. that he wrote that he would march at 1 A.M. on the 6th. He stated his force, after deduction of a garrison left at Pressburg, at a little over 13,000 men. His last orders were to rest three hours at Marchegg, but now there was no time to spare for this, so, at 2 A.M. on the 6th, orders were despatched to him to march straight on through Ober-Siebenbrünn.

Napoleon's orders of this night appear all to have been verbal.[1] There is some disagreement as to what they were in the case of Davout, but, on the whole, the accounts of Pelet and Laborde seem more reliable than that of Koch, who says Davout was ordered to make an outflanking attack on Markgrafneusiedl.

Accepting Pelet's account, we find that Davout was ordered to draw rather closer to the centre, calling in his detachment from Grosshofen. Masséna was to move, at 2 A.M., towards Aderklaa, leaving only Boudet to cover Aspern and the bridges. The Emperor was, in fact, concentrating towards his centre, so as to be ready, as the Austrian intentions became clearer, to move in any direction; it was the strategical "bataillon carrée" applied to tactics.

According to Pelet, Napoleon's design at first was for Davout to take Markgrafneusiedl, Oudinot the heights between it and Parbasdorf, which place was to be stormed by Marmont. Macdonald would follow the same direction as on the previous evening, and Bernadotte would attack Wagram. The whole attack would be frontal only. Yet he wished to make no final decision till the last moment, till he saw more plainly the condition of affairs. Wrede, who was still in the Lobau, kept asking for orders and being put off. He got them at last, namely, to cross from the Lobau, but to hold fast for the moment at Enzersdorf, till he got further orders.

The Austrian attack broke out first from the extreme left where Rosenberg, at 4 A.M., as ordered, led forward the IV. corps,[2] which he divided into three columns. Six battalions marched across the Russbach on Grosshofen, 16 more took Glinzendorf as objective. Ten battalions and 8 squadrons formed the advance guards of these columns, half in front of each, but the whole advance guard was commanded by Radetzky. The 3rd column, of 38 squadrons under Nostitz, was ordered to outflank the enemy's right, and form a link

---

[1] Unfortunately Col. Saski's collection of official documents does not yet extend beyond the battle of Essling. On the other hand, it is generally observable that written orders in the French archives are infrequent on days of battle and probably few were issued, if any.

[2] Including Nordmann's advance guard, which was put under Rosenberg when it fell back from Essling on the 5th.

with the Archduke John when he arrived. Nostitz sent a detachment of hussars under Fröhlich to Ober-Siebenbrünn, as on the previous day. Riese, with 11 battalions and a heavy battery, remained in the position as reserve. Rosenberg, with his main body still behind the Russbach, directed Radetzky, who had driven in Davout's outposts, not to hurry his advance too much. As for Davout, when the storm broke on him he was on the move towards the centre. Friant's left and Gudin's right were in Glinzendorf, Puthod was in Grosshofen. Between the two villages were artillery and skirmishers.

The light cavalry on Davout's right moved out in part to meet Nostitz in front, whilst part made for Ober-Siebenbrünn, so as to threaten his flank and rear.

It was about 5 A.M. when the Austrians, after some time spent in skirmishing with the French, advanced to the attack of Grosshofen and Glinzendorf, into the nearer parts of which they penetrated.

This early attack on Davout was somewhat surprising, and seemed to point to the early advent of John on the field. Napoleon at once sent Nansouty's and Arrighi's (late Espagne's) cuirassiers to Davout's assistance, and even marched the Guard in the same direction, whilst Nansouty's horse artillery opened on the right flank of the advancing Austrians.

Charles had prescribed a fixed hour for Rosenberg's advance, thinking that by that time both the attack of Kolowrat and that of Klenau would have begun, and John would be nearing the field. But there had been delays; the Austrian right was still a long way off, and John not likely to be up for hours, if at all. Therefore, Charles, whose intention was to begin the attack with his right, sent orders to Rosenberg to return to his position. But that general was already too deeply involved with Davout to allow of his withdrawal without the appearance of defeat. His main body was already involved in support of the advance guard, and Davout was making a vigorous counter-attack. When, therefore, they found the Austrians retiring the French naturally pressed forward. Radetzky covered the retirement, losing 1000 men in doing so. The whole affair was over by 6 o'clock, and Rosenberg's force was back beyond the Russbach.

Napoleon, being now assured that there were no signs of John, resolved to send Davout to a front and flank attack on Markgrafneusiedl, which was one of the keys of the Austrian position on the Russbach. Davout required two hours to prepare the attack, as he had to get two of his divisions across the Russbach lower down, out of range of the Austrian guns, for the flank attack. Napoleon left Arrighi's cuirassiers to support him, but again withdrew the Guard and Nansouty to the centre, whither he himself returned. Davout was quite safe to be trusted with an affair of this sort.

The Emperor directed Eugène and Oudinot to be prepared to storm the heights in front of them, so soon as Davout's flank attack was developed. When he got back to his centre, he found the Austrians had occupied Aderklaa, which was of vital importance to himself.

Bellegarde, with 15 battalions and 8 squadrons, had moved on Aderklaa soon after 3 A.M., leaving Dedowich behind with 7 battalions. About 4 A.M. Bellegarde's advanced troops observed the Saxons evacuating Aderklaa, no doubt under Bernadotte's orders. The Austrian advance guard occupied the place unopposed, and their main body took post between it and Wagram. By 6 A.M. the grenadiers also had come up and taken post on the opposite side of the village. The Reserve cavalry (less one cuirassier regiment sent to the II. corps) stood in rear of the infantry. But there were still no signs of the Austrian right wing, the III. and VI. corps, which had been delayed in various ways.

A tremendous cannonade was maintained on both sides, and Bernadotte, whose flank was exposed towards Aderklaa, felt it necessary to draw back his Saxons. Masséna was not coming into line, and Napoleon, thoroughly appreciating the serious loss to his line in the Austrian occupation of Aderklaa, just at the angle between his wings, ordered Masséna and Bernadotte to retake it, and then, when Davout should have passed Markgrafneusiedl, to storm Wagram. He was, at this time, entirely ignorant of the approach of the Austrian III. and VI. Corps. His attention was directed chiefly to the square tower marking the position of Markgrafneusiedl. When the line of smoke in that direction should show that the village was taken by Davout, he knew that the Austrian left would have been turned, and the whole position, from Wagram to Markgrafneusiedl, jeopardised. Then would be the time to storm Wagram and the line of heights.

Masséna entrusted the attack on Aderklaa to Carra St Cyr. That general pressed forward with his division in closed columns, whilst Bernadotte's Saxons advanced on his right, suffering terribly from the fire of the Austrian artillery on their right flank.

On Carra St Cyr's right were his Hessian battalions, which behaved splendidly under the great trial of the Austrian artillery fire. The attack had been delayed by Carra St Cyr, though the recapture of Aderklaa was of supreme importance. Masséna was furious at the delay. He had himself been disabled two days previously by a fall with his horse, but had insisted on commanding his corps from a carriage, with which he pressed into the very centre of his troops, launching them against Aderklaa. The village was carried triumphantly; not only that, but the 24th and 4th regiments poured out of the farther side in hot pursuit of the fleeing Austrians. Presently the two regiments, finding themselves almost in the midst of Bellegarde's troops without support, halted and began firing, whilst the Austrians, rallying from their panic, attacked them furiously in front and on both flanks. They could do nothing but fall back on Aderklaa, into which the enemy followed them.

But there had been moving for some time across the plain east of the Bisamberg a glittering line of bayonets, the Austrian III. and VI. corps. At about 8 A.M., the III. corps was on the line Breitenlee-Süssenbrünn, whilst the advance guard of the VI. had driven Boudet's outposts back between Stadlau and Aspern, and the main body was surging through the space between Hirschstetten and Stadlau.

Charles, posted on the heights of Wagram, had been witness of the French attack on Aderklaa and galloped to this critical spot. It was by his orders that Bellegarde, with the Reserve cavalry and the grenadiers supporting him, had again advanced to the recapture of the lost village. Before him he drove Carra St Cyr and the Saxons, and, after a desperate fight, finally remained master of the place; for Masséna could not support his leading division, on account

of the threatened attack of Liechtenstein on one flank, and
the fire of Kolowrat's batteries from north of Breitenlee on
the other. The French left wing was in imminent danger had
the Austrians followed up their victory, as the French themselves would have done. But that was not the Austrian way,
and they proceeded to draw up their line with Bellegarde
between Aderklaa and Wagram, whilst the grenadiers occupied a line from Aderklaa towards Breitenlee.

Masséna, still hoping to recover Aderklaa, sent Marulaz
and Lasalle against the two batteries which the Austrians had
in front of it. The light cavalry rode down the Austrian gunners and captured the batteries; but the threatening attitude
of Liechtenstein's cavalry compelled them to fall back again.
Then Molitor attempted to storm the place. The fighting in
the streets and houses raged with the fury of that of Aspern
and Essling seven weeks before. Finally, the French fell back
in confusion, leaving the Austrians in possession of the hotly
contested village.

As a temporary measure to support the French left,
Eugène turned Macdonald's corps and most of his guns westward, whilst the news of the serious danger was sent to Napoleon, who was farther east intently watching the progress of
Davout's attack on Markgrafneusiedl. He at once galloped
back to Masséna and was instrumental in stopping, by his
presence, the flight of his troops. It was 9 o'clock when the
Emperor first became aware of the danger which threatened
him on the left, in the advance of the Austrian III. and VI.
corps. There was not a moment to lose, for Kolowrat's right
was already in Breitenlee, whilst his left touched the
grenadiers. Klenau, too, with the VI. corps, had attacked
Boudet about Aspern, and his hussars by a happy charge on
Boudet's artillery, forming that general's right wing, had
captured the whole of it. Boudet himself, deprived of the
support of his guns, was driven into the bridge-head on the
Mühlau. Thus, between 9 and 10 A.M., two fresh Austrian
corps were advancing against the empty space between the
Stadlau arm and Neu-Wirtshuas. Klenau even had posts in
Essling. The Austrian right wing was advancing almost in
rear of the French centre and left.

It was well for Napoleon that he held his reserves massed

in the centre, whence he could move them to either wing, or
to fill a gap.

Once more, as at Eylau, the Emperor decided to use his
heavy cavalry to gain time. Bessières was ordered to charge,
with the cuirassier divisions of Nansouty and St Germain
(late St Sulpice), and the cavalry of the Guard commanded
by Walther. Bessières, charging at the head of these great
lines of cuirassiers and carbineers, made for the point of
union of Liechtenstein's grenadiers and the left of Kolowrat.

Whatever may be said of the inefficiency of Napoleon's
cavalry as purveyors of intelligence, no one has ever doubted
their bravery and efficiency on the battlefield, at least in
these days when the horses obtainable were still good. Again
and again the line of mail-clad warriors descended upon the
Austrians between Süssenbrünn and Aderklaa. In one
charge Bessières' horse was shot under him, and his men
rushed with redoubled fury to the rescue of a leader to
whom they were devoted. At one moment they had again
overwhelmed the Austrian batteries in front of Aderklaa,
which were only saved by their infantry. Heavily as the
cavalry lost, their charges were effectual in forcing back the
right of the grenadiers and the left of Kolowrat, whose advance they brought to a standstill.

Screened by them, Napoleon was busy completing the re-
arrangements necessitated by the new state of affairs. Obviously, the first thing to be done was to provide a force to
meet the movement of Kolowrat and Klenau against the
French left and rear. For this Masséna must be used, and his
corps must make a flank march of extreme difficulty across
the front of Kolowrat, under fire of his artillery. To Masséna
were attached the light cavalry of Lasalle and Marulaz and
the cuirassiers of St Germain. Next to him was Bernadotte,
and the movement of these two southwards would leave a
gap in the centre which must be filled. In the first line there
the Emperor ranged on an arc of a circle an immense battery
of 100 guns, made up of those of Macdonald's corps and of
the Guard. These were opposite the space between
Süssenbrünn and Breitenlee. Macdonald and the Guard infantry formed behind them, and Wrede was hurried up to
Raasdorf. Liechtenstein had just had orders to attack when

the deployment of this great line of artillery effectually
stopped his doing so. But Napoleon, though his attention
was now largely concentrated on the centre, did not neglect
his attack on the Russbach position. Davout was urged to
press on his attack on Markgrafneusiedl, whilst Oudinot was
told to hold the Austrians with artillery fire for the present.

The Austrian offensive had now nearly exhausted itself.
Klenau contented himself with re-occupying the works at
Aspern and Essling, his main body, very slightly in advance
of the line Aspern-Breitenlee, awaiting the development of
affairs in the centre. In the moment of victory the enterprise
of the Austrians failed. Klenau's inactivity gave time to
Masséna for his flank march.

We must now look to what was happening on the extreme
left of the Austrian line. It was about 10 A.M. when Davout
was ready to attack. The tremendous cross fire of artillery
which he had brought to bear on the Austrian guns at and
about Markgrafneusiedl had almost reduced them to silence.
To the east of the village, Montbrun, Grouchy, and Pully,
having driven Fröhlich from Ober-Siebenbrünn, were moving towards Sichdichfür. Arrighi was in the centre of the
right wing. On their left, the divisions of Morand and Friant
marched against the heights north of Markgrafneusiedl on
the left bank of the Russbach, whilst Gudin and Puthod advanced on the village from the right bank. To meet this
double attack, Rosenberg had thrown back his second line
and his cavalry "en potence" on his left. In vain he sent for
help from Charles and Wimpffen in this position, which he
felt to be doubly dangerous after the collapse of his artillery
before that of Davout. Davout himself led the frontal attack
across the Russbach. The fighting was very severe, for the
Austrians made a brave defence of Markgrafneusiedl, but by
11 A.M., the French had stormed the village and were pushing up against the square tower in its rear which the Austrians had fortified. The tower, threatened in rear by the
advance of Morand and Friant, was stormed and the Austrian counter-attack against it failed. The fighting at the
tower was desperate; on the Austrian side Vecsey and Nordmann met their death, and four other generals were

wounded. Davout's horse was killed under him, and Gudin, close beside him, was wounded four times. Whilst Davout, with Puthod and Gudin, was advancing northwards, Morand and Friant were capturing the heights facing east. Morand was at first repulsed, but then, supported by Friant, he reached the heights. Friant, too, only succeeded on his second attempt in mounting the curtain and driving the Austrian infantry out of their half completed entrenchments. As the Austrians formed a fresh line in rear, Arrighi charged them with his cuirassiers, but was repulsed with loss.

At this juncture, Charles arrived in person, bringing up, from Hohenzollern's corps (II.), a reinforcement of five batallions and two cavalry regiments (one of cuirassiers). The II. corps had, so far, only had to oppose Oudinot's artillery fire, and had had rather the better of the duel. Therefore, it was able to spare these reinforcements. With the cavalry thus collected, including that of Rosenberg, Charles sought to defeat the dragoons and light cavalry on Davout's right, and to threaten the right flank of his infantry. But the cavalry attack was mismanaged, and, instead of the whole force of over 40 squadrons attacking the French dragoons and light cavalry, only one regiment of dragoons and one of cuirassiers charged them. The first line drove back the French first line and captured 10 guns, but then the French second line charged, drove back the Austrians, and recaptured the guns.

It was noon when Davout had crushed in the Austrian left, and Napoleon saw that he was debouching from Markgraf-neusiedl. That was the signal for the decisive manœuvre by which he hoped to break the Austrian centre and secure victory.

As for the attack on his left by Klenau, he had done more than sufficient in sending Masséna to deal with it, and obviously his own success in the centre must cause it to collapse completely. Binder v. Krieglstein considers that, with the armies of Austerlitz and Jena, he would not even have sent Masséna. But his troops were not what he had in 1805 and 1806, and there was the fear that they might not stand as the news reached them of the enemy in rear, threatening their retreat to the island.

For the great effort in the centre Macdonald was selected, mainly, probably, because he happened to be in the right position.

It was noon when the Emperor saw that Davout had possession of the tower at Markgrafneusiedl. At once, an officer was despatched at his topmost speed to tell Masséna to attack "and that the battle was won, since the Archduke John had not yet appeared." Oudinot was ordered to storm the heights in front of him. Macdonald's column, which had been prepared behind the great battery, was of an extraordinary formation. In front, eight battalions, of the divisions of Broussier and Lamarque, were deployed one behind the other. Behind the right were the six remaining battalions of Broussier in column of battalions. Lamarque's seven remaining battalions were in similar formation behind the left. The rear of this great square was closed by Serras' nine battalions. The battalions were extremely weak, for the whole thirty only amounted to 8000 men.

The attack was covered on the right by Walther with the cavalry of the Guard, on the left by Nansouty's cuirassiers and carbineers. It was directed, as had been that of the cavalry, on the point of junction of Kolowrat (III. corps) and the grenadiers. In front of this tremendous column the Austrian first line could but yield; yet it was not routed, and the regiments fell back on either side of Macdonald's column, into both flanks of which they poured a terrible fire, whilst the second line treated its front in like manner. Macdonald could not get forward, even with the help of attacks by his cavalry. He complained bitterly of the cavalry not doing all they might have done. He was in very evil plight, and the numbers of his infantry column were presently reduced to some 1500 men.

Meanwhile, however, Davout had been making rapid progress, once he had debouched from Markgrafneusiedl and begun to roll up the Austrian left on the centre. As their extreme left fell back before Davout's cavalry threatening their rear, it became necessary for those above the Russbach, between Markgrafneusiedl and Parbasdorf, also to retreat on Bockflüss. That in turn compelled Hardegg, who had so far successfully held Parbasdorf against Oudinot's attacks, to evacuate the village and seek safety, partly towards the Helmahof, partly towards the IV. corps at Bockflüss.

Masséna, too, had made rapid progress against Klenau, who, by 2 P.M., had been forced to evacuate even Aspern, and to commence his retreat along the Danube.

Where was John all this time? We know that Napoleon was satisfied that he was not near enough to be a serious danger. From Marchegg he wrote, at 10.30 A.M., to Charles that he had arrived there with part of his corps, but was still awaiting its rear, and especially the artillery which was behind. He could not hope to recommence his march before 1 P.M., twelve hours after he had left Pressburg. He hoped at the latest to reach Leopoldsdorf by 5 P.M. That, however, was much too late for him to be of any use to Charles.

Soon after 2 P.M., Napoleon had poured up reinforcements to the assistance of Macdonald's shattered column. Pacthod's division of the Army of Italy was ordered to attack Wagram on Macdonald's right, whilst Durutte on the left was to storm Breitenlee. To the direct support of Macdonald Wrede was sent, and how seriously Napoleon thought of the situation is shown by his words to the Bavarian general: "You see the unfortunate position of Macdonald. March! save the corps, and attack the enemy; in fine do as seems to you best."

Even the Young Guard was ordered to Macdonald's assistance, and, as he sent them off, Napoleon said to Reille: "Do not risk anything; for I have nothing as a last reserve but the two regiments of the Old Guard." Marmont was marched into the gap on Oudinot's left.

But the end had almost come; for Charles recognised that there was now no hope of John's arrival in time. He had seen, too, the successful advance of Davout against his left, of Masséna against his right. To save himself from decisive defeat, he must retreat at once, and his orders for that were, Bellegarde with the I. corps, to fall back towards Gerasdorf, whilst Liechtenstein remained with the cavalry on the plain in front of that village covering him. Kolowrat moved back towards the heights of Stammersdorf; the grenadiers on Hagenbrünn; Klenau between Gerasdorf and Leopoldau.

Charles himself would go to Stammersdorf. The IV. corps was ordered to take post by evening to the west of Pyrawarth.[1]

Just as the retreat was beginning, Napoleon's fresh advance started. Pacthod, moving against the I. corps, had a severe struggle, in which he was assisted by Tharreau, the left division of Oudinot. The other divisions only came into contact with the enemy as he retreated through Sässenbrünn and Breitenlee. At Gerasdorf, where the I. corps was to make a stand, there was more severe fighting. The French cavalry were driven off momentarily, and then the retreat was continued, before the infantry, to the Stammersdorf heights.

Thither also had retreated Klenau, hotly pursued by Masséna's cavalry under the intrepid leadership of that "beau sabreur" Lasalle. As he led one of the many cavalry charges, Lasalle fell dead with an Austrian bullet in the middle of his forehead. His was the last of the many grievous losses which Napoleon suffered amongst his favourite leaders in the two great battles before Vienna.

On the French right progress had been easy since the capture of Markgrafneusiedl and its tower. As Davout advanced across the open plateau on the left bank of the Russbach, Oudinot joined his left. Oudinot's left division (Tharreau) carried Wagram, and, as already mentioned, brought aid to Pacthod. The other two divisions, north of Wagram towards Helmahof, drove the Austrians before them across the upper Russbach, this time from the left to the right bank.

On Davout's right, Montbrun and Grouchy could not penetrate beyond the edge of the wooded heights about Auersthal and Bockflüss. Friant attacked and captured Bockflüss about 6 P.M.

By 8 P.M. the battle was over along the whole line. The French army at that hour stood thus:—

From the Danube near Jedlersdorf through Leopoldau stretched Masséna's corps, his two divisions of light cavalry, the Saxons, Wrede's Bavarians, and Eugène's army. Nansouty and the Guard cavalry were about Gerasdorf. Marmont and the divisions of Gudin and Puthod were at

---

[1] Six or seven miles north of Bockflüss near the source of the Russbach.

Wagram, with Oudinot between them and the Wendling-
erhof. Davout had Morand's and Friant's divisions, and the
cavalry of Grouchy, Pully, and Montbrun to the south-east of
Bockflüss and Auersthal. What remained of Dupas' division
was at Raasdorf, collecting fugitives and stragglers. Napoleon, as usual, encamped in the midst of the Guard infantry.

The day had been oppressively hot, and many men had
been struck down by sunstroke, for the plain was waterless in
most parts. All were exhausted, and, in addition to this,
Napoleon still feared the arrival of John, whose force he
erroneously estimated at 30,000 men. Therefore, no attempt
was made to pursue that night. Another reason against pursuit was the defensive strength of the Austrian positions on
the heights of the Bisamberg, and of those about Bockflüss.

As for John, he had started from Marchegg, according to
promise, at 1 P.M. and endeavoured with his cavalry to get
into touch with Rosenberg. He found, however, that that
general had retreated, and, finally when he reached Ober-
Siebenbrunn about 5 P.M., he received a message from
Rosenberg that all was over and he was too late. He was
isolated on the plain, his men had marched 26 miles since 1
A.M., and he could do no good, either by moving towards the
Lobau or by attacking the French rear, seeing that he had
but 13,000 men. Therefore, he resolved to let his men rest
till dark and then to return to Marchegg, which he reached
at 7 A.M. on the 7th. So bad was the state of the French army
that the appearance of some of John's cavalry created a
panic, and thousands of men fled towards the Lobau.[1]

At nightfall the rest of the Austrian army stood thus: V.
corps at Strebersdorf; VI. north of Stammersdorf; III. corps
on the right of VI., with the I. behind it; Cavalry Reserve
between Seiring and Hagenbrünn; Grenadiers at
Hagenbrünn; Nostitz's cavalry division between Enzersfeld
and Königsbrünn; main body and II. corps at Enzersfeld;
IV. corps, and 11 battalions of II., on the heights across the
Brünn road, with Radetzky and 4 battalions south of them.

Charles, having no intention of fighting a third day's battle, proposed to start during the night on his retreat into

[1] It was these men whom Dupas had to rally and collect.

Bohemia again. At 8 P.M., orders were issued for retreat at 10, to the heights north of Korneuburg, covered by Klenau, standing till midnight on the line Am Spitz—Stammersdorf—Erdesbrünn.

The losses in this great battle of two days are, as usual, difficult to estimate accurately. The Austrian returns are confusing, as they relate to the period 29th June to 11th July. They are, however, much more reliable than the French, which Napoleon always intentionally reduced.

Binder v. Krieglstein has devoted a great deal of care to working out the losses as nearly as possible. Without following his details, we may accept the following table of Austrian losses as a fair approximation:—

	LOSSES OF ALL SORTS.	PERCENTAGE OF STRENGTH.
Advance guard................	7,000–7,500	50
IV. corps	5,600–6,000	30
II. corps.....................	9,500	30
I. corps......................	7,000	30
Grenadiers	1,769	16
Cavalry Reserve	1,877	21
III. corps....................	1,900	11
VI. corps	2,500	15
	37,146	26

The Austrian account gives 31,335 killed, wounded, and prisoners, besides several thousand missing, who rejoined later. This does not differ widely, when these missing are included, from the Prussian writer's estimate. Four generals (Wukassowich, Nordmann, D'Aspre and Vecsey) were killed and 13 wounded, including the Archduke Charles himself. The French accounts only allow of a guess at their losses.

Binder v. Krieglstein, after careful consideration of all available sources of information, including Martinien's nominal lists of officers killed and wounded, estimates the loss in killed and wounded alone at 27,500, or about 15 per cent. on a total of 180,000, inclusive of artillery and departmental troops.

The Austrians lost, in killed and wounded, about 24,000

officers and men, 16 per cent. on a total of 150,000. Of French and allied generals no less than 40 were killed or wounded, amongst whom the death of Lasalle was the most notable loss.

Perhaps the most significant fact in the losses is the proportion of officers to men in the killed and wounded. The Austrians lost, according to their own account, 730 officers, whilst we know, from Martinien, the French loss was 1822. In the former case one officer killed or wounded to every 32 men, in the latter one to every 14. The French had more officers proportionately, but these figures still point to the probability that the French officers had to sacrifice themselves more freely on account of the quality of their troops.

The total loss on both sides in the two days' battle, including prisoners and missing, will probably not be overestimated at between 65,000 and 70,000, out of a total of about 320,000 engaged.

The Austrians carried off 7000 prisoners, and, curiously enough, they had more trophies to show than the conquerors; for they had 12 eagles or standards and 21 guns, whilst the French had only 10 or 11 of the former and 20 guns.

"The Battle of Dresden," from *Napoleon's Last Campaign in Germany, 1813*

The Campaign of 1813 was a complex, bloody affair in which Napoleon ultimately confronted virtually all of Europe. In a superb display of his strategic abilities, he managed to stave off defeat by repeated use of the central position. But his enemies were far too strong for him, his army no longer composed of battle-hardened veterans and his commanders growing tired after the long years of war. But he remained a dangerous foe. For if he could not win the campaign, he was certainly capable of inflicting repeated defeats upon his enemies. The campaign fell naturally into two phases. From February through early June, Napoleon managed to keep his Russian, Prussian, and Swedish enemies at arm's length, inflicting several serious, but by no means fatal defeats upon them. Then, on June 4, an armistice was concluded during which both sides built up their forces. But Napoleon's enemies gained more from this respite than he did: when the Armistice expired on August 16 Napoleon found Austria ranged against him as well. The renewed campaign opened at Dresden, in Saxony, not far from the Austrian frontier, from whence an Allied Army of some 200,000 men debouched, intent upon seizing the important city from its French garrison before Napoleon could march to its support. The result was the Battle of Dresden, August 26–27, 1813, which was a fine example of Napoleon's abilities in adversity, as well as one of the last instances of the French use of ordre mixte on a large scale.

THE 26TH AUGUST

First Period, up to noon.—The first of the allies to attack were the Prussians advancing from the south against the nearest part of the Grosser Garten. The French had evacuated Strehlen at 4 A.M., an hour before Ziethen, supported by Pirch, moved from it against the Grosser Garten. The Prussians made but slow progress, and it was only as Roth, with the Russian advanced guard, came to their assistance, by attacking the north-eastern corner of the garden, that they were able to push slowly forward.

Roth appears to have attacked between 7 and 8 A.M., and, by the latter hour, when they had been already fighting for three hours, the Prussians had only mastered the outer half of the garden as far as the palace in its centre. By 9 A.M. they had got about half-way from the palace to the city end of the garden. Here they were ordered to break off the fight for the time. On the right of the Prussians the Russians began their advance between the Grosser Garten and the Elbe between 7 and 8 A.M. As they advanced from the Blasewitz wood they suffered severely from the artillery fire of the Marcolini fort on the right bank of the Elbe. They could make little progress till the Prussians, aided by Roth, got forward in the garden, and the Russians coming from Striesen planted a strong battery on a slight elevation, the Windmill height. Covered by this, they succeeded in capturing the building known as Engelhardt's, near the Elbe. An attempt to advance on the Hopfgarten was repulsed. No further progress was made before the general lull in the battle, which began about noon. On the Prussian left between Zschertnitz and Räcknitz operations up to noon were confined to an artillery duel with the opposite French lunettes.

The Austrian attack towards Plauen began about 6 A.M. By 9 they had driven the French back past the Feldschlösschen, which was stormed, and on to redoubts Nos. IV. and V. From the Feldschlösschen the French artillery fire from redoubt IV. failed to drive the Austrians, as, the walls of the building being of lath and plaster, the French shells passed straight through them without setting fire to the building. A serious mistake had been made by the French engineers in not destroying this building before the battle. On the other hand, Austrian advances against redoubts IV. and V. were driven off by the fire of those forts, supported by the guns of one of the bastions of the old enceinte.

Thus when the fighting died away about noon the allies had attained the following positions. The Russians on the right stretched from Engelhardt's to the Grosser Garten, of which about three-fourths of the length was in possession of their own left and the Prussians. In the centre no progress had been made. On the left, up to the Weisseritz, the Austrians were close in front of the French redoubts IV. and V. Beyond the Weisseritz the Austrians had driven the French out of Lobtau. On the extreme left, Meszko's division had met with little opposition, and had succeeded in getting as far forward as Schusterhaüser on the Elbe.

In Dresden, meanwhile, the early attacks spread the greatest alarm among the inhabitants, who were aware that the allied troops were especially bitter against them, on account of alleged ill-treatment of Russian and Prussian prisoners. Confidence was to a great extent restored by the appearance of Napoleon between 9 and 10 A.M. Men began to say, "There is Napoleon. Things will soon be very different." There was no longer any talk of abandoning homes and escaping across the river. The Emperor was still reputed invincible in Germany.

Leaving Stolpen in his carriage at 5 A.M. he had mounted his horse as soon as he came in sight of Dresden from the hills above. At the Marcolini (Meissenberg) fort he stopped to watch the Russian advance, and to direct more artillery on them. Then he galloped into Dresden, paid a visit of a few

moments to the king, and hurried off to inspect the defences. St Cyr found him, between 11 and 12, on the French
left, on foot in the midst of the horse artillery, which at the
moment was not firing, as the pause in the battle had commenced. Then the Emperor rode along the defences towards
the right. The garrison was terribly weak. Behind the garden
walls in many places there was only one man to every ten
paces. At the Dippoldiswalde road he went farther forward
to observe the enemy. Arrived at redoubt IV., he was annoyed to find the Feldschlösschen in the enemy's possession
and ordered St Cyr to retake it. The battalion sent for the
purpose succeeded for a moment, but was driven out again.
Having passed along the whole of his line, Napoleon returned to the Schloss Platz, where he took his position at the
head of the stone bridge, watching the arrival of his troops
and directing them to their posts in the line. Teste, with eight
battalions, arrived first, and was sent to Friederichstadt,
where Murat was put in command of this infantry, of the 1st
cavalry corps, when it arrived at 2 P.M., and of Pajol's cavalry
of St Cyr's corps.

Next came Decouz's and Roguet's Young Guard divisions
under Mortier. These were sent to the suburbs on the left.
Two more divisions of Young Guard, under Ney, went to the
Dippoldiswalde and Falken "schlags," left and right of redoubt IV. The Old Guard remained in the city in reserve,
sending only one regiment to each of the suburbs of Pirna
(on the left), Falken (centre), and Freiberg (on the right).
The Guard had marched 90 miles in the last seventy-two
hours, and that not on good roads but alongside of them, for
Napoleon kept the roads for his guns and wagons, whilst the
infantry and cavalry marched on a broad front across country. Latour-Maubourg's 78 squadrons went to behind
Friederichstadt, where the public slaughter-house now
stands, and there also were Pajol's 46 squadrons—23,000
cavalry in all. The rest of Teste's division, when it arrived,
followed the first 8 battalions to Friederichstadt. It was between 3 and 5 P.M. when Roguet's 14 battalions and Barrois'
10 of the Young Guard arrived. These went to the suburbs
on the right bank of the Weisseritz. The general reserve of
Old Guard, under Friant and Curial, counted 10 battalions

and 30 guns in the Altstadt, besides the 3 regiments sent as special reserves to the right, centre, and left. These were all the troops Napoleon could expect for this day's battle. We have somewhat anticipated in noting their arrival.

On the side of the allies, the Tsar and the King of Prussia stood, about 11 A.M., on the heights of Räcknitz in company with Jomini,[1] Moreau, and their other advisers and staff. They could clearly see the stream of Napoleon's soldiers hurrying to Dresden by the Bautzen road beyond the Elbe. Yet, the glow of bivouac fires towards Stolpen in the previous night should have warned the allied leaders that a great army was approaching. Jomini, clearly realising that the capture of Dresden was now hopeless, counselled retreat to Dippoldiswalde, and the Tsar agreed with him. But the King of Prussia thought otherwise. Hours of discussion followed, ending in the decision to countermand the general attack fixed for 4 P.M. Whether Schwarzenberg deliberately neglected to give the counter-order, or whether there was a misunderstanding, it is certain that the three guns, the prearranged signal for attack, were fired and the battle recommenced.

Second Period, from 4 to 6 P.M.—It was towards 4 P.M. when Napoleon was informed that the allies appeared to be preparing for a general attack. Galloper after galloper was dispatched to hurry the march of the approaching French reinforcements.

The Russians on the allied right were still much annoyed by the French artillery beyond the Elbe, and, farther to their left, hampered in their movements by the Landgraben. French troops, too, had been pushed out along the Elbe, sheltered by an embankment constructed to restrain floods, and by several villas and farms. Nevertheless, the Russian right advanced for some distance victoriously from En-

---

[1] Jomini had been Ney's chief of staff at Bautzen. He went over to the allies just before the end of the armistice. His defence of his conduct attributes it largely to Napoleon's refusal to let him leave his service in 1810, and to his disapproval of Napoleon's ambition. But it is difficult to avoid the suspicion that, had Ney's recommendation of him for appointment to a division after Bautzen been accepted, he would not have gone over. His case is different from Moreau's, inasmuch as he was a Swiss, not a Frenchman.

gelhardt's, capturing Anton's and Lämmchen. In the centre
they got little beyond the windmill height. On the left, between the Landgraben and the Grosser Garten, they pushed
close up to redoubt II., but all their efforts to storm it were
repulsed.

The Prussians in the Grosser Garten also arrived in front
of redoubt II., which they attempted to storm along with the
Russians on their right. They, too, were driven off here, as
well as from the adjoining Prince Anton's garden, which was
protected by a wall with a ditch in front of it.

Kleist, with his Prussians, advanced from the Rothe Haus
against the Bürgerwiese and the Hospital garden.[1]. In the
attack on the latter they were joined by the right of the Austrians. Kleist had arrived within ten yards of the Dohna suburb when the Austrians on his left gave way before the
terrible fire. At this juncture, too, Serurrier, with St Cyr's
44th division, broke out from the Bürgerwiese, compelling
Kleist to retire.

The signal guns for the general attack were followed immediately by the advance of numerous Austrian columns in
the space between Kleist's left and the right bank of the
Weisseritz. As the Austrian right advanced against the Hospital garden and redoubt III., they found their movement
facilitated by the ditches and channels which then scored the
slopes below Tschertnitz and Räcknitz.

The fate of the extreme right in this period has been
noticed above in connexion with Kleist's attack. Two columns
farther to the left were directed on redoubt III. Notwithstanding the support of their own and of Russian guns
pushed forward with them, the Austrians were almost
stopped by the terrible fire of the redoubt and the French
batteries on either side of it. The two leading Austrian lines
had already given way, when suddenly the work was silent.
The supply of ammunition had given out. Seizing their opportunity, the Austrians dashed forward once more, mounting the parapet of the redoubt and engaging in a desperate

---

[1] On the outer edge of the Dohna Schlag to the east of redoubt III. The
Bürgerwiese is the open space cutting into the Schlag. Prince Anton's
garden is directly behind the Grosser Garten.

hand-to-hand conflict with its defenders, who were nearly all killed or wounded before the remains at last retreated and sought shelter in the gardens behind.

The next Austrians on the left nearly got possession of the gardens; a few, indeed, penetrated into them, but the latter were turned by French reserves. In one of these attacks on the gardens several hundred Austrians, hemmed in against the walls by the French reserves, were compelled to surrender. So desperate was the fighting in this part that it is said that in redoubt III. alone 180 French and 344 Austrian dead were found in the evening, after its recapture.

The attack on redoubts IV. and V. was less successful. In redoubt IV. the allies' artillery fire wrought such havoc that 96 of its small garrison were *hors de combat,* and the fort was deserted for the moment. As the Austrian infantry rushed forward from the Feldschlösschen to seize it, French reserves issued from the "schlags" in rear and drove the enemy back to their starting-point. Two attacks, from Kohler's Garden and the "Meisterei," on redoubt V. likewise failed before the steady fire of the French. A third attack from the Tharandt road met with the same fate. Beyond the Weisseritz, on the signal for the general advance, Bianchi pushed on towards Friedrichstadt from the positions gained before noon. He was met by a heavy artillery fire in front from the Freiberg road, and by a flanking fire from redoubt V.

On the extreme left, Meszko's men were in front of Cotta and Schusterhaüser, and a small party even got along below the Elbe bank to nearly opposite Uebigau. Thence, however, they had to fall back hurriedly, to avoid being cut off by French reserves and cavalry.

Napoleon, in Dresden, had been anxiously marking the course of the battle during this period, waiting for all the troops he could collect before making his counter-attack. By 5 P.M. he had some 70,000 men in the Altstadt and in the line of defence. The allies had about 150,000 on the field, but they had acted throughout with want of decision, and had kept nearly two-thirds of this great army in reserve.

Alarm had once more taken hold of the unfortunate citizens as they saw great masses of the allies pouring down from the heights, and the shells began to burst in all directions in the suburbs. Many houses were in flames. There was a general rush for safety in the cellars.

The streets were full of French troops, especially the open spaces in the suburbs where reserves were massed, ready to move at a moment's notice to any gravely threatened point. Amongst these troops the bursting shells produced only a feeling of exhilaration and eagerness. They were to fight under the immediate command of a leader whom they still believed to be invincible.

Aster tells a curious story of a battery which received orders to be ready to move into the fighting line. The men were dust-stained and untidy after their long march. The moment they heard of the order, each man began to get out of his haversack his parade uniform, which it was thought suitable to don on such an occasion. Comical scenes ensued, as men, in the act of changing their trousers, had to skip off as they might to avoid a shell about to burst. All were laughing and cheery, as if about to go to some fête. Such was the spirit of Napoleon's soldiers.

Third Period, from 6 P.M. till dark—The tide of the allied advance had reached its height towards 6 P.M. Their front line is shown on the plan, and it was one which made matters look very black to the uninitiated. Not so to Napoleon, who, between 5 and 6 P.M., had issued orders for the counter-attack which commenced at the latter hour. Ney, who had been ordered to take command in the Falken and Blinde "schlags" behind redoubt IV., had no fresh charger up. The Emperor, seeing his difficulty, turned to Caulaincourt saying he could lend Ney his horse. The Duke of Vicenza hesitated for a moment. "Descendez," was Napoleon's brief, stern order, and Caulaincourt instantly dismounted and changed chargers with Ney.

As soon as the orders for the general advance were issued, the Emperor left the Schloss Platz to watch their execution. First he went to the bridge of boats above the stone bridge, thence he was guided by Count Nostitz to the Rammischer "schlag," near the Elbe on the French left. Hence he passed through the Pirna and See "schlags," so close to the foremost line of the enemy that one of his orderly officers and several of his suite were wounded. It was 8 P.M. before, being finally satisfied that everything was going as he wished, he returned to the king's palace.

Meanwhile, on Napoleon's extreme left, the 3rd and 4th divisions of the Young Guard under Mortier began to issue, about 6 P.M., from the Ziegel "schlag" close to the Elbe. At that moment an ammunition wagon blew up, and the terrified horses dashed wildly amongst the troops. For a moment they were delayed, then Roguet advanced close to the Elbe, whilst Decouz attacked the Russians at Engelhardt's, driving them back on the Windmill height, which, after a desperate hand-to-hand struggle, was taken at 7 P.M. By 8 P.M. the French on this wing had driven the Russians back into the Blasewitz wood and Striesen.

Wittgenstein was now so hard pressed that he personally rode over to Barclay to ask for reinforcements. Klüx's Prussian brigade was sent up to behind Striesen, which village the Russians evacuated only at midnight.

Simultaneously with this advance, three more columns of Mortier's troops issued from behind redoubt II., and from Prince Anton's garden, driving back Wittgenstein's left and the Prussians, whose attack had just failed. By 7 P.M. the French had driven the allies through half the length of the Grosser Garten to the palace. Here the fight swayed backwards and forwards till, at 8 P.M., the Prussians, still holding the palace, were separated from their antagonists only by the width of the central cross avenue. At that hour the turmoil of the struggle gave place to a still more ghastly silence, broken only by the groans of the wounded.

About redoubt III. the counter-attack began very soon after the Austrians were in possession of it. It was facilitated by the threat to the Austrian flank, due to Ney's advance by redoubt IV., to be described presently. The attack on the captured redoubt was commenced by a column of the Young Guard from the west of the Hospital garden. The first attempt failed, though about 50 men got in through a gate in the gorge of the work which, being closed behind them, left the little party isolated in the midst of about 500 Austrians. Refusing the enemy's calls to surrender, the gallant band held firm against tenfold numbers. As no officer was with them the drum-major took command, brandishing his baton, with which he promptly felled the Austrian leader. Help was at hand, and this little band of heroes held their ground till what remained of them was rescued by a fresh irruption, through the palisading, of their comrades, now reinforced by two regiments led by Berthezène. The redoubt was now recaptured, and some 400 Austrian prisoners were taken in it.

Ney, from the Falken and Blinde "schlags," had begun to advance about the time the Austrians took redoubt III. He passed on both sides of redoubt IV., threatening by his movement the flanks of the Austrians in front of redoubts III. and V. His right column marched from the paper-mill on Kohler's garden, from which it drove the Austrians. The left column, charging along the upper Plauen road, failed in its first attempt to retake the Feldschlösschen. The second succeeded in taking it at the point of the bayonet. After this the Austrians in this quarter fell back fighting towards Plauen till darkness stopped the combat. In the low ground on the right bank of the Weisseritz the enemy, now reinforced by Chasteler's grenadiers, still held on, though suffering heavily.

During Ney's attack, Dumoustier issued from the Freiberg "schlag," drove the enemy in front of him across the Weisseritz, and recaptured the Chaussée Haus near the crossing of the Freiberg road. The Austrians retired to Riesentzien's garden, which they still held, destroying the wooden bridge near it.

Beyond the Weisseritz, Teste's infantry, with part of Dumoustier's, issued from the Lobtau "schlag" against Altona and the neighbouring buildings, but were eventually driven from all but a small inn at Klein Hamburg, which they evacuated at midnight. In this combat even Pajol's cavalry took part. As darkness fell, the Austrians on the Tharandt road withdrew behind Lobtau and bivouacked south-west of it. The village was occupied by neither party during the night, but the Austrians still held Cotta, Dölzschen, Nauslitz, Rossthal, Wolfnitz, and Nieder- and Ober-Gorbitz.

As a result of the day's fighting, the line of French outposts, marked on the plan, shows that they had regained practically all that they had lost earlier in the day.

Between 9 and 10 P.M. there were brought to Napoleon at the Royal Palace 700 Austrian prisoners, most of whom had been captured in or near redoubt III. After inspecting them by torchlight, the Emperor distributed crosses to the battalion of Young Guard escorting them.

The day had been fine, but towards midnight rain began to descend in torrents, which continued for the rest of the night, and during the whole of the next day.

If terror still reigned amongst the citizens, the French troops were jubilant over the great success which they had undoubtedly gained against vastly superior numbers. Moreover, their spirits were further raised by the knowledge of the approach of strong reinforcements, and by the fact that they were amply supplied with food and drink in the midst of the magazines and resources of Dresden.

During the night there was a constant stream of reinforcements pouring into the Altstadt over the three bridges across the Elbe.

In the evening of the 26th August Napoleon was inclined to believe that the allies would retreat in the night, but he issued orders for his troops for the next day, in the event of a fresh battle, should the enemy decide to maintain his position. During the night there arrived

II. corps (Victor), 36 battalions, 2 squadrons, 68 guns.

VI. corps (Marmont), 40 battalions, 8 squadrons, 78 guns.

Guard cavalry (Lefebvre-Desnoettes), 10 squadrons, 6 guns.

These raised the total available on the 27th to 180 battalions, 137 squadrons, 486 guns. At most, after allowing for losses on the 26th, these could not amount to more than from 120,000 to 125,000 men. The allies, on the other hand, had 158,000 men (less the losses of the 26th) actually on the field, and expected the arrival of 21,000 more with Klenau early next morning.

Nevertheless, the feeling in their camp was one of general despondency. They had gained little or no ground as the result of the day's fighting. This was attributable mainly to Schwarzenberg's indecision, and the confusion of his orders. It was almost impossible to say whether he aimed at a general attack, or merely at a reconnaissance in force. He had missed the great opportunity for storming Dresden before Napoleon's arrival with reinforcements. There had been no unity of command, no co-operation of the various columns. Amongst the troops all confidence had disappeared; they were filled with the dread of Napoleon's presence. Moreover, they were very short of food and drink, owing to the wild confusion prevailing amongst the supply columns on the miserable roads between Dresden and the Erzgebirge. The best road, that by Peterswalde, was already threatened by Vandamme. That general, crossing by the Königstein bridges, had, by 5 P.M., got across 34 battalions and Corbineau's cavalry, but no artillery. With these he had attacked the inferior observing force under Prince Eugene of Würtemberg. Though Eugene's men held out bravely till dark, they were obliged by their weakness to evacuate during the night the whole Pirna plateau, and the town itself. Eugene's appeals to headquarters for reinforcements had resulted in nothing but his supersession in the command by Osterman Tolstoi, who was ill and unfit for the task.

Eugene, seeking above all things to protect the rear of the army at Dresden, had abandoned the Peterswalde road and fallen back to a position north and south of Zehista, facing the Elbe. This was known both to the allies and to Napoleon.

At the council of war at allied headquarters there were again many differences of opinion and lengthy discussions, which ended in a decision to hold on next day to the heights before Dresden.

THE BATTLE OF THE 27TH AUGUST

When day broke on the 27th, the rain was still descending in torrents, and it was almost dark; a depressing outlook for all, especially for the allies, conscious as they were of failure on the previous day. Moreover, their commanders felt themselves handicapped by being able to see through the mist but a small area of a country which they knew indifferently, whilst Napoleon knew it thoroughly.

At 6 A.M. Mortier, on the French left, began his advance with Roguet on the left and Decouz on the right. The Guard cavalry followed the former.

By 7 A.M. Roguet had taken Blasewitz without serious fighting, and was proceeding to clear the Blasewitz wood. South of the wood Decouz was supported by Ney's two divisions, advancing on his right along the north edge of the Grosser Garten, from which the Prussians had retired at daybreak. The Russians, driven from Grüna, retired on Seidnitz, and, as Roguet with the French left swung round from Blasewitz, the whole of the Russian advanced guard (Roth) fell back to a position extending north-eastwards from Seidnitz to the Elbe.

The French were now pivoting on their right at Seidnitz, their left moving on Tolkewitz, threatening to surround Roth's right. Wittgenstein now ordered Roth, who was making a stubborn resistance, to retire on Reick and Prohlis, so as to join the right of the allied main position at Torna. He still held firmly to Seidnitz, where his left repulsed several French attacks.

As soon as the Russians had evacuated Tolkewitz, the French cavalry passed through it towards Laubegast, and drew up south of it in two lines, facing the Pirna road.

Meanwhile the French had at last taken Seidnitz, whence Roguet set out to attack Gross- and Klein-Dobritz. The cavalry, at the same time, advanced towards Leuben. Nansouty, by passing Leuben and wheeling to his right, threatened the retreat of the Russians in Dobritz, and determined them, after repulsing several of Roguet's attacks, to retreat to Reick and south-east of it. This movement Nansouty made no attempt to harass with his cavalry, as apparently he might have done, seeing that the infantry were unable to fire their muskets in the wet. On the other hand, the allies had 62 squadrons on their right, which might have annihilated Nansouty's 28. Possibly the difficulty of seeing any distance in the blinding rain may account partially for the inactivity of the cavalry on both sides.

Whilst Mortier was thus getting forward on the left, Ney had reached Grüna. St Cyr, on his right, had taken Strehlen, between 8 and 9 A.M., without much difficulty, since it was only defended by one Prussian battalion, which presently retired to Leubnitz, where the Prussians still held the right bank of the Kaitzbach. St Cyr had not yet moved the main

body of his corps beyond a position between the Grosser
Garten and Strehlen, but he had posted a powerful battery
on the rising ground just east of the latter place, with which
he was firing heavily on Tschertnitz and Leubnitz.

Such was the position at 11 A.M., when Napoleon reached
Leubnitz. The Emperor had betaken himself, at 6 A.M., to a
post just behind redoubt IV., where a great bonfire was
lighted for him, and a tent pitched. Here he remained till 10,
waiting for news of Murat's attack with his right beyond the
Weisseritz. At that hour he received a report which satisfied
him that all was going well in that direction, and that he
might now go to look after his left. Riding through the Pirna
suburb and the Grosser Garten, he reached Seidnitz about
11 A.M., and at once ordered an attack on Reick. The village
was strongly protected on the north and east by the Landgraben, here about 8 feet deep, flowing in a channel 6 to 8 feet
wide at the top. The channel ran along an embankment 10 to
12 feet high, and 18 to 20 feet thick. The French attack was
made on both sides of the angle where the watercourse turns
from north-east to north-west. Meeting the Russians in front
on the embankment, and charged in left flank by Russian
and Prussian cavalry, the French were driven off with heavy
loss. The attack was renewed with reinforcements, but the
defenders would not yield till a French shell fired the north
part of the village and reduced them to the southern part. In
the smoke the Russians failed to see that the French had
almost surrounded them, and when they attempted to retreat on Prohlis, they found themselves cut off. Then they
sold their lives as dearly as they could in a fierce hand-to-
hand struggle in the houses. It was not till noon that the
French were finally in possession of Reick, where the horror
of the scene was enhanced by the burning of many in the
raging fire.

The remains of Roth's force fell back on Torna. Beyond
Reick the French advanced but a short way after noon,
though they continued to bombard and set on fire the villages in front of it. After witnessing the storming of Reick,
Napoleon betook himself to St Cyr's corps. This he now
found with its right in Strehlen, and left in contact with Ney's
right at Grüna.

Presently the relief of the Prussians in Leubnitz by the

Russians induced a belief that they were retreating, and an attack was at once made on the village from Strehlen. The French got into the nearer part of it, but, swept with grape by two guns at the church, and then charged with the bayonet by two Prussian battalions, they were driven out again. A second attack failed before it reached Leubnitz.

It was at this juncture that Napoleon arrived on the scene. He was furious at the failure of the attacks, and ordered a third, to support which he had added horse artillery guns to the battery east of Strehlen. This attack was nipped in the bud by a storm of artillery fire directed on the French as they issued from Strehlen. Skirmishing continued along the Kaitzbach till evening, when the French surprised, and got into the north-east corner of Leubnitz, whence they were promptly ejected again.

It was 1 o'clock when Napoleon, disgusted with his failure at Leubnitz, started on his return journey to redoubt IV. On the way he ordered a horse artillery battery forward to fire on the enemy's battery near Räcknitz. After a few rounds it stopped firing, and, on his inquiring the reason, he was informed that the object battery had withdrawn. He then ordered his own battery to fire on a group of horsemen a little to the left of Räcknitz. The first shot fired had momentous results; for the ball hit Moreau as he was riding just in front of the Tsar. It tore through his right leg above the knee, passed through his horse, and shattered the left leg also.[1]

Before this, the Tsar, seeing things going badly on the right, had, on the advice of Jomini and Moreau, directed Barclay and Wittgenstein to attack Mortier's front with all available reserves, whilst Kleist and Miloradowich attacked his right towards Strehlen and Grüna. The plan was good; but Barclay objected that, if it failed, he would lose all his artillery, as, in the muddy state of the country, he could not get his guns up the hill again. This remonstrance arrived just

[1] Moreau behaved heroically, calmly smoking a cigar, whilst both his legs were amputated by the Tsar's surgeon, Wylie, at a farm a short way in rear. "I am done for," he said, as Alexander spoke to him, "but how good it is to die for the good cause, under the eyes of so great a monarch." He was carried, suffering great agony, to Laun, in Bohemia, where he died a week later. His body was embalmed and taken to St Petersburg, where it was buried with great pomp

as Moreau was wounded, and in the confusion no reply was sent. Barclay, therefore, did nothing; and the counter attack never came off, though Danilewski and Jomini say Kleist and Miloradowich had actually changed front to the right ready for it. Perhaps, too, the ardour of headquarters for this move had cooled in consequence of the news just received, that Vandamme, at Pirna, had driven Eugene of Würtemberg off the Peterswalde road. The news, perhaps, did not reach Napoleon till later, as the Saxon general, Gersdorf, who had received it, had been sent to inform the King of Saxony of the impending victory of the French.

Marmont's troops, all along the line from redoubt III. to the Weisseritz, had been heavily fired on since early morning by a long line of Austrian guns, extending almost continuously along the heights from Räcknitz to above Plauen. On his right the French had driven the Austrians from all the gardens and houses right up to Plauen. Beyond this, nothing happened on Marmont's front.

We must now describe the course of events beyond the Weisseritz. The Austrian main position on this side rested its right on the gorge of the Weisseritz at Dölzschen. Thence it passed through Nauslitz, Rossthal, Neu Nimptsch, and Nieder Gorbitz, almost up to Leutewitz.

Murat started his advance against this line between 6 and 7 A.M. Victor's corps (II.) assembled opposite the Weisseritz woodyard, near the bridge on the Freiberg road. Thence they were to spread out fanwise in four columns moving towards Nauslitz, Rossthal, Wolfnitz, and Nieder Gorbitz. The artillery was in advance covered by skirmishers, the corps cavalry followed the main body of the infantry.

Teste's division assembled behind the rising ground at Lobtau. Pajol's cavalry took post between Victor and Teste, whilst Latour-Maubourg's squadrons came up on Teste's right, having the Saxon Guard cuirassier regiment on his extreme outer flank moving towards Leutewitz.

Victor's artillery, pushing forward, opened a heavy fire on Nauslitz and the Austrian guns there, whilst the infantry advanced in four columns. The 1st, on the left, followed the small ravine (perhaps better described as a hollow road) which leads up the slope to between Rossthal and Dölzschen. The 2nd column attacked the gardens about Nauslitz, the

3rd went by the right of Nauslitz, the 4th moved by the Freiberg road against Wolfnitz and Nieder Gorbitz. The cavalry followed in rear of the infantry.

The 1st column, covered by the ravine and the orchards on either side of it, had little difficulty in reaching its head, where it found itself close to the Austrian position between Rossthal and Dölzschen.

The 2nd column was not so fortunate, and had to make several attacks before it was in possession of Nauslitz. Thence it followed the two ravines which lead, one into Rossthal, the other rather to the left of it. The ravines were admirably suited to the French infantry, adepts in the use of cover, and as the 1st and 2nd columns issued from them, the Austrians between Dölzschen and Rossthal gave way, retiring partly on each of these villages. The 1st column now turned to its left, hemming the now separated right of the enemy against the great ravine of the Weisseritz. At the same time, the 2nd column turned to the right against Rossthal, which they stormed, taking 300 prisoners.

From Rossthal the 2nd column attacked the right flank of the Austrians opposing the 3rd column, and drove them partly towards Neu Nimptsch and partly on Pesterwitz. Neu Nimptsch was also stormed by the 3rd column. The 4th column, advancing on Nieder Gorbitz, had stormed Wolfnitz. The defenders of Nieder Gorbitz were surrounded and captured in a ravine between Neu Nimptsch and Alt Franken with the aid of Victor's cavalry, which was now up on the height between Neu Nimptsch and the Austrian reserves of Messery towards Pesterwitz.

During the attacks on the other villages, Meszko's troops had fallen back from Nieder to Ober Gorbitz and to the west of it, where Mumb's brigade had joined them.

About noon the Austrians from Wolfnitz, and those now driven out of Ober Gorbitz, were in considerable disorder in the open space between the latter village and Neu Nimptsch. Victor's cavalry was preparing to charge them, so they formed themselves into four squares as far as possible. Their muskets, however, would not to go off in the rain, and they were ridden down by the French cavalry. Many were cut down, a great many more taken prisoners, and only a few got away to Pesterwitz.

The capture of Ober Gorbitz had cut Meszko completely from Alois Lichtenstein's division at Neu Nimptsch, so that the Austrian line was now pierced in two places, between Dölzschen and Rossthal, and between Neu Nimptsch and Ober Gorbitz.

As soon as Victor's cavalry had destroyed the four squares as above described, Pajol's cavalry had moved along the Freiberg road.

Whilst all this was happening in the Austrian centre and right, between the Freiberg road and the Plauen gorge, Murat, with the main body of the French cavalry and Teste's infantry, had advanced against Meszko's left and Mumb's brigade west of Ober Gorbitz. The Austrians fell back, as they were bound to do, after the ruin of the troops in the centre. Indeed, by this time, when it was too late to save a disaster, Weissenwolf had ordered a general retreat. His left was to make its way by Pesterwitz to the Weisseritz in rear below. Czöllich, with the right, was to reach the same point by Potzschappel.

The French cavalry followed Meszko. Teste's right moved round Gompitz to Pennrich, which they easily took, as Meszko's attention was fixed in front of him. He and Mumb retreating in squares, now found themselves with their retreat by Pennrich cut off by Teste's infantry there, and attacked by the cavalry of Murat and Pajol on the other three sides. The Austrian infantry, unable to fire their muskets, and threatened by cavalry and artillery, laid down their arms and surrendered.[1] Four entire regiments were captured here, with Meszko and Mumb. The Saxon cuirassiers who, during the fights at Wolfnitz and Nieder-Gorbitz, had marched from Leutewitz to Ober Gorbitz, had already taken two Austrian squares of 2000 men.

[1] Marbot, no doubt, refers to this part of the battle in his famous story of Bordesoulle riding up to an Austrian square, and calling on it to surrender as it could not fire. When they replied that his cavalry equally could not charge in the heavy mud, he clinched the argument by opening out and showing a battery of artillery ready to fire. The Austrians at once gave in. The story may or may not be true.

The neighbourhood was an unpropitious one for the Austrians, for it is within two miles of Kesselsdorf, where they and their Saxon allies were so badly beaten by the "Old Dessauer" in 1745, though, it is true, very few Austrians actually fought that day.

We must return for a moment to the Austrian right, which had been hemmed against the gorge at Dölzschen by Victor's left column. Protected in front by a garden wall facing towards Rossthal, they had behind them as means of retreat nothing but a very difficult and steep footpath from Dölzschen down to the Weisseritz at the point where the Felsenkeller brewery now stands, and a bad steep road from their left along the face of the cliff.

For some time they managed to keep the French off, but about 2 P.M., a shell fired Dölzschen, and the village was rushed in the consequent confusion. Some of the defenders, pursued by the French fire, got away by the path or the road, and attempted to scale the opposite heights, which are in many places sheer precipices. Those who got so far narrowly escaped drowning in the swollen Weisseritz. One battery succeeded in getting down the bad road, but could not cross the stream short of Potzschappel, as the bridge had been destroyed. Numerous prisoners were taken in Dölzschen. Here the French infantry broke into the wine cellars and indulged in what Aster calls a "Bacchus-feast," which might have cost them dear had there been any Austrians to make a counter attack. There were plenty in sight, just across the gorge, where the reserves stood; but they were compelled to look idly on at the destruction of their comrades, to whom they could bring no help in time.

By 2 P.M. the whole Austrian left beyond the Weisseritz had been practically destroyed. The number of prisoners taken was enormous, Aster thinks 15,000 is not too high a figure to take.[1]

What remained of this unfortunate left wing got into the

[1] With regard to prisoners, the author found the following returns in the Paris records—(1) One showing 1407 prisoners received at headquarters up to midnight on the 26th, and 4209 more up to 7 p.m. on the 27th. (2) Prisoners in Dresden on the 29th August, 12,535.

These two returns give rise to a suspicion that the numbers taken at Dresden may have been exaggerated. But there is a later return showing the total number received up to the 8th October at 23,518 (over 15,000 Austrians). The greater part of these must have been taken at Dresden, for there were few other large captures of prisoners by the French. Of the 590 others who deserted from the allies only sixteen soldiers were Prussians, and not a single officer! 478 are classed as "miscellaneous," *i.e.* neither Russians, Austrians, nor Prussians.

Weisseritz Valley about Potzschappel, whence they reached the Dippoldiswalde road by Rabenau, far in rear of the allies' main position. Some who tried to escape to Freiberg were followed by French cavalry and lost many prisoners. They probably hoped to meet Klenau, but that general had marched by Tharandt. When he heard of the disaster to the Austrian left, he at once moved to his right to the Dippoldiswalde road.

Victor's cavalry had found Alt Franken still occupied by Austrians. They were shelled by horse artillery, and the village was stormed by French infantry from Ober Gorbitz, just as its garrison was retiring on Pesterwitz.

All fighting on this side of the Weisseritz was over by 3 P.M., though the French cavalry continued the pursuit as far as Herzogswalde, taking many prisoners and some guns.

In the rear of the allies, Vandamme had not done very much on the 27th August. Even on that morning he had not got his corps completely across the Elbe at Königstein, but Mouton-Duvernet was able to occupy Pirna, and the plateau above it, whilst Phillippon's division took post to the left of Krietschwitz, and Corbineau's cavalry advanced to between Langen Hennersdorf and Berggieshübel. A battalion was placed on the Kohlberg, the hill at the junction of the Gottleuba and Seidnitz Valleys.

Vandamme, deceived partly by the thickness of the weather, partly by the reports of a doctor who had been captured from the enemy, believed he was not strong enough to attack till the whole of his corps was up. At 4 P.M., hearing of the progress of the battle at Dresden, he prepared to march next day on Berggieshübel and Hellendorf.

At 3 P.M. the battle at Dresden was nearly over, the artillery fire had ceased. At 4 P.M., Napoleon, wet to the skin, with the famous cocked hat reduced to pulp by the rain and hanging limply about his ears and down his neck, rode through the Dippoldiswalde suburb to the palace. Behind him marched 1000 Austrian prisoners. Later on 12,000 more came in from beyond the Weisseritz, including Meszko, two other generals, sixty-four officers of high, and many of lower rank. Fifteen Austrian standards were borne by the grenadiers of the Old Guard; twenty-six guns, and thirty ammunition wagons followed. Save the one battery which escaped from Dölzschen, practically the whole of the Austrian artillery of the left wing was there.

"When an army of 120,000 men, in the presence of 180,000 enemies, deploys from a bridge-head, then surrounds the enemy on both wings, and seriously damages both; when it compels a whole division to lay down its arms in the open field, when it brings in immediately from the battlefield 13,000 prisoners, fifteen standards, and twenty-six guns, that is a quite undeniable victory." So says von Caemmerer, thinking apparently of less honest historians, who would attempt to deny that at Dresden Napoleon gained one of his most remarkable, though almost his last, great victories.

Could he have carried out his original plan of holding the allies before Dresden, whilst he, with 100,000 men, instead of Vandamme with 40,000, issued by Königstein on their rear, the result would perhaps have been decisive of the whole campaign. But the weakness of Dresden diverted him from his purpose, and as it was, he owed much to the irresolution of the allies, to their postponement of the attack on the city till the 26th, and to its general feebleness during the hours in which he was bringing up his reinforcements. Yet it is tempting to speculate what might have happened had he kept to his original plan, and sent 40,000 of his nearest troops to support St Cyr, whilst with 100,000 he himself crossed at Königstein. Would not St Cyr, with another 40,000 men, have been able to hold on at least to the Altstadt behind the old enceinte, for the scaling of which the allies had made no preparations? Would the allies have dared to continue their attack on Dresden after the 26th, perhaps even after noon on that date? By that time they might well have learnt, from Eugene of Würtemberg, that Napoleon himself was crossing at Königstein. Would not that have sent them hurrying back to Bohemia, harassed and delayed by St Cyr with 60,000 men? Napoleon at Stolpen, be it remembered, was nearer to Königstein than he was to Dresden, and he had at least as good a road. Latour-Maubourg and the Guard were also nearer to Königstein than to Dresden; Victor and Marmont no farther from one than from the other.

However, this is mere speculation, and we must return to actual facts. These were, that the allies had been badly defeated at Dresden, that they had lost probably at least 25,000 men, that the Peterswalde road was already intercepted by Vandamme, and the next best road, by Freiberg, was in Murat's hands. They were practically confined to the bad tracks between the two, on which their movements, hampered by the congestion of trains, must be slow. By the Peterswalde road Napoleon could be across the Erzgebirge and in Bohemia, ready to meet them there as they debouched from the difficult passes of the mountains. We shall see presently how he lost his chance. On the 26th and 27th August his genius flashed forth, he was the Napoleon of Austerlitz, Jena, and Friedland; on the following days he relapsed into the declining energy of 1813.

His unerring appreciation of the advantages to himself of the separation of the allied left by the Plauen gorge recalls his similar estimate of the position of the Russian left at Friedland, separated by the smaller obstacle of the mill stream from the centre and right. His bold resolve to attack on both wings, notwithstanding his inferiority of numbers, was a novelty with him. The only question is whether he might not have still further weakened his centre in order to strengthen his left, and break in the allied right; that is, whether he might not have added at least half of St Cyr's corps to his left.

He owed much, no doubt, to the faults of his enemy, to the massing of the allied army on its centre, to the neglect of the right, and especially to the collection in the centre of the great mass of their cavalry, where it was useless. If the support of Dresden rendered Napoleon's centre safe, the allies equally were safe in their centre. Possibly their action may have been due to their belief that he would always make his great effort to break the centre. That was an idea held by St Cyr, as we have already seen when that marshal discussed the plan for Bautzen. Still, Bautzen itself should have warned them that he allowed himself to be tied down by no such hard and fast rule.

Again, they committed a grave error in leaving their exposed left wing miserably weak both in guns and cavalry, the two arms which could do most in the pouring rain of the 27th August, in an age when neither breech-loaders nor even percussion caps had been invented to do away with the necessity for primings, which could not be kept dry.

One thing must be said in favour of the allies' treatment of their left wing, namely, that they had good reason to believe Klenau would have joined it early in the morning, nearly doubling its strength. They had not reckoned on that commander's slowness, due doubtless to the terrible meteorological conditions, and had been content to accept his assurance that he would be up in time. It is not, however, clear why Klenau should have gone by Tharandt instead of by Kesselsdorf. He started that move before he knew of the ruin of the allied left. Surely the allies should have known that Klenau was delayed in time to repair their error to some extent by sending reinforcements, from their reserve at Gittersee, across the Weisseritz to the left wing.

When their right wing was hard pressed, the proposal for a strong counter attack with Kleist and Miloradowich came to nothing, partly on account of Barclay's rather weak objection, partly on account of the depressing effects of Moreau's mortal wound, and the news of Vandamme's progress at Pirna. The former, however it may have affected Alexander, was after all only an incident, the latter was an additional reason for attempting to clear the Pirna road, as well as for the despatch of reinforcements from the centre to Osterman at Zehista.

For the counter attack on Napoleon's left, cavalry might also have been sent up to the right from the centre, where it was standing idle. It may also be remarked that the Russo-Prussian cavalry, already available on the right, might well have displayed more activity than it did against Nansouty's.

"The Battle of Hanau," from *Napoleon's Last Campaign in Germany, 1813*

Napoleon's victory at Dresden was marred by the ineptitude of one of his generals, who bungled the pursuit, permitting some 30,000 French troops to fall prisoner to the enemy. In the weeks after the battle Napoleon's enemies avoided his main army, concentrating on

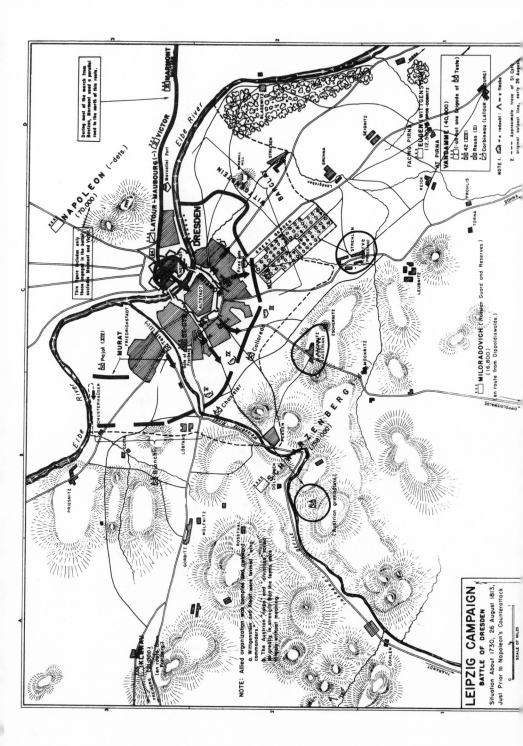

LEIPZIG CAMPAIGN
BATTLE OF DRESDEN
Situation About 1730, 26 August 1813,
Just Prior to Napoleon's Counterattack

SCALE OF MILES

NOTE: Allied organization and composition, especially
a. Wittgenstein's and Kleist's commanders, vary
greatly in strength; both the names listed
here without meaning.
b. The Austrian Korps and divisional names are
here without meaning.

NOTE I. ⌐⊏ = redoubt; ∧ = fleche
2. --- = Approximate trace of St. Cyr
original outpost line, early 26 August

VARRAMME (40,000)
□ 42 ⟨XXX⟩   ⊠ Reuss ⟨II⟩
⊠42 ⟨XXX⟩   ⊠ Corbineau (LATOUR-MAUBOURG)

EUGEN WITTGENSTEIN
(12,500)

MILORADOVICH (Russian Guard and Reserves)
(16,800)
(en route from Dippoldiswalde)

NAPOLEON (-dels.)
(70,000)

LATOUR-MAUBOURG (-)   VICTOR

MURAT
⊠ Pajol ⟨XIV⟩

subordinate forces under several of his marshals. This wise strategy led to several victories and gradually forced Napoleon to concentrate his forces in the area between Dresden and Leipzig if only to prevent portions of them from being destroyed in his absence. And during the days October 16–19, there occurred in the vicinity of Leipzig "The Battle of the Nations." With but 190,000 men against some 300,000, Napoleon had little hope of victory, but made a determined effort to secure one anyway. In the end, pressed from virtually all sides, and with some of his Allied contingents deserting to the enemy, he opted for a retreat. The retreat began smoothly and it looked as though the Battle of Leipzig would go down in history as a well-conducted rearguard action when the only practicable bridge across the Elster River across the French line of communications was blown up by a panic-stricken engineer officer, before much of the army could get across. Hundreds died on the bridge, and hundreds more drowned trying to swim the river, while thousands more became prisoners of war. Napoleon's retreat became a desperate race to get to the Rhine and France. A series of tough rearguard actions ensued, as the Allies attempted to impede the French retreat. In these, the French gave as well as they could. But their forces were gradually whittled down by losses and by Napoleon's ill-advised policy of placing garrisons in scores of fortresses. Nevertheless, by the end of October the main body of the French Army was virtually out of danger. Indeed, the only obstacle between Napoleon and France was a combined Allied-Bavarian Army of 30,000 men under General Count Karl Philip Wrede. The Bavarians and Wrede had both formerly been in French service, but had gone over to the enemy after Leipzig. The ensuing Battle of Hanau, October 30–31, 1813, was Napoleon's last victory on foreign soil, and a useful illustration of Napoleon's personal capabilities as a general, so that despite having under his command greatly outnumbered, exhausted, demoralized troops, he secured a smashing victory over excellent, veteran troops under an inept leader.

It is curious to find Wrede, who certainly owed his military advancement as well as his title of Count to Napoleon, now becoming the bitterest enemy, after Blücher, of the man he had followed since 1805. Even German writers seem to look rather askance at his conduct.

It was perhaps due to his well-known favour with Napoleon that he had earned a reputation in Austria which led to his being appointed to the chief command of the army, with which he moved, south of the Main, to intercept such of the beaten French army as might be making for Frankfort and Mayence. With the details of his march we are not concerned.

On the 27th October, he was under the impression that he had only to deal with a flank column of 18,000 or 20,000 men, and that Napoleon was farther north on the road to Coblence. With some trifling successes on the 28th and 29th, Wrede became still more confident. He was at Hanau by 2 P.M. on the 29th with all his troops, except Rechberg's division, which he sent ahead to occupy Frankfort. His army had dwindled, owing to hard marching and detachments, including one he had to leave before Würzburg, which he had failed to take. He had at Hanau about 30,000 men and 58 guns.

Hanau, then a town of some 15,000 inhabitants, stands in the angle between the Main and the Kinzig, a tributary reaching it from the north-east. The town was still surrounded by a wet ditch, though the fortifications had fallen into disrepair. The Kinzig, which flows in a semicircle round the northern side of the town, was, especially in the rainy autumn of 1813, a serious obstacle, passable for all arms only at the bridge north-west of Hanau, and at that a mile or so to the east, near the Lamboi forest. The forest comes down to within a mile of Hanau on the eastern and northern sides. The main road from Erfurt to Mayence passes north of the town, without crossing the Kinzig.

Still under the impression that Napoleon was far away, Wrede, on the morning of the 30th October, posted his army east of Hanau and across the great road, to bar the retreat of the French. His left was astride of the road, facing its issue from the forest. This wing consisted chiefly of cavalry, and of 28 guns. A few squadrons watched northwards on the Friedberg road. The centre stretched from the road to the Kinzig (which was behind it) at the Lamboi bridge. The right was south of the Lamboi bridge. The position was so bad as to justify Napoleon's remark, "Poor Wrede, I made him a count, but I could never make him a general." The separa-

tion of the front by the Kinzig, the position of the centre with
its retreat barred by that stream, and the facilities offered by
the forest to the approach of the French, were the chief
defects of the position. If the enemy could seize the Lamboi
bridge, the right would be hopelessly separated, and the ruin
of the centre and left was almost certain. Napoleon had but
16,000 or 17,000 men available for the moment, but they
were sufficient, under him, against Wrede with nearly double that strength.

By noon, after some fighting with the Bavarian advanced
troops in the forest, Victor, supported by Macdonald, was at
the outer edge of the wood opposite Wrede's centre. Even
then Wrede had only just realised that he was opposed to the
Emperor. He now called over a brigade from his right to
protect the Lamboi bridge. Napoleon had decided to attack
in superior force against Wrede's left. Drouot had reported
the feasibility for artillery of a track he had discovered
through the forest north of the road. The wood opposite
Wrede's left was cleared about 3 P.M. by two battalions of Old
Guard, and Drouot gradually collected a battery of 50 guns
in that direction, whilst the 2nd cavalry corps and the Guard
heavy cavalry assembled behind him. Wrede's 28 guns were
soon mastered, and then the French cavalry charged that of
Wrede's left, who were carried away and driven off the field.
Wrede's centre, hard pressed by Drouot's guns, and with the
French cavalry now descending on it from the left, held out
for a time, but was presently compelled to retreat. With the
Kinzig barring direct retreat, it had to move to its left, an
operation in which it naturally suffered heavily. The last
three battalions were cut off and driven into the Kinzig,
where several hundreds were drowned. The remains of
Wrede's centre and left assembled at Gross Auenheim.

When Wrede saw the danger to his left and centre, he
tried to bring help from his right across the Lamboi bridge.
The first brigade, called over earlier, was already retreating
when the second succeeded, for the moment, in driving the
pursuers back to the wood. Then the tide turned again, and
both brigades were pushed in confusion on to the bridge,
which was insufficient for their passage. Here again several
hundreds were drowned in the Kinzig.

That night Wrede bivouacked with his right on the Lamboi bridge, his centre and left along the Aschaffenburg road and holding Hanau.

Napoleon, having driven Wrede across the Kinzig, had no desire to pursue him. He continued his retreat on Frankfort, leaving a rearguard to keep Wrede from interfering with the remainder of the army still behind.

At 2 A.M. on the 31st Hanau was bombarded, and presently Wrede evacuated it, leaving it to be occupied without resistance by Bertrand when he arrived at 8 A.M.

With Bertrand in Hanau, and Marmont preventing his issue over the Lamboi bridge, Wrede could do nothing against Napoleon's troops passing along the road beyond. By 3 P.M. all had passed and Marmont followed with the III. and VI. corps, still leaving Bertrand with the IV. to cover the retreat.

When Wrede again advanced he completely failed in his attack on the Lamboi bridge. In storming Hanau itself, he was badly wounded. An attack on the Kinzig bridge beyond the town, to which the French retired, failed, and there was now no further obstacle to Napoleon's retreat to Mayence through Frankfort, which had been evacuated by Rechberg as the French approached.

In the four days, 28th to 31st October, Wrede lost about 9250 officers and men. The French loss in killed and wounded was probably less, but during this period there fell into the hands of the enemy, in small detachments or as stragglers, 5 generals, 280 officers, and about 10,000 men.

There is not much to be said about the battle of Hanau. The position taken up by Wrede was hopelessly bad, and he suffered the penalty of taking it. He seems to have realised what was coming when he learnt that he was in the presence of his late master, for he remarked that he was bound to fight, and that he and his men must just do their best. On the whole, he might consider himself fortunate in saving any part of his centre and left, which had to pass round the northward bend of the Kinzig before reaching a passage at the bridge of the branch road joining Hanau to the main road.

Napoleon had, with unerring instinct, instantly seized the

features of the battlefield and the weaknesses of Wrede's position. He could not avoid fighting. He was probably not anxious for another battle, though he felt satisfaction in reading Wrede, who after all had treated him with considerable ingratitude, a severe lesson.

Here we close the history of this campaign, for it is unnecessary to follow the course of the operations of the allies against the fortresses still held by Napoleon's garrisons in Germany. A few words may, however, be said about the fate of Dresden and St Cyr. It has already been told how Napoleon, after deciding to take St Cyr north with him and to abandon Dresden, made that fatal change which deprived him of the I. and XIV. corps, which he so badly needed at Leipzig. Not only that, but he also insisted on keeping Magdeburg, Torgau, and Wittenberg, the garrisons of which and of Dresden would have given him at least 50,000 more men at Leipzig, and might even have changed the result of the battle of the 16th.

St Cyr at Dresden, blockaded by Russians and Austrians after Leipzig, made some ineffectual attempts to escape down the right bank of the Elbe. Then, the garrison and the inhabitants being reduced to the greatest straits by starvation, he accepted a capitulation under which the garrison was to be sent back to France under promise not to serve again in the war. The capitulation was signed on the 11th November, and the garrison was already on the march to France, when it was announced that Schwarzenberg had refused to ratify it. Though the allies offered to replace St Cyr in Dresden in exactly the same position, as to arms, provisions, etc., as he held when the capitulation was signed, he considered it useless to return, and he and his army became prisoners of war.

Under all the circumstances, the conduct of the allies in this matter seems open to censure.

V

Petre as Military Critic

F. Loraine Petre not only sought to explain accurately the course of the campaigns of Napoleon, but also attempted to analyze them, striving for fundamental lessons which might prove useful to the professional student of military affairs. The selections which follow are examples of Petre's best efforts at evaluation and analysis of military operations, demonstrating a healthy lack of bias toward his subject, and considerable talent as a military critic, as he examines two of Napoleon's most interesting campaigns, that against Austria in 1809 and that in France in 1814.

"The Strategy and Tactics of the Campaign of 1809," from *Napoleon and the Archduke Charles: A History of the Franco-Austrian Campaign in the Valley of the Danube in 1809*

Napoleon, at St Helena, writing with the object of proving his own military infallibility, said: "The battle of Abensberg, the manœuvre of Landshut, and the battle of Eckmühl are the boldest, the most brilliant, the ablest manœuvres of Napoleon."

The verdict of modern military criticism is not quite so favourable as this. Whilst admitting to the full the brilliancy

248

and soundness of many of the Emperor's orders and movements, it points out that there were others far short of the
standard of excellence exhibited in 1806. All are agreed that
nothing could be better than his orders for the strategical
deployment of his army on the defensive, according to the
date on which the Austrians might commence their advance
over the Bavarian frontier. Unfortunately, the orders fell for
execution to a man who was more or less of a machine,
capable only of carrying out hard and fast directions, incapable of appreciating the principles which inspired them. We
have sufficiently explained how Berthier's poverty of comprehension and imagination resulted in the pitiable confusion of his mind, and the dispersal of the army of a
commander with whom concentration was the alpha and
omega of his military creed.

There is equally but one view as to the general excellence
of Napoleon's measures for the remedy of the almost desperate situation in which his Chief of Staff had involved him on
the 17th April. The blot on them was the miscalculation of 24
hours as to the arrival of Davout and Masséna within supporting distance of one another and of the centre.

As for Davout, his flank march by the right bank of the
Danube was, on the face of it, dangerous. It was based on the
Emperor's misapprehension of the strength of the Austrian
"column of Landshut" which, till some time in the night of
the 17th–18th, he believed to be merely an advance guard of
a single corps, instead of, as it really was, the main body of
the Austrian army. Had he known that when he issued his
orders to Davout on the 17th, he would perhaps have
hesitated. Nevertheless, there was really but a very small risk
if the march from Ratisbon to Abensberg had been carried
out on the 18th, as Napoleon intended. He was not very clear
as to the exact position of Friant, though he probably did not
intend that general to move round by Ratisbon; for Napoleon knew he was still a long way from there. Everything, his
separate mention of Friant, and his order to him to leave
detachments on the Altmühl, treating it as a great
bridgehead to Ingolstadt, points to his intention that Friant
should march across the Altmühl to the Danube, not that he

should leave it on his right, sending detachments off in that direction to the passages of the river. At Neustadt or Kelheim Friant would cross the Danube and join Davout who, meanwhile, would have marched by the right bank. If, however, as we believe, that was Napoleon's intention, his orders were far from clear, and Davout, who was certainly not wanting in intelligence, misunderstood them.

In the case of Masséna, the Emperor was again misinformed as to the state of dispersion of his corps. The Masséna of former days would have done something to expedite the concentration, but nothing could have enabled the corps to be at Pfaffenhofen on the evening of the 18th.

When, at last, Davout was able to start his march on the morning of the 19th his position differed widely from what it would have been on the 18th. The Archduke Charles was already marching against him, and few generals have ever had such an opportunity of cutting off one-third of the enemy's army as Charles had on the 19th. With Lefebvre's letter of the 18th before him, as well as Davout's own orders for the march, he had every information he could desire. Yet he failed to destroy, or even seriously to injure Davout. Instead of keeping to his left, so as to meet the head of the marshal's columns, he sent nothing further west than Thann and he spread his army over much too broad a front. Liechtenstein, marching down the valley of the great Laber, must inevitably pass outside even Montbrun's flaking column. At noon he was within a couple of miles of Rosenberg's battle, yet Charles took no measures to call him in to fall on the flank and rear of Davout with the 15,000 men he had.

Rosenberg was allowed to fritter away his battalions, till he ended by meeting Montbrun with only half his available force.

Hohenzollern, too, detached too many flank guards and had only 17,000 men left to fight between Hausen and Teugen. Finally, Charles himself stood all the day idle with at least 10,000 grenadiers, besides some of Rosenberg's troops, on the heights of Grub. From those heights one can look right down on the slope above Saladorf in front of Hausen. Davout with 30,000 men (St. Hilaire, Friant, Petit, and Montbrun) might have been opposed by more than 50,000

Austrians,[1] whereas he only met Hohenzollern's 17,000 and half of Rosenberg's men.

Davout's own conduct of the battle on the ridge was excellent, and the way in which Montbrun, with 2000 infantry and 3000 cavalry, kept at bay far superior numbers till evening was beyond all praise. Davout's action in sending Morand and Gudin to Saal, where they did nothing, is not so easy of explanation. It is true he was anxious about his baggage column in the defile, and he is said to have intended bringing the infantry divisions back up the Feking brook against the left flank of Hohenzollern. Nevertheless, one cannot help suspecting that he felt his position to be a desperate one, and that he had better try and save at least these two divisions by hurrying them through the still remaining gap to join Napoleon and Lefebvre.

General Bonnal was apparently unaware of the fact that Davout's orders had fallen into Charles's hands,[2] but, even without that, he considers Davout's situation on the morning of the 19th as strategically almost desperate. Yet, even if Charles had brought the whole of his available forces against Davout, it is not certain that the tactical superiority of the French, especially in a wooded close country, in which the genius of the French soldier shone, would not have retrieved the strategical situation.

In urging Liechtenstein on to Ratisbon, Charles was hankering after supposed moral advantages, which would have been much more surely gained by driving Davout into the Danube. The Archduke must have known that Davout could have left little, if anything, in Ratisbon, and that the place, bombarded by Kolowrat's artillery on the heights above Stadt am Hof, could not hold out more than a few hours.

Why did not Davout, after his success on the 19th, move the rest of his corps, after Morand and Gudin, towards

---

[1] Hohenzollern 17,000; Rosenberg 13,000; Grenadiers 10,000; Liechtenstein 15,000.

[2] Binder v. Krieglstein's book, which shows this, was not published till the year after the "Manœuvre de Landshut," and the fact of the capture of the orders is not mentioned by Von Angeli. On the other hand, Binder v. Krieglstein does not appear to have read Bonnal's book. He neither refers to it, nor mentions it in his bibliography.

Abensberg? General Bonnal finds the answer in the wretched condition of the roads, the fatigue of the men, and the necessity for collecting and caring for the wounded.

Napoleon's designs were perfect up till noon on the 19th. He calculated on having for the 20th Davout at Neustadt, Lefebvre at Geisenfeld, Masséna and Oudinot at Pfaffenhofen. If Davout and Lefebvre were attacked the Austrians would have their left and rear exposed to Masséna and Oudinot; if the attack were on Lefebvre and Masséna, Davout would be within striking distance of the enemy's right flank. At noon on the 19th, the Emperor, at Ingolstadt, had not heard the guns at Hausen. He was nearly 30 miles away and the intervening woods and hills would deaden the sound. It was now that he began to fall away, and to indicate his intention of sending at least a large part of Masséna's force to Landshut, to threaten Charles' communications with the Inn. That idea was, General Bonnal holds, dictated by the dominating desire to move direct on Vienna and to keep Charles in front of him on that line. Thus he wanted, by manœuvring, to bind Charles to that line of retreat. It was no part of his programme to drive the Austrians to the north of the Danube, whither he had no intention of following them. To do so would be to abandon for the time the advance on Vienna. With his forces in the positions hitherto contemplated, the union of the whole army within striking distance would be complete; now the Emperor was himself going again to disperse it, by sending Masséna in a direction from which he would not be able to take part in a battle on the Abens. He was even exposing Masséna to the risk of Charles' turning back against him, and, behind the screen of the Isar, defeating him before the Emperor could succour him.

When he heard of Davout's success, the Emperor's view was this. Charles would be driven back by Davout, on the 20th, towards the south, or at least checked in his northward advance. Then the attack of Napoleon's column on his left from Abensberg would compel him to retreat on Landshut, where he would find Masséna ready to complete his destruction. Here the Emperor's undue optimism again appears. He thinks of the hard-fought battle at Hausen as a second Auerstädt, and he writes of Masséna being at Landshut at 3

P.M. on the 20th, more than 24 hours before he actually reached it. He contemplated the prospect of the whole Austrian army standing in the angle between himself and Davout, attacked in front and left flank and driven on Landshut. He never allowed for Charles' actual movement from left to right to the eastward of Davout and then northwards to Ratisbon.

He decided, therefore, to push forward on the 20th with Lefebvre, Vandamme, Morand, Gudin, and the cuirassiers, from the Abens towards Landshut, calling up two of Masséna's divisions, and sending the other four by Freising and Moosburg on Landshut. Davout, he seems to have presumed, would move southwards; therefore, he sent him no orders, and Davout, who knew the Austrians were doing something quite different from what the Emperor expected, spent the day without serious action.

As Napoleon drove the Austrians before him with ease on the road to Landshut, he was under the impression, though the slight resistance should have shown him otherwise, that he was driving the greater part of the Austrian army into the cul-de-sac of which the farther end would be closed by Masséna. He refused to believe Davout's reports indicating a movement on Ratisbon, and, even on the 21st, he assured Davout that he had nothing in front of him but a weak screen of three regiments. Davout knew better, but it was only at 2 A.M. on the 22nd that Piré's arrival at last convinced the Emperor that he had been employing the greater part of his own army in defeating less than one-third of what Charles commanded on the two banks of the Danube, which were now united for the Austrians by the surrender of Ratisbon.

By the evening of the 21st, Napoleon had driven the remains of Hiller's 42,000 men through Landshut towards the Inn. But Masséna had failed him, and left the end of the cul-de-sac open at Landshut. The Austrian left wing was driven away from the rest, but the Emperor is romancing when, in the first bulletin, he sets out that that had been his object in the advance from the Abens. His excessive optimism is again apparent when he compares Abensberg to Jena, and multiplies the number of prisoners taken by three or more.

Once he is disillusioned by Piré, at 2 A.M. on the 22nd, he

returns to the true faith and acts with immense energy. Now he is all for making an end of the Archduke on the 22nd, and so bringing the war to a conclusion. But it was too late now; he had missed his chance of decisive battle, though he had been fortunate enough, owing to Davout's excellent conduct on the 21st, to escape a disaster to his left.

Charles, too, had again missed his opportunity of destroying Davout on the 21st, for he had shown no symptoms of the offensive, and had sent Kolowrat from Ratisbon on a useless tramp to Hemau and back, instead of keeping him to help in crushing Davout, for which purpose Bellegarde might also have been called up. What Charles' motive for sending Kolowrat to Hemau was is far from clear. When he decided to fall on Davout with over 70,000 men on the 22nd, it was too late, and the scheme was abandoned the moment the appearance of the head of Napoleon's column from Landshut was signalled. The attack on Davout was given up, though Charles failed to ride forward, as he should have done, to Eckmühl to see for himself the position of affairs.

The battle of Eckmühl, so much vaunted by Napoleon, was in reality nothing more than a rearguard action, fought by Rosenberg with the IV. corps against a greatly superior enemy attacking him from west, south, and east. In only telling Rosenberg to get out of his position as best he could, Charles failed in his duty, a failure due perhaps to a natural tendency to indolence.

Count Yorck von Wartenburg,[1] who has little fault to find with Napoleon's earlier movements, condemns his failure to pursue Charles in the night of the 22nd, during which the Austrians got the greater part of their army ready to cross the Danube at Ratisbon. Lannes is said to have counselled pursuit; the other marshals held that the troops were too fatigued. Lannes' corps had marched 22 miles from Ergolding to Eckmühl, and, by the route it followed, it would be another 17 miles on to Ratisbon. The cuirassier's horses were so done up that they could not charge at more than a trot. Davout and Lefebvre, it is true, had not covered much ground, but they had had much fighting, both on the 22nd

---

[1] *Napoleon as a General,* ii. 57.

and the 21st. Masséna's men, owing to the length of the column on a single road, were behind, and had had more marching than even Lannes. Finally, the Emperor had only fought two Austrian corps,[1] and the probabilities were in favour of those behind them being able to offer a strenuous resistance. Moreover, Ratisbon itself was a serious obstacle, and, even if the pursuit were carried up to its walls, that would not have prevented the Austrian passage of the stone bridge, or the throwing of a pontoon bridge. On the whole, it would seem hardly justifiable to accuse Napoleon of want of energy in not pursuing in the night after Eckmühl.

But the case is different when we come to his refusal to follow Charles across the river on the 24th, except with Davout's corps, which observed rather than pursued the enemy. On this question there are diversities of opinion. Jomini, in his *Life of Napoleon,* puts into the Emperor's mouth the following defence of his action. "Some have blamed me for not having, on the contrary, pursued the then scattered army of the Archduke Charles. I was deterred from this by several reasons; first, the woody chain of the Böhmerwald mountains offered to the enemy positions of great advantage; secondly, the Archduke Charles had written me a letter showing a desire on his part to treat. By pursuing Hiller I might complete his ruin and dictate a more advantageous peace at Vienna. On the other hand, attacking the enemy in the mountains of Bohemia, Hiller, with the Archduke John and Chasteler coming from Italy and the Tyrol, might collect 80,000 fresh troops on the Danube, at the instant when the Archduke Charles, reinforced by the landwehr of Bohemia, would charge me in front."

To this it may be replied that the difficulties of the country were not in the least likely to stop French troops; on the contrary, the country was one in which the tactical advantage would be all with the French, just as it was in the wooded country south of Ratisbon. The Archduke's letter was certainly meant as a feeler regarding peace negotiations, but it did not reach Napoleon till the 1st May, when his army was already far on its way to Vienna, and he himself on the

[1] The IV., supported later by the III.

Salzach. As for Hiller, the Emperor had plenty of troops to keep him on the move towards Vienna, without interfering with the pursuit of the main Austrian army. Chasteler had but a small force, still many days' march from the theatre of operations, and, on the 22nd, the Archduke John was marching on the Adige and Verona, after defeating the Viceroy of Italy at Sacile.

It was the very absence of serious pursuit which enabled Charles to gather in the Bohemian landwehr. Had he been hard pressed, the very fluid landwehr battalions would probably have broken up without joining him.

Charles we shall see had made up his mind, if pursued, to fight at Cham on the Bavarian side of the frontier. He had 90,000 men, but only two of his corps were untouched and he had to reorganise his army. The idea of fighting at all was only a counsel of despair, a less desperate alternative than to allow his army to disperse in the difficult and ill-provisioned Bohemian mountains. A letter from Grünne to the Prince de Ligne, written after the war was over, deals with this question from the Austrian point of view. It is given in full by Saski, but we must confine ourselves to a summary and a few quotations. Grünne almost commences by speaking of "the mistake which, in my opinion, Napoleon made in not having followed us after the battle of Ratisbon." He says the army was retreating sore stricken, having lost two-thirds of its artillery, with execrable roads behind it, and these covered with stragglers. The troops were bivouacking in snow and mud, supplies no longer arriving. "I ask if that army, even reinforced by Bellegarde's corps, could have resisted the victorious Napoleon, if he had pursued it 'l'epeé dans les reins'? He would have thrown it into the forests of Bohemia, where it would have disbanded for want of supplies; the landwehr, which afterwards furnished 60,000 men, would not have formed, our depots of recruits would have dispersed, and in a fortnight Napoleon would have become master of, and disposed of all our resources." He goes on to affirm that Napoleon, in conversation with Wimpffen, admitted his error, adding that he had believed it impossible for the Austrian army to rise, like the Phœnix, from its ashes.

Yorck von Wartenburg, on the other hand, concurring

with Jomini, considers that, once Charles had been allowed
to escape after Eckmühl, it was too late to pursue him, that
he would be able to offer serious resistance in the Bohemian
forests, and that a direct march on Vienna was the only way
for the Emperor to reach the capital before the Austrians.

General Bonnal's opinion is decided, and, as we venture to
think, beyond doubt correct. He holds that Napoleon, after
first losing his chance on the 20th April of compelling
Charles to a battle in unfavourable circumstances, again lost
it on the 26th, by not following him to Cham. He desired a
decisive battle, no doubt, but his predetermined movement
on Vienna put it off till the 5th–6th July. He twice relin-
quished the substantial chance of battle for the shadowy possibilities of a strategic manœuvre. "But," says Bonnal, "every
strategic manœuvre aiming at great results without recourse
to battle is deceptive, when one has before one an energetic
enemy; it retards the decision of the war, and, as a consequence, necessitates much greater sacrifices than those it
would have been wise to accept at once."

The Austrians had, since 1805, vastly improved in every
way, an improvement for which Napoleon's overweening
pride did not suffer him to make allowance. Still, the French
infantry, and their allies following in their footsteps, had to a
great extent maintained their tactical supremacy, though the
gap between them and the Austrians had been sensibly di-
minished. In Davout's battle of the 19th April, and again on
the 21st, Austrians were pitted against the very pick of the
French divisions, and that largely in wood fighting, where
the French were sure to show to the best. Some of Davout's
battalions were entirely broken up into groups of skirmishers. That would have been contrary to the Austrian
drillbooks, which laid down hard and fast rules as to the
proportion of skirmishers to the battalion, and the time for
their withdrawal on the main body. Probably no Austrian
battalion could have stood the strain of this breaking up into
skirmishers without entirely going to pieces. There were constant instances in the "battue" of Abensberg where defeat
resulted almost at once in panic flight, without any attempt to
rally. Later on, we shall see Austrian troops, and those not all
of the same excellence as the men of the Ratisbon campaign,

fighting on open ground better suited to their system. Then, as might be expected, the French superiority to a great extent disappeared.

In marching capacity there was still no comparison possible between the two armies. The Austrians took 7 days to cover unopposed the 63 miles from the Inn to the Isar. In the 4 days from the 19th to the 22nd April the divisions of Morand and Gudin covered no less than 81 miles, and that included some fighting on the march to Landshut, and in the capture of that place, besides a good deal of marching straight across a rain-soaked country. The French infantry soldier of 1809 carried less weight on his back than his successor of to-day, and his burden and accoutrements appear to have been distributed so as to cause him the minimum of fatigue and discomfort.

Regarding the artillery, it is well to remember that the field batteries had attained very little mobility, and that it was only the horse artillery which could move faster than a walk, or a very slow trot for a short distance. The limbers and guns had no seats on them, and the ammunition waggons, having tops in the form of a roof, could equally not be used to carry the men.

In numbers the Austrian guns were superior to the French, and during all the earlier part of the battle above Teugen Davout had but three pieces to oppose to the Austrian guns on the crest.

On the 24th April, the Archduke Charles wrote to Francis I. that he was retreating to Cham, there to unite his army, including the corps of Kolowrat and Bellegarde. At Cham he would be guided by circumstances as to whether he would fight a battle, or would continue his retreat.

On the 27th, he wrote again from Cham. He was now assured that Napoleon was marching direct on Vienna, and meditating no serious pursuit of the defeated army on the north bank of the Danube. Charles considers that three operations are open to him.

(1) An advance on Ratisbon with the object of falling on Napoleon's rear. The objections to this were the difficulty, owing to loss of pontoons, in crossing the Danube, the

further difficulty of subsisting in the now exhausted country south of Ratisbon, and, finally, the danger of a battle fought and lost with the Austrian front towards Vienna. Charles felt that meant the end of the House of Habsburg, as well as of Austria, and he quailed before the responsibility.

(2) A bolder plan would be to move westward by Suabia towards France. To that the objection was that Napoleon would be at Vienna long before Charles could reach Paris.

(3) To retreat by Budweis, to rejoin Hiller, and resume the offensive against Napoleon.

The two first plans Charles considered impossible of execution, and he had decided to adopt the third as the safer.

Of the retreat we need not speak further, unless to call attention to Charles' unnecessary sensitiveness for his rear, which induced him to send Kolowrat back to meet a possible advance from Saxony, and afterwards to leave him with a whole army corps to meet Bernadotte. Charles' use of strong flank guards on his right had the effect of deceiving Davout who, till a very late date, suspected him of barricading himself in Bohemia.

Davout's great caution is very remarkable. It seems clear from his actions that he did not agree with the Emperor's decision to march on Vienna, disregarding Charles once his retreat into Bohemia was certain. Napoleon was convinced as to Charles' direction long before Davout was satisfied on the point, and the marshal's doubts induced the Emperor, on several occasions, to leave his subordinate some discretion as to the rapidity of his advance by the right bank.

There was always the danger that Charles might yet break back across the Danube in rear of Napoleon, and unite with the Archduke John and Chasteler to fight that battle "à front renversé," the issue of which must be almost as momentous for Napoleon as for Francis. That was what Davout evidently feared when he thought Charles was stopping in Bohemia. It was the plan which, in a modified form, the Austrian commander-in-chief contemplated when he sent Kolowrat towards Linz, and ordered John to co-operate with him from the south. Who can doubt that it is the one which Napoleon himself, in Charles' position, would have followed?

Napoleon, too, clearly shows how much anxiety the safeguarding of his long line of communications caused him. His frequent orders to Lefebvre to act vigorously in the Tyrol, his eagerness for the commitment of John to a retreat on Hungary, his orders for the construction of an almost impregnable bridge-head opposite Linz, his instructions to Beaumont and the new reserve division at Augsburg, and to Kellerman and Jerome, all point in the same direction. Once he was assured that Charles was marching towards Vienna, or Moravia, with the greater part of his army, that John was bound for Hungary, that Chasteler and Jelacic were driven out of the Tyrol, he felt little anxiety about Kolowrat, whose attack of the 17th May on the Linz bridge-head was easily disposed of by Vandamme and Bernadotte. In his inmost soul Napoleon perhaps regretted the advance on Vienna, even before Essling. After that repulse, with its disclosure of the greatly increased strength of Charles, it is difficult to doubt that he must have done so. Even Wagram was too little of a decisive victory to obliterate the memory of Essling.

After Essling, Napoleon's position was one of extreme anxiety. The news of the reverse spread like wildfire throughout the continent, offering every encouragement to the brave spirits who were for a bold stroke for liberty. The news from Spain, and the gallant fight of the Tyrolese peasants, gave them still further encouragement. Perhaps their worst enemy, and Napoleon's best friend, was the feeble and selfish Frederick William of Prussia. Even Russia must have been a source of anxiety to Napoleon, for her alliance was, to take it at the best, but half-hearted.

For the defeat of Essling the Emperor had himself to blame. He had certainly been careless in his preparations for the crossing, once more a result of his unbounded pride and his contempt for his enemy. He had been amply warned of the dangers of a sudden rise of the Danube, the fate of the Austrian bridge at Mauthausen should have warned him of the danger to a bridge of boats from barges and other masses floated down the rapid stream. Yet he trusted his army to a single bridge of boats without any protection by stockades, or by boats cruising about to arrest such floating masses above the bridge. His information regarding Charles' position seems to have been bad and to have led him not to expect serious resistance immediately after the passage. Even on the morning of Essling, his cavalry had failed to detect the advance of the whole Austrian army.

Napoleon was always preaching the advantages of field fortification; yet he neglected it before Essling. It is true he at once began a bridge-head at the northern end of his last bridge, but he took no measures to fortify the greater bridge-head of Aspern-Essling and the line between them. Had he spent the night at that work, it is doubtful whether the Austrians would ever have effected a lodgment in either village. The church and churchyard at Aspern might have been rendered almost impregnable, and the same may be said of Essling.

Perhaps Napoleon's escape from still greater disaster at the battle of Essling was due as much to the Austrian failure as to his own efforts. Charles devoted all his energies to the attack on the two strong positions of Aspern and Essling, almost neglecting the attack on the weak, and weakly held, curtain between them. A successful attack on the centre would have broken the Emperor's army in two, and, possibly, have resulted in annihilation of everything on the left bank on the 21st May. As it was, the more or less disjointed attacks on the two villages were never completely successful, and Napoleon was able, thanks to the splendid conduct of Masséna's men on the one flank and Lannes' on the other, to retire in good order to the Lobau. His desperate attack on the Austrian centre, on the 22nd May, narrowly missed success, and that thanks, to a great extent, to Charles' personal valour and influence. It is all very well to blame him for playing the part of a regimental officer, instead of a commander-in-chief, but it must be remembered that he had had unpleasant experiences of the rout into which an Austrian repulse was apt to degenerate, and he probably felt that the crisis was approaching which would convert an orderly retirement into a panic flight, ending in the separation and ruin of his army. Essling was the first great success of an Austrian army against Napoleon in person. Still, a great deal more was made of it than it deserved; for, after all, it was but a partial success, gained by immensely superior forces, which should have been able to absolutely destroy the 22,000 men whom alone Napoleon was able to utilise on the first day of the battle. On the other hand, Napoleon had no justification for attributing his defeat solely to the breaking of the bridge. His attack on the Austrian centre was fairly beaten off before the arrival of Davout became hopeless.

Charles' proposed attacks on the Lobau after Essling were palpably a make-believe, and could not possibly have succeeded.

There is no clearer proof that Napoleon realised his own rashness in the first crossing than the infinite care which he bestowed on his preparations for the second, and the perfection with which they were carried out. The thoroughness of the way in which he turned the Lobau into a great entrenched camp, the success of his endeavours to deceive Charles as to the point of passage, are admirable. The Austrian general had seen the results of Napoleon's failure to fortify the Aspern-Essling position, and had not failed in the same way. Where he did fail was in presuming that the Emperor would dash his head against the front of an almost impregnable fortified position, when Charles had left the bank opposite the whole eastern side of the island practically undefended. The Emperor would not even have had space to deploy in front of the works at Aspern-Essling. Napoleon of course saw all this and determined to turn the fortified position, to debouch by the eastern side of the island, and to unfold his army like a fan, turning the Austrian left. To conceal his real intentions, he resorted to every possible device. By keeping Davout and Eugène before, or to the east of Pressburg, and then marching them to Ebersdorf by a circuitous route, he succeeded in making Charles believe, almost up to the last moment before Wagram, that the real crossing was to be above or below Lobau, where there would be nothing but a feint. When it was no longer to be concealed that the crossing was to be from the Lobau, the Emperor still withdrew the Austrian attention from the real point of passage by ostentatiously moving the greater part of his troops on the island towards the old bridge. Then Legrand was sent over to the Mühlau as a further evidence of his intention to cross there. The bridges and boats for the crossing of the lower part of the Stadlau arm were all kept carefully hidden behind the islands in it.

At the Austrian headquarters divided counsels ruled. Charles disagreed with Wimpffen and Grünne as to the place where Napoleon would cross. He wrongly persisted in expecting a crossing elsewhere than at Lobau. Then, again, the two parties disagreed as to whether, if the crossing were from Ebersdorf, the enemy should be attacked in the act of crossing, or whether he should be left to deploy on the Marchfeld, and then received in a defensive battle in the strong positions of the Russbach and the hills on the north and west of the plain. Here Charles seems to have been in the right, but the result of his failure to firmly impose his own views was that he was almost insensibly drawn into following those of Wimpffen. His situation resembled that of Brunswick in 1806, when Massenbach was striving to commit him to crossing to the right bank of the Saale.

Napoleon's arrangements for the crossing of the lower Stadlau arm worked perfectly smoothly. Jomini has remarked that there was very nearly being fearful confusion, owing to the crossing of Davout's and Oudinot's corps on the left bank. The blame is thrown entirely on Berthier, who is supposed to have miscopied Napoleon's orders. Any stick seems to be considered good enough to beat this poor dog with! It seems to us, however, doubtful if the responsibility must not rest on other shoulders.

Jomini does not point out that the orders provided for a good deal more crossing of corps. Oudinot passed on the extreme right, though destined for the centre in the deployment beyond the river. By the next bridge on Oudinot's left passed Masséna's infantry, destined for the left in the deployment. The next bridge on the left of Masséna's infantry was assigned to Davout, who had to take the extreme right beyond the river. On Davout's left was the bridge for Masséna's cavalry and artillery. Thus Davout would,

(1) pass between Masséna's infantry and cavalry, or,

(2) he would cross right into Masséna's infantry if they had advanced as far as Davout's bridge when he crossed, or,

(3) at the best, he would pass across the rear of Masséna, and very close to it.

It seems difficult to attribute all this crossing of corps to a clerical error of Berthier. What we would suggest is this: Napoleon's whole scheme depended on the first crossing being made on the extreme right. At the same time, he wanted to have Masséna and Davout, his two most trusted commanders, on his wings at the critical points. To send Davout across on the right was out of the question, for Oudinot was already there, and he was to have mastered the passage before Davout could even reach his bridge. Masséna, equally, could not be sent across on the right if he was to take the left beyond the river. Therefore, Oudinot must pass on the right.

Why not send Masséna's infantry over the bridge which was assigned to Davout? The reasons probably were, (1) that the great bridge, swung in one piece, was only for infantry, and, therefore, would not have taken Davout's cavalry and artillery; (2) that, if this transposition had been made, Davout and Masséna's infantry might have crossed on the Lobau, at least if there was any delay on Masséna's part. For these reasons we think that the throwing of the blame on Berthier is not justified.

Napoleon probably realised the objections to the arrangement, but expected Masséna to be clear of Davout's bridge before the latter crossed.[1] As for Davout and Oudinot, the risk could not be avoided under all the circumstances. It must be accepted, in the hope either that Oudinot would have reached his place in the centre before Davout crossed his line, or else that Davout would have crossed Oudinot's front in time to avoid confusion. As it was they met, and it

---

[1] This is probably what happened, as there is no mention of danger of confusion between Davout and Masséna. The author has been unable to ascertain exactly where, relatively to Masséna's infantry position, Davout passed. That will perhaps be cleared up when Col. Saski's fourth volume is published.

Count Yorck, without stating his authority, says that Masséna, by 4.30 A.M., was opposite the northern end of the Ile Alexandre, well beyond Davout's bridge. Oudinot only moved into line at 8 A.M., after Davout had reached his place on the right (*Napoleon as a General,* ii. 89).

was only the good sense of men and officers which saved the difficulty.

On the Austrian side the view prevailed which favoured retirement, before decisive action, to the strong positions in rear of the Marchfeld; yet, as a result of the mere existence of divergences of opinion on this matter, a half measure was adopted. The fortified line Aspern-Essling-Enzersdorf was occupied by a force of some 30,000 men, with instructions to hold it as long as possible. There was very little use in this, for the holders of this line were to be left unsupported, and there could be no doubt that nothing but defeat could lie before them. The capture of the position from a force of this strength was a foregone conclusion, especially when it had been turned by the direction of the French crossing. The rather feeble defence of Enzersdorf seems to point to the realisation by the Austrian advance guard of the hopelessness of their exposed position.

Charles would probably have done much better to insist on following his own scheme of attacking the French in the act of crossing, or before they could deploy, as they did unmolested, on a line facing north. But if he did so the attack should of course have been with his whole force, not with an isolated corps. Once Masséna was established on the left flank of the fortified position, its garrison was powerless to delay the French deployment, covered as it was by the overwhelming fire of the batteries on the Lobau. The only result of the defence of the line was the retreat of two beaten forces, one towards each wing of the Austrians, placed respectively on the Russbach position and that of the Bisamberg. Charles, instead of using all his available forces on the battlefield, left the V. corps and a brigade of the III. on the Bisamberg heights. Any serious attack in that direction was improbable, looking to Napoleon's system. Schustekh might have been called up from Krems, but he paralysed Vandamme's larger force opposite him, and was therefore, perhaps, better left where he was.

Up till 6 or 7 P.M. on the 5th July there was no hindrance to the French worth mentioning. The attack which then took place on the line of the Russbach was manifestly mismanaged. Time pressed, if a decisive result was to be obtained before dark, and each corps was hurried into action irrespective of the others. The position was a strong one, the attack on it, owing to want of time, was simply frontal, and, though success was nearly attained at one moment, the French were beaten off all along the line, and there was a disgraceful panic.[1]

The Austrian right wing could do nothing in time to help the left, a fact which, no doubt, led Charles to the decision to have no more to do with Wimpffen's "pair of pincers" scheme.

The 6th July began with an event very fortunate for the Austrians, the abandonment of Aderklaa by Bernadotte and its occupation by the enemy. It was of extreme importance to Napoleon, but he was unable to get permanent possession of it again till the close of the battle. Each side, on this second day of the battle, endeavoured to turn the enemy's left. Napoleon's new attack on the Russbach position was to be by Davout marching against its left, by the left bank of the stream, with part of his corps, whilst the rest of the corps attacked Markgrafneusiedl in front. The frontal attack on Davout's left was only to be pushed home when the Duke of Auerstâdt had broken down the support of the Austrian left by the capture of Markgrafneusiedl. For the advance of the III. and VI. corps from the Bisamberg against his own left, the Emperor does not seem to have been prepared. He apparently thought Boudet, in the Aspern-Essling position, was quite sufficient to guard the bridges in that direction, as well as to keep off any enterprises against his left and rear. He had moved the rest of Masséna's corps farther to the right. Yet he was careful to keep his reserves in mass towards his centre, whence they could most easily be sent in any direction required. He actually, at one moment, was moving the Guard to Davout's support. Finding it not required there, he took it back, to be employed later in the centre. The attack of the III. and VI. corps necessitated the flank march of Masséna to the left, and the 100-gun battery seems to have been intended as much to protect that operation as to make a

---

[1] There was another after the battle was won on the 6th; clear evidence of the deterioration of the French troops.

breach in the enemy's centre, into which the Emperor could pour his infantry and cavalry.

Though his scheme now was to break through the Austrian centre, he still kept his eye constantly on the progress of Davout's advance, designed to roll the Austrian left back upon the centre. The Austrian left was the point to which he looked for the decision of the battle, and, as he saw the line of smoke from Davout's muskets pass west of Markgrafneusiedl, he said to an aide-de-camp: "Gallop! Tell Masséna that the battle is won, since the Archduke John has not yet appeared." Charles, too, saw, as Davout and Oudinot moved westwards, that there were but two alternatives left to him, to retire defeated but not annihilated, or to make a last effort for victory, with utter ruin staring him in the face if he failed. Napoleon would, perhaps, in Charles' place, have accepted the latter alternative. Charles seeking, not for the conquest of fresh empires, but for the preservation of his country and his House, wisely chose the first. By retreating he could still keep in hand a respectable army, capable of further action, and of gaining terms which from a Napoleon victorious as in 1806 he could never expect. He had attacked on a widely extended line, the necessary consequence of a turning movement such as his. Napoleon, on a shorter line, holding his masses in a central position, was able to break through the weakened Austrian line.

The battle ended in victory for Napoleon, but not decisive victory such as he gained at Austerlitz and at Jena.

Immediate pursuit there was none, and, tired though his troops were, its absence seems to point to a decadence in Napoleon's thoroughness.

The Archduke John was, throughout the day, on Napoleon's mind. His arrival, with the force he actually had, would probably not have turned the scale in the Austrian favour; but Napoleon believed he had a very much larger army, and his own reserves had been largely drawn upon. When he sent Reille with the Guard to Macdonald's aid, he said to him, "Do not run risks; for I have nothing with me as a last reserve but the two regiments of the Old Guard." Though John might not have saved the battle, that is no excuse for his delay in arriving. Charles, in his report on the battle of Wagram, blames his brother's delay in starting from Pressburg, and asserts that his arrival at Ober-Siebenbrünn would have protected the left of the army against Davout.

The consequence of the absence of immediate pursuit was that, for two days after Wagram, Napoleon was in uncertainty as to the direction of Charles' retreat. When he sent Davout and Oudinot towards Nikoloburg, he was ignorant that only one corps (Rosenberg's) was in that direction. When Charles had decided to stand at Znaim, Napoleon had moving against him only the weak corps of Marmont from Laa, and Masséna's echeloned far along the road to the Danube.

Marmont's attack on the Austrian left at Znaim, on the 10th July, was certainly rash, and exposed him to the risk of very severe treatment at the hands of a more enterprising enemy. His conduct generally at this time was very rash and negligent, and he could not justly complain of the severe terms in which Napoleon censured his neglect in leaving the passage of the Thaya, at Laa, in his rear, absolutely unprotected against any stray body of cavalry. On the 11th, Napoleon was able to bring to his support a strong body of cavalry, but, even with that, it was not possible to hope for any decisive result. Masséna, too, arrived from the south, though, for the first part of the day, he had only Legrand's division available, and, later, only that and Carra St Cyr's. Napoleon saw clearly that, until Davout and Oudinot should arrive, he was powerless to defeat the six [1] Austrian corps in position about Znaim. The French reinforcements could hardly be ready for action before the early hours of the 12th. The Emperor could not even hope to prevent the Austrians from retreating on Iglau; if they did so, as Charles intended, the French army would be once more drawn far to the north, away from Vienna. That was probably what induced Napoleon to accede to Liechtenstein's demand for an armistice. Had he seen his way to holding Charles at Znaim till the 12th, it seems certain he would not have granted it.

With the armistice of Znaim the campaign was at an end,

---

[1] V., I., and III. in first line, II. and Grenadiers in second line, VI. on the road to Iglau.

though it took several months of negotiation before peace was finally concluded.

Brilliant as many of Napoleon's manœuvres had been, the campaign differed very widely in the degree of its success from its predecessors of Austerlitz and Jena. Its comparative failure must be attributed largely to Napoleon's preconceived idea of marching on Vienna, irrespective of the enemy's movements, an idea to which he obstinately adhered when Charles retreated through Ratisbon into Bohemia. Had Napoleon followed him to Cham with the corps of Davout, Masséna and Lannes, it is difficult to doubt that the result must have been the defeat of the Austrian army, with its complete break-up in the Bohemian Forest. Hiller could have easily been dealt with by Bessières' force and Lefebvre, behind whom the Guard was beginning to arrive.

With the army of Charles destroyed, Napoleon might have marched on Vienna as he marched on Berlin in 1806. "There is nothing better than to march on the enemy's capital after a decisive victory; before it, no!"

The failure to gain a decisive victory over Charles in April led only to the barren occupation of Vienna, to the repulse of Essling, to the indecisive victory of Wagram, and to the armistice of Znaim.

It seems remarkable that, with the incompleteness of his success, Napoleon should have in the end been able to dictate such terms as those of the Treaty of Schönbrünn. Francis and his friends of the war party would have renewed operations had they dared, but they had thrown away, by the dismissal of the Archduke Charles, their best, perhaps their only general, and probably they felt that a renewal of the struggle could but end in fresh and more decisive defeat, with the inevitable consequence of the obliteration of Austria from the map of Europe, and of the House of Habsburg from the list of reigning families.

"The Strategy and Tactics of The Campaign of 1814," from *Napoleon at Bay, 1814*

The campaign of 1814 has been greatly admired, and has even been held up as the greatest effort of the Emperor's genius.

If, on the one hand, we think this estimate places it too high, on the other, it is certainly a wonderful example of what Napoleon's genius could do in circumstances which, since the great defeat of Leipzig, had become so desperate that no other general of the time would have even attempted to make head against them. To find a parallel we have to go back to Frederick the Great in his struggle against almost all the rest of Europe.

Napoleon had lost practically the whole of the great army of 1812, and that had been replaced in 1813 by another of inferior quality, which he had conjured up as if by magic. Now that, too, had nearly disappeared, except for the garrisons left behind in the German fortresses. For Napoleon these were as much lost as the dead, disabled, and prisoners of Lützen, Bautzen, Dresden, and Leipzig.

But the spirit of the great leader was still unquelled, though he found it impossible to raise from exhausted and discontented France the new troops he wanted. Time was his most urgent need, and the allies seemed determined to give him that, by delaying their advance and negotiating for a peace which, perhaps, they never intended to grant, or Napoleon to accept.

Still, the Emperor had not sufficient time; for he was bound to Paris by the immense labours of organization and of government, which he alone could control. When, at last, he tore himself away to return to the front at Châlons, he was a week too late to be able to fall upon one of the allied armies, Blücher's for choice, before they could unite. Their union had been effected, though it was still by no means complete, and there was yet a chance of inflicting a heavy blow on Blücher before he was fully supported by the slow-moving corps of the army of Bohemia. Napoleon's attack on Blücher at Brienne was the most natural course for him to take; but it failed, and henceforward he must have known that he had to reckon also with a large part of Schwarzenberg's army. Here he made his first great mistake, in waiting too long about Brienne, until he could not avoid the battle of La Rothière in which, with his inferior numbers and poor position, he could not reasonably hope for success. He was saved from complete ruin by the faults of the allies, which were numerous.

Forgetting that it is never possible to be too strong on the decisive battlefield, Schwarzenberg wasted Wittgenstein's corps, and perhaps Yorck's also. Even Wrede would have been sent off after Wittgenstein, but for his own suggestion crossing Schwarzenberg's orders. The limitations of Blücher's command were bound, as for political reasons they were intended, to prevent the realization of the full fruits of victory. Blücher himself failed to perceive that Napoleon's left, not his centre, was the point on which the main effort was required. His own centre, with the Guards and Reserves behind it, was safe from any counter-attack Napoleon could make on it.

The pursuit on the 2nd February was tardy and inefficient, and another great mistake was made in the separation of the armies of Silesia and Bohemia. As has already been pointed out, Blücher, at this time, had no prospects of reinforcement to a strength much exceeding 50,000 men, a number which would not give him any marked superiority to the force Napoleon would be able to bring against him.

Napoleon, having failed to cut off Blücher as he had hoped, had now to recommence that system of "va et vient" marching alternately against each of the hostile armies, of which he was so great a master. For his purpose of containing one enemy with a portion of his force, whilst he fell on the other with the rest, the river system of Champagne was of the greatest advantage. The Seine and its tributaries in particular facilitated defence against an enemy advancing on that side. The main road by which Schwarzenberg was advancing from the plateau of Langres had first to pass the Aube at Bar-sur-Aube. Then it met the Seine at Troyes where a defence was possible. The great northward bend of the river between Troyes and Montereau necessitated a second passage of the river at Nogent or Bray. Schwarzenberg could in this part only advance on the south bank; for the roads on the north bank were bad, and moreover the Aube had to be crossed. Moreover, any attempt to pass round the bend would expose the allies to attack in left flank by Napoleon holding the passages of the Seine. Below Nogent Schwarzenberg could move by both banks, but his force on the south bank would encounter the lines of the Yonne and

the Loing. Moreover, the French, destroying the bridges of
the Seine as they passed, and leaving others intact behind
them, might at any moment attack the enemy on one bank
with strong forces, leaving only a weak one to contain him on
the opposite bank.

The Marne, too, was a good line for the defence of Paris.
The main road from Germany to Paris crossed it at Châlons,
at Château-Thierry, at La Ferté-sous-Jouarre, and yet again
at Trilport.

Napoleon's movement against Blücher in the second and
third weeks of February was, as we have said, his most successful manœuvre of this campaign; but we have also endeavoured to show that much of its success was due to
fortuitous circumstances, and to Schwarzenberg's removal of
the connecting link between the two armies, without inform-
ing Blücher. Both the prescience often attributed to Napoleon, and the incapacity alleged to have been displayed by
Blücher in disseminating his forces require to be discounted
considerably. Napoleon had no certain knowledge of the dispersion of the army of Silesia until he reached Sézanne.
Blücher's great faults were, first, in not keeping in better
touch with Seslawin's movements, and secondly, in trying to
combine two incompatible objectives at the same time,
namely, the rallying of Kleist and Kapzewitch, and the pursuit and envelopment of Macdonald. The first fault was one
of constant occurrence in the allied armies and was, perhaps,
inherent in a divided command.

It is hardly possible to give too much credit to the leaders
and troops of the Silesian army for the wonderful way in
which they pulled themselves together at Châlons after the
very severe handling they had had.

When Napoleon, having beaten but by no means destroyed Blücher, returned to his containing force on the
Seine, he decided to meet the enemy in front, not to march
against his right flank and rear, as he did in the latter part of
March. His strength, combined with that of the containing
force, was little more than half that of the army of Bohemia.
The proportion of forces was generally the same throughout
the campaign, and consequently the Emperor was never able
to provide a reasonably large containing force, and at the

same time to carry with himself an army even equal in numbers to the hostile army against which he moved offensively. He had to rely largely on the real value and the prestige of his personal presence at the head of troops.

The success of his movement against Schwarzenberg, in the second half of February, was, as he complained bitterly, marred by his want of the means of passing the Seine at Nogent, in pursuit of the enemy. Had he been able to do so, it might well have gone hard with Schwarzenberg's advanced left wing. As it was, Napoleon owed a debt of gratitude to Pajol for his brilliant cavalry action at Montereau, which secured for the Emperor the bridges over the Seine and Yonne at their junction.

When Schwarzenberg got back to Troyes, he was in a difficult position for a leader of his character. The country in which he stood was poor at the best, and now its resources were exhausted. Napoleon, on the other hand, had at his back the richer country towards Paris. Schwarzenberg, therefore, must either fight a decisive battle or must fall back to Langres. He would dearly have loved to return to the eighteenth-century system of manœuvring, but that was not possible with an adversary like Napoleon, or in an exhausted country. There cannot be a shadow of a doubt that, from a military point of view, Schwarzenberg should have fought a great battle, in which, with Blücher to help him, he could have opposed the Emperor with more than twofold forces. He appears to have made up his mind to fight until the news of Augereau's advance from the south alarmed him for his communications with Switzerland, and decided him in favour of a retreat towards the plateau of Langres, and a fresh separation from Blücher. He also weakened his own army by the despatch of Bianchi and a large force to Dijon.

Napoleon had hoped for a battle about Troyes, though, as we have seen, his chances of success in it were small. We have already commented on his apparent reluctance to believe that Blücher was again marching on Paris, until the Prussian had already gained a considerable start of him. Still, Napoleon kept his main body at Troyes ready for all eventualities, either to support the pursuit of Schwarzenberg or to follow Blücher, according to circumstances.

Marmont and Mortier (the former was chiefly responsible) deserve great credit for their little campaign on the Lower Ourcq, during the period before the Emperor reached La Ferté-sous-Jouarre, and during his detention there, owing to his want of the means of throwing bridges. Nevertheless, Blücher succeeded in escaping across the Upper Ourcq, and it may be said that when Napoleon at last crossed the Marne on the 3rd March, he had practically lost all chance of compelling Blücher to fight before he was joined by Winzingerode and by Bülow. Of the latter's whereabouts Napoleon was in complete ignorance.

It may be thought that the Emperor would have done better, instead of waiting for the repair of the bridge at La Ferté-sous-Jouarre, to have marched direct to Château-Thierry, and crossed there as Victor actually did. But he could feel no certainty that he would not find the same difficulty in crossing at Château-Thierry that he had already found at La Ferté-sous-Jouarre. Moreover, he must have felt nervous as to the period during which Marmont and Mortier could maintain themselves on the Ourcq, and prevent Blücher's march on Paris. Lastly, the roads to Château-Thierry were very bad, as he knew from experience three weeks earlier. Once Blücher had been reinforced by Winzingerode and Bülow, his strength was more than double that of Napoleon, who could hardly hope for success in a battle against such odds. What happened at Craonne and Laon we know, and the Emperor probably owed his escape from ruin after the latter battle largely to Blücher's physical breakdown.

The march on Reims, and the defeat of St. Priest were very brilliant affairs in Napoleon's best style, and had important political results in restoring the Emperor's fading prestige in Paris, as well as the military result of again severing all direct communication between Blücher and Schwarzenberg.

Having just dealt with the movement on Arcis and against Schwarzenberg's communications, we need not refer further to the subject.

We have not said much of Napoleon's attempts to harass the allies by raising the country against them. But for the conduct of some of the allied troops themselves, especially the cossacks, it seems probable that the Emperor would have had little chance of raising the country people to armed resistance. They were tired of the years of war, which had carried off their sons and husbands to supply the constant demand for conscripts, and they would no doubt have watched almost with indifference the progress of an invasion conducted with humanity. But the atrocities of the cossacks and others, though they were little, if at all, worse than those committed in the past by French troops in Germany, exasperated the inhabitants, and prepared them to respond in desperation to the Emperor's calls to rise and defend themselves. There were frequent encounters with armed peasants, and many stragglers of the allies, or small parties, were cut off, and either massacred or captured. Convoys were also cut off, if not strongly guarded. In this way the allies were undoubtedly hampered, and compelled, as Napoleon had been compelled in 1813, to take special precautions. But it cannot be said that the general course of the war was seriously influenced by popular risings.

As for the negotiations, which commenced from Frankfort in November, 1813, and continued off and on till the middle of March, 1814, it is difficult to believe that either side was in earnest. On the whole, it is more probable that the allies, with the divergent views and aims of their different groups, would have welcomed peace than that Napoleon would have accepted terms which, if they were to lead to permanent peace, would have shorn him of all his conquests, and put an end to his dreams of universal empire. Generally speaking, he was only open to reason when affairs were going badly with him. A success, such as that against Blücher in the middle of February, or the subsequent victories over Schwarzenberg, at once raised his hopes and his terms, and set him definitely against peace. Caulaincourt, who saw more clearly that in peace lay the only chance of recovery, was unable to influence his Imperial and imperious master. In this campaign Napoleon's insane optimism constantly blinded him to actual facts, even more than was the case in 1813. It seems almost as if he believed that the fall of the conqueror of Europe was an unthinkable contingency.

Weather played an important part in this campaign. Continued alternations of frost and thaw rendered the roads almost unpassable, and the rivers unfordable everywhere. On the whole, probably, this was an advantage to Napoleon; for the wonderful marching powers of even French recruits gave him an advantage over the slower moving allies. This advantage was increased by the fact that Napoleon, operating in his own country, was generally able, as before Champaubert, to get willing help from the peasantry and their farm horses in dragging his guns over roads which it seemed almost impossible for them to traverse, as well as in food supplies.

It has been said that Napoleon's great want in 1813 and 1814 was cavalry. Yet, in the latter year, it may be remarked that he was often proportionately stronger in cavalry than his enemies, whose total numbers throughout were generally double his. When he marched against Blücher on the 9th February, one-third of his force was cavalry, an arm in which Blücher at the moment was weak. It must be admitted that much of the French cavalry was of the poorest description: that many of the recruits had never been on a horse till a fortnight before their first battle, that they could only just hold their reins in one hand and a sword in the other, and that both hands had to be used when they wanted to turn their horses. Still, the Emperor had some good cavalry, especially the cavalry of the Guard, and the squadrons of Treilliard and Sparre, veterans of the war in Spain. What his cavalry was still capable of under his command was seen at Vauchamps. If Sebastiani's troopers yielded to panic at Arcis in the morning of the 20th March, they nobly redeemed their reputation in the charge of the same night.

The artillery, too, was of very varied quality, some of it atrociously bad and untrained, some of it, especially the famous artillery of the Guard, as good as ever. In this arm Napoleon's most powerful enemy was the Russian artillery, which, always good and well led, made it a point of honour not to lose guns.

The French infantry ranged in quality from the splendid veterans of Spain and of the Old Guard to the poor recruits of Pacthod's National Guards, and some even less trained. Yet even these covered themselves with glory, and died fighting to the last, in the bloody actions near Fère Champ-enoise.

When all was over, both Napoleon and his troops might well have said, with François Ier after Pavia, "Tout est perdu fors l'honneur."

Bibliographic Note on the Napoleonic Works of F. Loraine Petre

Napoleon and the Archduke Charles: A History of the Franco-Austrian Campaign in the Valley of the Danube in 1809.
London and New York: John Lane, 1909; London: Arms & Armour Press, New York: Hippocrene Books, Inc., 1976.

Napoleon at Bay, 1814.
London and New York: John Lane, 1914; London: Arms & Armour Press, New York: Hippocrene Books, Inc., 1977.

Napoleon's Campaign in Poland, 1806–1807.
London: Sampson Low, Marston, 1901; London and New York: John Lane, 1907; London: Arms & Armour Press, New York: Hippocrene Books, Inc., 1975.

Napoleon's Conquest of Prussia, 1806.
London and New York: John Lane, 1907; London and New York: John Lane, 1914; London: Arms & Armour Press, New York: Hippocrene Books, Inc. 1972; London: Arms & Armour Press, New York: Hippocrene Books, Inc., 1977.

Napoleon's Last Campaign in Germany, 1813.
London and New York: John Lane, 1912; London: Arms & Armour Press, New York: Hippocrene Books, Inc., 1974; London: Arms & Armour Press, New York: Hippocrene Books, Inc., 1977.

Bibliography

This bibliography lists only works of some note which have appeared on Napoleon, the Wars of the French Republic and Empire, the armies of France and her enemies, and the conduct of war in the period 1789 through 1815 since the original publication of the works of F. Loraine Petre.

Adlow, E. *Napoleon in Italy, 1796–1797*. Boston: W. J. Rochfort, 1948.

Balkoski, Joseph. "Ney vs. Wellington: the Battle of Quatre Bras, June 16, 1815," *Strategy & Tactics* No. 74 (May–June 1979), pp. 4–11.

Calvert, Michael, and Peter Young. *A Dictionary of Battles (1715–1815)*. New York: Mayflower Books, 1979.

Chandler, David. *Atlas of Military Strategy*. New York: The Free Press, London: Lionel Leventhal, 1980.

———. *The Campaigns of Napoleon: The Mind and Method of History's Greatest Soldier*. New York: Macmillan, 1966.

———. *Dictionary of the Napoleonic Wars*. New York: Macmillan, 1979.

Chorley, Katherine. *Armies and the Art of Revolution*. Boston: Beacon Press, 1973.

Clausewitz, Carl von. *On War*, edited and translated by Michael Howard and Peter Paret. Princeton: Princeton University Press, 1976.

Connelly, Owen. *Napoleon's Satellite Kingdoms*. New York: The Free Press, 1965.

Corvisier, André. *Armies and Society in Europe, 1494–1789*. Bloomington, Ind.: Indiana University Press, 1979.

Delderfield, R. F. *The March of the Twenty-Six*. London: Hodder & Stoughton, 1962.

———. *The Retreat from Moscow*. New York: Atheneum, 1967.

Duffy, Christopher. *Borodino and the War of 1812*. New York: Scribners, 1973.

———. *Fire and Stone: The Science of Fortress Warfare, 1660–1860.* London: David & Charles, New York: Hippocrene Books, Inc., 1973.

Dupuy, Trevor N. *The Battle of Austerlitz.* New York: Macmillan, 1968.

———. *The Evolution of Weapons and Warfare.* Indianapolis and New York: Bobbs-Merrill, 1980.

Earle, Edward Meade, editor. *The Makers of Modern Strategy.* Princeton: Princeton University Press, 1943.

Esposito, Vincent J., and John R. Elting. *A Military History and Atlas of the Napoleonic Wars.* New York: Praeger, 1964.

Fuller, J. F. C. *The Conduct of War, 1789–1961.* New York: Minerva Press, 1968.

Glover, Michael. *The Napoleonic Wars: An Illustrated History, 1792–1815.* New York: Hippocrene Books, Inc., 1978.

———. *Wellington's Peninsular Victories.* New York: Macmillan, 1962.

Glover, R. C. *Peninsular Preparation: the Reform of the British Army, 1795–1809.* Cambridge: Cambridge University Press, 1963.

Griffith, Paddy. *Forward to Battle.* London: Anthony Bird, New York: Hippocrene Books, Inc., 1981.

Heriot, A. *The French in Italy, 1796–1799.* London: Chatto & Windus, 1967.

Herold, J. Christopher. *Bonaparte in Egypt.* New York: Harper & Row, 1962.

Hughes, B. P. *Firepower: Weapons Effectiveness on the Battlefield, 1630–1850.* New York: Scribners, 1974.

Keegan, John. *The Face of Battle.* New York: Viking Press, 1976.

Koontz, John E. "French Tactical Columns, 1808–1815." Unpublished monograph, 1982.

Lachoque, Henri, and A. S. K. Brown. *The Anatomy of Glory: Napoleon and his Guard.* New York: Hippocrene Books, 1978.

Liddell Hart, Basil Henry. *The Ghost of Napoleon.* London: Faber, 1933.

McElwee, William. *The Art of War, Waterloo to Mons.* Bloomington: Indiana University Press, 1974.

McNeill, William H. *The Pursuit of Power: Technology, Armed Force, and Society since A.D. 1000.* Chicago: University of Chicago Press, 1982.

Manceron, C. *Austerlitz.* New York: Norton, 1966.

Nofi, Albert A. "Napoleon's Art of War," *Strategy and Tactics,* No. 75 (July–August 1979), pp. 11–19.

———. "Napoleon at Waterloo," *Strategy and Tactics,* No. 42 (January–February 1974), pp. 21–34.

Oman, Charles W. C. *A History of the Peninsular War.* 7 vols. Oxford: The Clarendon Press, 1902–1930.

———. *Studies in the Napoleonic Wars.* New York: Scribners, 1930.

Palmer, Alan. *Napoleon in Russia.* New York: Simon and Schuster, 1967.

Paret, Peter. *Clausewitz and the State.* Oxford: Oxford University Press, 1976.

———. *Yorck and the Era of Prussian Military Reform, 1807–1815.* Princeton: Princeton University Press, 1966.

Parker, Harold. *Three Napoleonic Battles: Friedland, Aspern-Essling, Waterloo.* Durham, N.C.: Duke University Press, 1944.

Phipps, Ramsey W. *The Armies of the First French Republic and the Rise of the Marshals of Napoleon I.* 5 vols. London: Oxford University Press, 1935–1939.

Quimby, Robert S. *Background to Napoleonic Warfare.* New York: Columbia University Press, 1957.

Roger, A. B. *The War of the Second Coalition, 1798–1801.* Oxford: The Clarendon Press, 1964.

Rogers, H. C. B. *Napoleon's Army.* New York: Hippocrene Books, Inc., 1974.

Ross, Steven T. "The Military Strategy of the Directory: The Campaign of 1799," *French Historical Studies,* V,2 (Fall 1967), pp. 170–187.

———. "The Development of the Combat Division in Eighteenth Century French Armies," *French Historical Studies,* IV,1 (Spring 1965), pp. 84–94.

Rothenberg, Gunther. *The Art of Warfare in the Age of Napoleon.* Bloomington, Ind.: Indiana University Press, 1978.

———. *Napoleon's Great Enemies: The Austrian Army and the Archduke Charles.* Bloomington, Ind.: Indiana University Press, 1982.

Scott, Samuel F. *The Response of the Royal Army to the French Revolution: The Role and Development of the Line Army, 1787–1793.* Oxford: The Clarendon Press, 1978.

Shanahan, William O. *Prussian Military Reforms, 1786–1813.* New York: Columbia University Press, 1945.

Sterwig, J. M. *Guineas and Gunpowder: British Foreign Aid in the Wars with France, 1793–1815.* Cambridge, Mass.: Harvard University Press, 1969.

United States Military Academy, *Campaign Atlas to the Wars of Napoleon.* West Point: USMA, 1973.

Van Creveld, Martin. *Supplying War.* Cambridge: Cambridge University Press, 1977.

Weller, Jac. *Wellington at Waterloo.* New York: Crowell, 1967.

————. *Wellington in the Peninsula.* London: Vane, 1963.

Young, Peter, *Napoleon's Marshals.* New York: Hippocrene Books, Inc., 1973.

Index